WETLAND
RIDERS

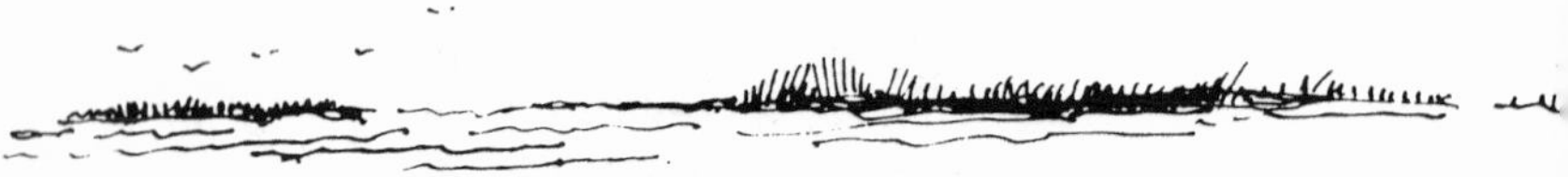

WETLAND RIDERS

ROBERT FRITCHEY

NEW MOON PRESS
GOLDEN MEADOW, LOUISIANA

Published by New Moon Press

2416 South Bayou Drive

Golden Meadow, Louisiana 70357

Drawings of fish on pp. 77, 185, 221, and 237 from "Fishes of North America" by Jordan and Evermann, 1898. Provided by the Smithsonian Institution.

The drawing on p. 9 is from a *National Fisherman* article illustrated by Jim Sollers of Augusta, Maine. A freelance illustrator since 1981, Jim contributes regularly to several commercial fishing and boating magazines.

All other illustrations are by Lee Roy Tooke. A fisherman and boatbuilder from Cedar Key, Florida, Lee Roy has lived in South Louisiana since 1972.

Photograph on p. 16 from Peabody Museum of Salem, Mass.; photo on p. 135 from New Orleans Historical Collection; photo on p.215 by Jonathan Blair, from National Geographic Society; photo on p. 281 by Bill Mutch, courtesy of *National Fisherman*; photo on p. 283 courtesy of Tidewater Administration, Maryland Department of

Natural Resources; photo on p. 313 courtesy of Florida News Bureau; photos on pp.298, 299 and 344 by Walter B. Sikora; photo on p. 332, top, courtesy of Florida Department of Commerce, Division of Tourism; photo on p.332, bottom, courtesy of Florida Sea Grant; photo on p. 333 by Nathan Benn, from Woodfin Camp; photo on p.345, top, courtesy of U.S. Army Corps of Engineers; photo on p. 345, bottom, courtesy of Coastal Restoration Division, Louisiana Department of Natural Resources; photo of author by Brian Gauvin; all other photos by Robert Fritchey.

ISBN 0-9636215-0-5

Library of Congress Catalog Card Number: 92-063214

Printed in the United States of America

For the men and women who work
on the front lines—
the coastal finfishermen

ACKNOWLEDGMENTS

For support while writing, thanks to my mother and to my father, a world-class sportsman who bore quietly the indignity of a son's having crossed the line to fish for money. I'm also in debt to my friends, Frank Cogswell, Tom Brown, Kenan and Linda Lupton, Carol Wells, Claude and Susan Pritchett, Adel Zaeeter, Bill Van Calsem, and Ron and Liz Anderson, whose generosity greatly facilitated the writing of this book. I must also say "Merci" to Russell and June Cheramie, Nolte, Ben and Don Griffin, Obelique "Crip" Broussard, Andrew and "Miss Eva" Cheramie, Ron Helms, Chaz Willyard and the many other good people from the Bayou who helped me along.

Editor Nancy Schoeffler and Kathleen Joffrion, who designed the book and cover, deserve special gratitude. Both ladies took time from their full schedules to devote to this project, without concern for reward.

Helen Sue Musser offered creative advice.

Finally, I'm grateful to Tony Barnes and the other employees at the New Orleans Public Library who so graciously responded to each of my frequent requests; and to Cahn Enterprises, for providing a bit of writer's habitat in the French Quarter.

PREFACE

A wide belt of salt marsh stretches across South Louisiana. The southern edge of this watery prairie melts into grassy islets, open lakes and bays, the Gulf of Mexico. The northern border reaches inland until, imperceptibly, the land rises, the water sweetens, and trees take hold to produce the familiar Louisiana swamp country of moss-draped cypress and tupelo gum.

Louisiana's nearly three-and-one-half million acres of coastal marshes would cover more than half of the state of Massachusetts. As if on a midwestern plain, one's vision flows freely across these grasslands to the horizon.

But here grow no amber waves of grain — these wetlands yield the greatest seafood harvest in America.

Each year, commercial fishermen land over a billion pounds of shrimp and crabs, oysters and finfish in Louisiana ports. More than 18,000 independents in coastal communities across the state support their families by fishing. Just as these fishermen depend on the production of this vast marshland nursery, net makers, boatbuilders, fishhouses, markets, restaurants and a variety of other coastal and inland businesses depend on the fishermen.

The coastal wetlands enable these traditional people to preserve a unique culture, which molds the spirit of South Louisiana.

Fewer than 2,000 of Louisiana's coastal fishermen are licensed to catch and sell finfish. Of these, many are primarily shrimpers, crabbers or oystermen who may sell a few fish when their own fisheries are closed or otherwise unprofitable.

Those who chase the fish through the summer and winter, spring and fall, number in the hundreds. These are the inshore finfishermen.

Unlike the offshore tuna or red snapper fisherman, the inshore finfisherman rarely loses sight of land. After an exhausting day of netting redfish or spotted seatrout from his open skiff, he returns to his wife and children.

The inshore netter rides the beaches, the shallow inside bays, and he rides the marsh, in search of fish. The water is read by eye for the signs of his quarry. While he searches, the meter runs; the engine burns up fuel and oil while the fisherman forces his boat into the out-of-the-way lairs that may hold fish.

If his hunches about where the fish will be are wrong too often, he's out. But if he's good enough to stay in this game, he has earned the right to call himself, proudly, a fisherman.

Yet, the immensely productive inshoreman finds himself in an ironic position: Though he fuels an industry that provides consumers with a commodity of Old World quality—wild-caught fish—he has relatively little to show for it. There are no wealthy inshore finfishermen.

"Freedom, that's what it's all about," says Charenton fisherman Ray Carline. "It's what our country was made of. It's not havin' to punch a clock. You work as hard as you want to work or as little as you want to work. That's the whole thing about it, that's what makes it so great...Bein' free."

In 1980, at age 30, I fell in with the fishermen. After completing my formal education, I had imposed some rigorous parameters on my life: "I'll earn my livelihood only from renewable resources, and I'll never work for another man."

Shortly thereafter, I found myself in a tent on the South Louisiana marshes. Though a lifelong sport fisherman, as a matter of survival, I learned to work with that prebiblical tool, the net.

By trial and error and by forging partnerships with other fishermen, I learned to fish in the style of a Cajun trammel netter. Each fisherman has his own specialty, be it trout or pompano, redfish or mullet. Because redfish is the staple of the Cajun *tramailleurs*,[1] I worked that marshland species.

As it turned out, the decade from the early 1980s to the early 1990s proved to be the most devastating in the long history of this little-known industry.

As the 1980s opened, fishermen worked freely, under few restrictions other than those imposed by nature. But earning a living as an inshore finfisherman became progressively more difficult—and finally next to impossible. What happened?

From down the Bayou, it was impossible to understand. In 1988, I moved to the French Quarter in New Orleans and began to write for *National Fisherman*, the trade magazine for the nation's commercial fishermen.

As I reported on fishery issues across the Gulf Coast, I soon learned that the plight of Louisiana's inshoremen is not unique; that coastal fishermen around America are rapidly disappearing.

Since he harvests fish whose life cycles require coastal wetlands, I suspected that the inshoreman's decline is associated with the rapid loss of this habitat. But the fisherman is not going out of business because there are no longer enough fish to support him. The fish may not be as plentiful as they used to be, but there are still more than enough to support a number of professional fishermen, particularly in Louisiana. Rather, the fisherman's problems stem from the manner in which the annual crop of fish is shared. With whom? Exploding numbers of sport fishermen.

Each year, biologists calculate the number of fish that may safely be harvested while leaving enough in the water to replenish the population. *How* the fish are allocated is not decided by biologists; without a thought to the consequences, it is being decided by politicians.

Commercial fishermen are often called "farmers of the sea." Like farmers, they harvest great quantities of food. Yet there are some key differences between the farmer and the fisherman.

When the orange grower's crop is threatened by a bitter Alberta Clipper, he lights smudge pots to warm the night air. When it is dry, he irrigates. His fortunes are susceptible to the vagaries of nature but the farmer can, at least, smooth out some of the bumps.

Not so the fisherman, whose fate is bound to the abundance and to the movement of his swimming crop, ever changing from season to season, day to day, hour to hour, according to the natural cycles-within-cycles of moon and sun, wind and tide, storm and calm.

The farmer's ability to buffer himself somewhat from extreme adversity stems from the control gained by owning his land. But the fisherman owns only his boat and gear. The water upon which he works is owned by the public. The seafood that he harvests from this water is also a common-property resource, technically "owned" by everyone in the state or nation, depending on whether it swims in inshore state waters or offshore federal waters.

Though he pulls his livelihood directly from the water, the common-property nature of the resource that the fisherman harvests opens the door to regulation by interests outside of his industry.

PREFACE

Since fishery regulations are most often imposed via the state Legislature and governor, the U.S. Congress, and the U.S. Department of Commerce, their passage hinges on the ability of the respective interest groups to influence these political bodies.

The recreational fishing industry is extremely powerful. Members of this industry do not sell fish for money; instead they market an incredible variety of goods and services to sport fishermen, who catch the fish for fun. Allowing commercial fishermen to harvest fish for the public to eat, rather than being caught by increasing numbers of sport fishermen, is viewed by members of this tourist-based industry as a restraint on its growth.

With money generated both from within the industry and from sport fishermen themselves, and with the aid of magazines and newspapers that sway public opinion in its favor, the recreational industry is convincing politicians to simply take the fish away from the commercial fishermen. Since they must sell fish to consumers in order to survive, inshoremen are at first impoverished, and then destroyed.

Like a Zydeco accordionist, the fisherman learns his trade from another. There are no books or schools that teach you how to catch enough fish to live. When the fishermen are gone, they are gone forever. Unfortunately, their value extends even beyond the food that they provide, the knowledge that they hold, and the colorful tradition they add to coastal cultures. As those who earn their livelihoods directly from the coastal marshes are eliminated, so too is their strong interest in protecting this threatened habitat.

R.S.F.
New Orleans
October, 1993

CONTENTS

PART IV

PART V

APPENDIX

UPDATE

Do you know what it is...to fish?
—Edville "Pagaie" Cheramie,
Cajun redfisherman

INTRODUCTION

In order to fully understand the controversy which has raged between these two warring elements, it is necessary that one spend considerable time on the coast fishing with a pole and line, and usually, as has been the case with the writers of this report, who would all be classed as sports fishermen, a fellow after spending several days at such fishing without catching anything perhaps but a few worthless catfish, perhaps a shark or two, and some sand trout, will observe a commercial fisherman pull up his net filled with a good catch of fine speckled trout, redfish, etc., and only then—and not until then—can one fully appreciate the feeling of the sports fisherman, and the resentment many of these boys seem to experience when they see the other fellow catching fish that they are unable to hook. While the closing of these waters to nets would in no way increase the supply of fish, that fact is unknown to the average sportsman, and when he sees a net fisherman make a good catch he is overcome in many cases with a feeling that must be experienced but cannot well be described.

—From a report by the Legislative
Investigating Committee on Saltwater
Fisheries and Marine Taxation, to the
Texas State Legislature, 1935

Louisiana's inshore finfishing industry is based upon an integrated fishery of seven primary species: red drum ("redfish"), spotted seatrout ("speckled trout"), pompano, black drum, sheepshead, striped mullet and southern flounder.

Just as there are for the farmer's crops, there are natural seasons for the harvest of each of these fish.

Flounder are targeted by only a handful of netters as they migrate from the marshes toward the Gulf in late autumn. Otherwise, finfishermen view flounder as *lagniappe*, a little something extra that sometimes appears in the net as bycatch. (Bycatch is any fish that is caught incidentally to that species for which the fisherman has set his gear.) By far, the majority of flounder entering the market are taken as bycatch of shrimp trawlers.

Mullet are fished primarily for the highly valued roe during an intense wintertime spawning run that lasts only about two months.

An increase in demand for fish in recent years has caused the price of sheepshead to increase many fold, from 10 cents per pound to as high as 65 cents. Because of its massive head and bones, which may total more than half the fish's weight, prices for this fine-eating fish never approach those of other species. Sheepshead are fished primarily during the winter and early spring.

Black drum have supported a sizable fishery for well over one hundred years, but catches increased dramatically during the 1980s. They are fished primarily during the late winter and spring.

Pompano are a delicacy, never abundant and always high-priced. These skittish fish are so reluctant to hit a net that they are usually fished at night. Fishermen who wish to participate in this specialized fishery must first thread their way at high speed through a maze of often unlit oil rigs and submerged oilfield debris. When they reach the grounds—nearshore and inshore banks—they flick on a "skipping light," a tiny 12-volt bulb that shines rearward, illuminating the boat's foamy wheelwash.

Navigating through the darkness, the captain zigzags the boat over the hard sand banks that lie perilously near the surface. As the breakers crash over the bars, the deckhand holds on, concentrating only on the dimly lit area behind, until, across the wheelwash streaks a deep-bodied fish..."Pompano!"

"See any more?," the captain shouts, above the noise of the engine and the crashing waves. "How big?"

"There's another one! And another one! Yeah, yeah, they're big ones. Let's get it!"

The captain doubles back to see for himself. If it looks promising, the net is hurriedly run into the water. With luck, some of the rapidly fleeing fish will hit it.

Pompano are available sporadically from the spring, into the fall. Probably fewer than two dozen of the state's fishermen have the skill—or the temerity—to chase "The Gold."

No fisherman earns his livelihood from any one, or any combination of these five species alone. If he has the equipment—and if the fish happen to show up in his territory—he may enjoy a short bonanza during the winter mullet run or the springtime black drum run. But always, when the brief flurry ends, he returns to the two species that are his bread and butter: the redfish and the spotted seatrout.

As with the others, there are seasons when these two species are most abundant. The skillful fisherman, however, can make a catch of reds or trout most any time of the year. In addition to their ready availability, they are highly valued by consumers. With the exception of the luxurious pompano, for which the fisherman may receive $3.50 per pound, they fetch the highest of prices, averaging well over one dollar.

Redfish and trout provide Louisiana finfishermen with the majority of their annual income. The value of the two species landed each year averages more than 60 percent of the total value of the inshore industry. They are the keystone of this industry; pull them out and the whole thing falls.

The recreational fishing industry is pulling them out—the two species happen to be the mainstay of this industry, as well.

Their good eating, year-round availability and abundance near shore help make them popular with sport fishermen in the coastal waters of Louisiana and other Gulf states. But what makes them most alluring to anglers is their game nature.

Unlike the vegetarian mullet or the nibbling sheepshead, both redfish and trout will strike an artificial lure with a thrilling jolt. Once on the hook, they strongly resist capture and, like a game boxer, they do not give up easily.

In sporting terms, whether a fish is "game" or not is a subjective decision. But there is nothing hazy about a fish's receiving the legal designation, "gamefish." A fish that has been declared a gamefish is off-limits to commercial fishermen and consumers—it may be caught only for fun, forevermore to be exploited solely by recreational fishermen.

Recreational industry members desperately seek to win gamefish status for redfish and trout. Since these fish are the property of everyone in the state, taking them from the public-at-large must be accomplished within the Legislature, and with the approval of the governor. The recreational industry's aggressive attempts to sequester these two valued species for its own use, and the commercial industry's efforts to thwart these attempts, have led to some of the most bitterly fought political battles in the legislative histories of Gulf Coast states. The first such fight took place in Texas.

The Texas coastline extends from the Louisiana line to the Rio Grande, a distance of 400 miles; if the winding shores of the many bays, lagoons and coves along this coast are included, the distance stretches to about 2,000 miles. Historically, Texas was the top producer of redfish on the Gulf Coast and second only to Florida in its speckled trout harvest, until the late 1970s and early 1980s, when a coalition that included sport fishermen, recreational industry members and the state's own wildlife and fisheries agency convinced the state Legislature to make redfish and trout gamefish.

The major players responsible for the enactment of that precedent-setting legislation continue to pressure other coastal states to "come in line" and adopt the same policy. Since they are meeting with success, and since this policy quickly led to the downfall of the commercial finfishermen of Texas, this book about Louisiana's finfishermen begins in the Lone Star State.

PART I

...and when they come to Austin they are listened to, but we poor devils, who have tried to supply Texas with fish, have no influence in any direction. We simply have to submit to what is put upon us, and the people of Texas do not know it.

The writer is making this statement to you in order that you may have some idea of the influence that is dominating the affairs of 6,000,000 citizens. Some day there is going to be a turn.

The words "recreation" and "future generations" have been propagandaed to such an extent that a lot of very fine people and others have begun to believe that God had no use for the hard working clerk or the man in the field, or the poor and lowly, or the hungry, a class of folks that must work all the time and cannot RECREATE, but must work under the burdens of the other class who are recreating; that God created all the good things in life for a favored class of folks. These folks with money and influence secure, through thoughtless legislation, favors that do not belong to them.

A big lot of folks have gone "hog wild crazy" on the subject of recreation.

    —C.W. Gibson,
     Corpus Christi fisherman,
     from a 1931 letter written to a
     Texas Senate committee

TEXAS GAMEFISH FIGHT

In 1887, while the Capitol of Texas was being built in Austin, a group of sport fishermen introduced a bill to prohibit the catching of redfish by commercial fishermen. They claimed that the fish were becoming depleted and endangered by the netters. Similar bills were presented in 1895, 1897, 1899, 1901, 1905, 1909...or, in nearly every one of the state's biennial legislative sessions.

In spite of the relentless sniping, the coastal finfishermen of Texas continued to harvest redfish and trout, enjoying the inevitable good years and enduring the bad. For well over a century they delivered their harvest to consumers in Houston and Dallas, Austin, San Antonio and Fort Worth, and as far inland as Lubbock, Amarillo and El Paso.

Through the years, laws and proclamations by the state did close up to 50 percent of the Texas coast to netting, according to a 1935 legislative committee report, "solely as a matter of expediency in order to settle the controversy and protect our commercial fisheries from being entirely exterminated through the political influence of a few wealthy citizens of the State." But it wasn't until the 1980s that the political climate in Texas finally enabled "a few wealthy citizens" to grab *all* the fish.

Nearly one thousand sport fishermen attended the victory celebration held at the Astro Village Ballroom in Houston. At the podium stood Senator O.H. "Ike" Harris and Representative Stan Schlueter, who had sponsored the sport fishermen's gamefish bills in the just-winding-down 1981 session.

As Harris raised a sheaf of legal-sized papers over his head, he shouted, "This is what you have been working for all these years. The governor signed it into law this afternoon!"

Rising as one, the sport fishermen shook the walls of the packed ballroom with their cheers. Hats flew into the air, the anglers hugged each other and, overcome with the emotion of it all, they cried.

Record high commercial landings preceded the ban on commerce in Texas redfish and trout. (Commercial landings are the number or poundage of fish unloaded at the docks by commercial fishermen.) Spotted seatrout landings in 1973 and 1974 approached two million pounds for the first time since the 1930s. In 1975 and 1976, redfish landings exceeded two million pounds for the first time since record-keeping began in 1887.

Not everyone was thrilled with the fishermen's success.

Galveston Senator A.R. "Babe" Schwartz, declaring that red drum stocks were in an emergency condition, called on Texas Parks and Wildlife Department biologist Howard Lee to draw up a bill that would include a total ban on the commercial harvest of red drum. Lee, however, could not comply with the request, he said, because he did not have the data to indicate that such a ban was necessary.

Following Sen. Schwartz's call for action on red drum, the Texas Parks and Wildlife Commission, which was responsible for directing policy within the Texas Parks and Wildlife Department, promoted Robert Kemp to director of fisheries, the first to be given supervisory powers over both the inland and coastal fisheries branches of TPWD.

An avid sport fisherman, Kemp had first been employed by TPWD in about 1950, as a freshwater fishery biologist. He was appointed assistant director of coastal fisheries in the mid-1950s but left the department a few years later to start a consulting business. Kemp was rehired in the early 1960s; prior to returning to TPWD, he had been selling insurance.

Kemp had maintained as early as 1957 that red drum was a threatened species. In a *Houston Post* article at that time he was quoted as saying, "It's time for Texas to quit closing its eyes to the cold fact that the redfish is almost a vanishing species on our coast."

As director of fisheries, Kemp soon began to push for tighter restrictions on the harvest of red drum, compelling Lee, who had himself been director of coastal fisheries from 1957 to 1961, to resign. Lee could not agree with Kemp and the commission, who he claimed were acting too hastily on a commercial ban without proper biological evidence.

According to a biologist who had been with Texas Parks and Wildlife at that time, Lee was not the only biologist who left after Kemp's promotion: "Kemp's first order of business was to purge the department. You were either pressured or forced to resign or if you didn't, minor charges were brought against you and you were fired. Besides Lee, three other employees who were prominent in redfish work left the department because of Kemp. Another, Ernest Simmons, who had more than 20 years of experience working on trout and redfish, was apparently too popular to fire. He was transferred from the coast to Austin to head freshwater fisheries."

By 1977, Kemp was able to produce the data that indicated that red drum populations were declining in all eight of the major bay systems of Texas, and that the decline was particularly noticeable in those bays still open to commercial net fishing. According to TPWD, redfish were showing classic signs of overharvest, such as a decline in their average age and an accelerated growth rate, as well as a decline in the numbers of fish caught by sport fishermen and in nets set by TPWD biologists. These data formed the basis for restrictions imposed by the 1977 Legislature.

Introduced by Sen. Schwartz, Senate Bill 624, which came to be known as the Red Drum Conservation Act of 1977, was a compromise from the ban on commercial fishing that was originally sought, and imposed restrictions on both commercial and recreational fishermen. A special red drum license of $50 was required for anyone taking reds commercially; to obtain a license a fisherman had to prove that at least 50 percent of his income came from such fishing. The new law limited finfishermen to no more than 200 pounds of redfish per day per boat. It also established an industrywide quota of 1.4 million pounds; when 90 percent of the quota was landed, the fishery was to be shut down until the following year. SB 624 also prohibited nets and trotlines[1] in the Galveston Bay system on weekends from Memorial Day through Labor Day. Daily bag limits for sport fishermen were established at 10 redfish per day.

The commercial fishing sector's outcry was immediate. The fishermen questioned the data that suggested the resource was declining. They claimed that they, themselves, were catching plenty of fish. After all, 1975 had marked an all-time record harvest for them and that of 1976 was a close second. They also regarded the daily quotas with considerable trepidation, explaining that there were many days when conditions did not allow them to even go fishing; when that day of 500 or 1,000 pounds did come along, they had to take advantage of it, to keep their operations profitable.

On the other side, sport fishermen cited the record high landings by commercial fishermen as additional proof that they were overharvesting the resource. They also suggested that the newly enacted law was not strong enough, that it would not adequately reduce the commercial harvest, or the growing problem of illegal fishing.

As more and more restrictions were imposed on the commercial fishermen, illegal fishing for red drum and trout increased in many areas along the Texas coast.[2] When, for instance, a fisherman's traditional territory was suddenly proclaimed as an area to be closed to netting but left open to recreational fishing, or when he was banned from pursuing his livelihood on the weekends in order that recreationists might better enjoy themselves, he felt he was being treated unfairly. The rough-and-tumble Texas fisherman, who had learned his trade from his father, felt that it was his God-given right to fish. In the context of the long history of closures, reopenings and reclosures, he tended to view additional restrictions that favored recreation over food production as impermant, if not frivolous. Many fishermen felt justified in simply ignoring the law and continuing to fish.

But their acts of civil disobedience against increasing regulation worked against them—Parks and Wildlife game wardens seized more of their gear.

Apprehensive and resentful over the fishermen's record harvests, and convinced that the netters would continue to disobey the law, a growing number of sport fishermen began to feel that some more stringent—and enforceable—measure was needed to reduce the red drum harvest and put an end to illegal commercial red drum fishing. That measure was to put an end to *all* commercial red drum fishing.

Though sport-fishing interests in Texas were already represented by several regional groups, these disgruntled anglers realized that they needed a stronger, more cohesive organization to exert the kind of pressure on the Legislature that they would need.

According to a 1981 *Field & Stream* article, "Winning the War on Netters": "In early March of 1977, a group of about twenty sportsmen, some wealthy and some not, met in Schero's Sporting Goods Store in Houston. They were convinced that excessive commercial fishing was killing sport fishing in Texas bays, and they determined to do something for the trout and redfish in much the same manner Ducks Unlimited[3] had done things for ducks. They named their group the Gulf Coast Conservation Association."

Walter W. Fondren, III, a Houston oil executive and EXXON heir was chosen to serve as chairman of GCCA's executive committee.[4] The committee included co-founder Perry R. Bass, a Fort Worth oilman/magnate.[5] Houston investor David Cummings served as GCCA president, and insurance magnate Clyde Hanks as GCCA vice president. Houston sport fisherman H.A. "Dusty" Rhodes served as dollar-a-year executive director.

GCCA had organized in time to assist in the passage of the Red Drum Conservation Act of 1977, which began to earn the group widespread recognition among the state's saltwater sport-fishing community. During the following winter, a few commercial fishermen played right into the budding GCCA's hand. Or, more accurately, its pocketbook.

"That's what got the fishin' closed, right there," declared a shrimper from the Galveston Bay fishing village of Smith Point, as he pointed to his photo album. The color snapshots showed heaps of speckled trout, piled knee-deep over the back deck of his trawl boat.

"That was back in February of '78 and it was super cold out there.

14

It'd been freezin' for three days and three nights and the fish were cold shocked. We was draggin' them deep holes right there in Galveston Bay.

"We'd go out in the evening, make one drag, dump it on the deck and just drop the anchor. The next mornin' we'd make one drag and go into the fishhouse and unload 'em. We sold 'em in the rough for 65 cents a pound. In three days' time we had a little over 12,000 pounds.

"There was only a handful of shrimp boats doin' it but then the sportsmen found out about it and they thought we overkilled the fish."

That "the sportsmen found out about it" was a Texas-sized understatement. The market was glutted to the point that Galveston fishhouses ran advertisements in newspapers urging locals to take advantage of the low prices by filling their deep freezes. The graven images of "their" trout killed by the shrimp trawlers and stacked like cordwood at the fishhouses infuriated sportsmen.

By the following spring, they were pointing to the highly visible "trout massacre" by the handful of Galveston Bay trawlers as a prime example of the "short-sighted greed" characteristic of *all* commercial fishermen. Momentum had been building steadily since the mid-1970s for a ban on the commercial harvest of redfish. After the "trout massacre," support for the proposed ban took a quantum leap. And now the ban was to include the spotted seatrout.

Sportsmen smelled blood and in a frenzy rushed to join GCCA at a minimum membership fee of $10, with special sponsoring memberships going for as much as $1,000. GCCA's first fund-raising dinner in May 1978 produced $120,000.

Galveston Bay trawlers with spotted seatrout in the 1920s

As the 1979 legislative session approached, GCCA had solidified into a politically strong organization and was prepared to return to the Capitol to lobby for even stricter measures on red drum and spotted seatrout. However, Texas Parks and Wildlife Commissioner Pearce Johnson urged J.C. Harlan, president of the Rockport-based Seafood Producers Association, to encourage his group to work with GCCA to try to resolve problems in the coastal area. SPA and GCCA did work together to combat illegal fishing by both recreational and commercial fishermen and, along with the Texas Shrimp Association, drafted resolutions to submit to Texas Parks and Wildlife, which would hopefully transform them into bills for the upcoming session.

One of the resolutions, to impose a first-ever 12-inch minimum size limit and a daily bag limit of 20 fish on spotted seatrout anglers, did not need legislative approval and was adopted by Texas Parks and Wildlife in December 1978. The measure was projected to reduce the poundage of trout pulled out of the water by recreationals by about 9 percent.

Another of their bills, introduced by Sen. Schwartz, called for a prohibition on trawling for redfish and trout during the wintertime. Trawling for fish during the wintertime had been perfectly legal; indeed fishermen had dragged Galveston Bay since the 1920s, if not before. But, with the massacre of '78, the fishery had clearly come to be regarded as "too efficient" for the inshore harvest of the coveted trout and redfish. The practice was easily banned.

The inshore finfishermen, who fished primarily with gill nets, trammel nets and trotlines, were subjected to no further restrictions in the 1979 session. As the Texas Parks and Wildlife Department delivered its annual report before the Legislature, however, it became clear that this session was only the calm before an approaching storm.

Commercial landings of redfish had fallen from the record of 2.1

million pounds in 1975 to 951,000 pounds in 1977, and then to 861,000 pounds in 1978. In addition to this 60 percent decline in commercial landings, Texas Parks and Wildlife demonstrated a steady decline in the success rate of sport fishermen since 1974. According to TPWD surveys, in 1978, it took a rod-and-reeler 50 hours of fishing to catch one redfish—80 percent longer than it did in 1974. It took an angler five hours to catch one speckled trout—45 percent longer than it had taken four years earlier. Aggravating the problem of less fish, was the fact that the numbers of recreational and commercial fishermen pursuing red drum and spotted seatrout had increased significantly and, the report concluded, major restrictions on the harvest of these two fisheries had to be considered if populations were to be maintained.

On June 6, 1979, TPWD fisheries chief Robert Kemp, addressing the newly-formed San Antonio chapter of GCCA, suggested the form that these "major restrictions" might take:

"Simply stated, there are too many people fishing a depleted resource. There no longer are, or will be again in my opinion, enough trout and redfish to meet the demands of both the commercial finfish industry and the tourist and recreational fishing industry. The solution is simple and logical. We should continue to allocate all the shrimp and the crabs and the oysters to the commercial fishing industry. These resources are a value to this state at more than $145 million annually. The shellfish make up more than 98 percent of the commercial fishing business. But we should then allocate the trout and redfish to the tourist and recreation industry. It's valued at $300 million annually. And, ladies and gentlemen, there's no other solution."

This was the first time an economic argument was used to justify the allocation of all Texas redfish and spotted seatrout to the recreational fishing industry.[6] Furthermore, by stating in public that he was in favor of a commercial ban on redfish and trout, Kemp put everyone on notice that the state's own fishery agency had picked sides in the gamefish conflict.

Commercial interests reacted immediately by attempting to remove him from his job.

The Texas Parks and Wildlife Commission, however, stood behind its man. The commission consisted of six members, appointed by the governor. Each member served a term of six years; terms were staggered which, ostensibly, reduced the political influence of a single governor and the special interests which backed him. Every other year, the governor designated one of the six members as chairman of the commission for a two-year term. The commission, in turn, appointed an executive director who served as the chief executive officer of the Texas Parks and Wildlife Department. The executive director's responsibilities included the appointment of division heads, law enforcement officers, park managers and all other employees. These employees, including the director of fisheries, served at the will of the executive director.

Gov. Dolph Briscoe, in 1977, had appointed Perry Bass to the commission. Though he resigned from GCCA's board of directors, Bass continued to support the group's political aims—with a $1,000 contribution in 1982, for example. In addition to Bass, the Texas Parks and Wildlife Commission in 1979 included Pearce Johnson, an Austin automobile dealer; John Green, a Beaumont oilman; Louis Stumberg, a wealthy San Antonio heir who traveled the world hunting and fishing; James Paxton of Palestine and Joe Fulton of Lubbock.[7]

"We've never had a commissioner on Parks and Wildlife that was a fisherman, or even related to the commercial fishing industry," explained commercial fisherman Bill Templeton, of Sargent. "These are political appointments and we've just never been strong enough politically—or rich enough—to get an appointment."

After two years of working with the Seafood Producers Association and the Texas Shrimp Association—and with Texas Parks and Wildlife squarely in their corner—GCCA leadership concluded that existing laws were ineffective in curtailing "overharvest" of redfish and trout. The consensus of the group was that commercial fishermen were not going to obey the laws or fully report their catches.

The industrywide commercial quota of 1.4 million pounds of redfish established by the Red Drum Conservation Act was broken down into nine regional quotas, one for each of the eight major bay systems and another for fish caught in the Gulf. When each quota was reached, that region was to be closed to fishing. But, due to extensive non-reporting of catch, none of the quotas was ever reached.

Consequently, GCCA leaders claimed that they could not depend on the fishermen to comply with regulations. The only solution remaining, they said, was to seek a total ban on the commercial harvest of red drum by eliminating the market for the species in Texas.

Originally, GCCA was a volunteer organization, but in 1980 it hired Richard Ingram, an Austin attorney working the state capitol for the Texas Municipal League, to replace Dusty Rhodes as executive director. Ingram, who commanded an annual salary of $50,000, was put in charge of a $500,000-a-year lobbying operation with five full-time staffers.

The same year, GCCA outlined the essentials of a bill that would address the issue of protecting the redfish and trout from "overharvest" by commercial netters.

The Texas Parks and Wildlife Department assisted GCCA in

designing a bill that the agency could fully support. Bob Kemp assisted in questions regarding the basis for the ban, statistician Gary Matlock assisted with biological analyses of the fish populations, and Chester Burdett, Chief of the TPWD Law Enforcement Division, addressed questions on the bill's enforceability. Although they drew up various drafts, each contained the same essential provision: Gamefish status for red drum and spotted seatrout.

The goal was to have their bills ready for the next legislative session, scheduled to convene in early 1981. In the meantime, the commission began to heat up the issue.

During the summer of 1980, it took "gamefish" on the road, holding several hearings across the Texas coast. The hearings addressed a series of regulations that the commission was authorized to enact on its own. Of the proposed regulations, the most controversial were a ban on the use of monofilament in commercial fishing nets and the classification of nine species of saltwater fish as gamefish.

In addition to red drum and spotted seatrout, these included striped bass, snook, tarpon, sailfish, blue marlin, white marlin and wahoo. The designation of gamefish by proclamation of the commission was not sufficient to take these fish off the market—a legislative mandate was required to ban the commercial harvest of a saltwater species of fish. Yet, the classification of these nine species as gamefish, if only in name, demonstrated to all that Texas Parks and Wildlife supported the concept.

At each hearing, advocates of the proposed regulations voiced their arguments, which mirrored Kemp's earlier statements, and those made in a July/August 1980 article in GCCA's publication, *Tide*, entitled "Gamefish status for redfish and speckled trout in Texas—why it should be established."

Those arguments were:

• TPWD data showed a significant decline in the populations of redfish and trout.

• TPWD figures showed a significant increase in the number of illegal nets that were being confiscated.

• There was an inability to control illegal fishing.

• Sport fishermen contributed more to the economy of the state than did commercial finfishermen.

• Finfish comprised only a small percentage of the commercial fishing industry.

• Of the finfish consumed by Texans, only a small percentage was red drum or spotted seatrout.

Commercial fishermen spoke up against the proposed restrictions at the hearings, but industry members did not do much to oppose the proclamations because they felt that it would be a waste of time and money. Texas Parks and Wildlife was simply carrying on its tradition of attempting to regulate the commercial fishermen out of existence while catering to the sport fishermen's whims, said fishermen. The agency had not listened to their concerns in the past and if the commissioners wanted to establish a regulation, they would, despite the commercial fishermen's objections.

The fishermen were right. The commission adopted the proposed proclamations. Not only did the new restrictions exacerbate the ill feelings between commercial and recreational fishermen, and between commercial fishermen and Texas Parks and Wildlife, they set the stage for increased illegal fishing.

A substantial amount of illegal netting already had been reported by TPWD law enforcement officers before the imposition of this latest round of restrictions. Between September 1978 and February 1979, game wardens claimed to have confiscated over 420,00 feet of gear from bays that had been closed to commercial fishing. With the ban on monofilament, more was to come.

Before monofilament webbing was introduced in 1960, fishermen used nets constructed of braided nylon. Made of clear plastic strands, "mono" nets are far lighter in weight, less susceptible to damage by crabs, and somewhat more difficult for fish to detect than nets constructed of nylon. The new technology caught on quickly among fishermen.

When the Texas Parks and Wildlife Commission banned monofilament nets, many commercial fishermen were faced with a loss of their investment. Since their netting was no longer legal, they reasoned, it didn't matter if it was confiscated. Those fishermen who were determined to ignore such regulations as weekend closures and baywide closures merely set out their nets at night and picked them up at dawn, harvesting fish until enforcement agents either caught them in the act or confiscated their gear.

The subsequent increase in the amount of illegal netting that TPWD law enforcement officers confiscated indicated that "overharvest" was also a law enforcement problem. This provided fuel to GCCA's argument that the only way to stop the illegal fishermen—who were rapidly becoming synonymous with *all* fishermen—was to kill the market for redfish.

At the same time GCCA was organizing the sport fishermen, commercial fishing interests, led by wholesalers and retailers, realized that the fishing industry needed to organize as well.

Commercial fishermen typically are highly separated from one coastal location to another. Isolated in their own remote coastal

GCCA's ad campaign implied that redfish were threatened with extinction if commercial fishing were not halted.

communities, the fishermen come to think of the surrounding waters as their own territory and regard intruders with suspicion. The fishermen's clannishness, combined with their highly independent nature, made the task of uniting the 14 already existing organizations under one banner a formidable one.

But in what was seen as an unprecedented and, say fishermen, a never-to-be-repeated accomplishment—they did it. The new group adopted the acronym PISCES, standing for the unwieldy, "Political Involvement of Seafood Concerned Enterprises."

By early 1981, GCCA boasted 7,000 dues-paying members and 30,000 affiliate members in other sportsmen's groups. Six satellite chapters, each with its own fund-raising dinners, helped fill the organization's coffers.

Fired up to an almost religious zeal, members signed new members and raised more money. All along the coast, bright red T-shirts, caps and windbreakers bearing the inscription, "Save The Redfish," were in evidence. Telegrams and letters with the same message poured into the offices of legislators.

Newspaper ads, some of which showed piles of dead fish in nets, carried headlines such as the ironic, "They Are Stealing Your Fish." One ad, illustrated by a fish skeleton above a tombstone framed by a boy's hand clasping his father's, was headlined, "DADDY, WHAT'S A REDFISH?"

Sport fishermen began to speak of the redfish as if it were the bison or passenger pigeon of the bays.

"Anyone who was not a fisherman would have believed the propaganda put out by GCCA," said Bo Cunningham, PISCES president and a wholesale seafood dealer from Seadrift. "It was real emotional, and it cost them a lot of money."[8]

As support mounted for GCCA's proposed ban on commercial fishing for red drum and trout, PISCES began to fight back. Its initial strategy was to attempt to remove key legislators who supported the ban.

During the re-election campaigns of 1980, Houston Rep. Gene Jones joined with Galveston Sen. Babe Schwartz on the red drum issue. They were quoted as taking a stand "to save redfish and trout for future generations by stopping those greedy netters."

Schwartz had sponsored the Red Drum Conservation Act of 1977, and he and Jones would likely be sponsoring GCCA's gamefish legislation in the upcoming session. If commercial finfishing was to stand a chance during the 1981 Legislature, these two politicians had to go.

PISCES actively campaigned against Schwartz and Jones, both of whom represented coastal districts. GCCA retaliated by mounting a campaign to rally sport-fishing voters behind the pair.

Whether because of the efforts of PISCES, or the Republican sweep of the 1980 election, voters rejected both Schwartz and Jones. A Democrat who had been in the Senate for years and who had chaired various committees, Schwartz was no friend of the fishermen. His upset by Buster Brown, an unknown whom the fishermen had strongly supported, was particularly sweet.

GCCA leaders were forced to seek new sponsors for their gamefish bills, whom they found in Sen. Ike Harris, a Dallas attorney, and Rep. Stan Schlueter, a rancher and builder from Salado, nearly 50 miles north of Austin.

During the 1980 campaign, SPORT-PAC, GCCA's political action committee, reported spending a total of $86,462 on 134 contenders for the 150-member Texas House and 32 candidates for the 31-

member Senate. In the House, 118 of GCCA's supported candidates won; in the Senate, 27 of its candidates were elected.

In contrast, PISCES spent only $6,900 for political purposes. "You can't fight money with peanuts, and that's all we had," lamented Bo Cunningham, explaining that the recent cascade of restrictions on their harvest—such as the Red Drum Conservation Act—had financially crippled fishermen.

All eight of the House candidates whom the commercial fishermen backed were elected; of the four Senate candidates whom PISCES supported, two were winners.

GCCA's contributions caught the attention of legislators, but even if the senators and the representatives went along with their plan, would the governor thwart their efforts with a veto?

"No way," assured Gov. William P. Clements.[9]

Clements, at a press conference and on television, told reporters that he had discussed GCCA's gamefish bill "by the hour with Texas Parks and Wildlife people" and "studied it extensively over the last six months." Clements said that he backed TPWD in its support of the bill and, if the Legislature passed it, he'd sign it.

The stage was set and in mid-February, Texas Parks and Wildlife and the Gulf Coast Conservation Association went to the Capitol to outlaw the commercial taking of redfish and trout.

On February 16, 1981, Sen. Harris introduced Senate Bill 139 before the Senate Natural Resources Committee and nearly 400 other people gathered on the floor and in the gallery of the chamber. The bill called for a total ban on commerce in red drum and spotted seatrout in Texas.

Testimony at this hearing was limited to those in support of SB 139. Texas Parks and Wildlife Department witnesses for the bill included fisheries chief Robert Kemp and Frank Dickerson. Dickerson was the law enforcement officer for Region 10, which includes Corpus Christi and the Laguna Madre.

Kemp testified that the ban on commercial fishing was necessary because the recent attempts by the commission and the Legislature to reduce fishing pressure on fish populations had not worked. These attempts included the Red Drum Conservation Act of 1977, the prohibition of the use of nets and trotlines on weekends, size and bag limits on red drum and spotted seatrout for recreational fishermen, closure of areas to the use of nets—such as the Laguna Madre—and the prohibition of the use of monofilament nets.

When new regulations were enacted, said Kemp, outlaw netters invariably stepped in to fill the gap left by the legitimate fishermen. (This point would be driven home a few weeks later when TPWD game wardens picked up over 18,000 feet of webbing in the lower Laguna Madre.)

The only way to eliminate this illegal harvest, stated Kemp, was to take away the fishermen's profit motive.

Kemp went on to state that the problem of uncontrolled commercial fishing was compounded by the rapid shift of human populations to coastal areas. He presented census data for 1980 that provided evidence that the population along the Texas coast had increased from approximately 2 million in 1950 to more than 4.5 million people. From this increase, Kemp projected that the numbers of recreational fishermen would increase from 800,000 to more than 1.15 million by the year 2000. Consequently, the recreational fishing effort would increase approximately 50 percent.

These recreational fishermen should be allocated all of the fish, said Kemp, because the public interest is aligned primarily with that of the recreational industry, not with that of the commercial fisherman or the consumer. He advanced this contention on the basis that recreational fishermen, who outnumbered commercial fishermen 800-to-one, spent far more money—on such items as suntan lotion, gasoline and beer—than commercial fishermen generated by selling their fish to consumers.

Kemp's conclusion to his testimony was succinct: "To put it all very bluntly, there are simply no longer enough fish on the Texas Coast to supply the demands placed on them. If we're going to maintain a fishery for trout and redfish, the only viable alternative is to prohibit the sale of those species."

After Kemp, Dick Ingram presented testimony for GCCA, and several recreational fishermen, representing themselves, testified in favor of the bill, saying that they simply were not catching the numbers of fish that they once did.

The following week, on February 25, commercial fishermen filled the Senate chamber, and it was definitely their day in Austin. Committee chairman Tati Santiesteban of El Paso was forced to halt testimony with more than 225 people still on the witness list against the bill.

Committee members heard from biologists refuting TPWD's claim that netting was to blame for the decline in numbers of redfish and trout; they heard seafood wholesalers and restaurateurs refute the department's claim that reds and specks were unimportant to their business; and they heard poignant testimony from the fishermen and their families who said they knew of no other way to make a living for their families, and who asked why bread should be taken from the mouths of their children so wealthy sportsmen might catch a few more fish.

Expert witnesses for the commercial fishermen included Richard

A. Frank, administrator of the National Oceanic and Atmospheric Administration[10] between 1977 and 1981, and Corpus Christi biologist Dr. Henry Hildebrand.

Fifteen separate organizations representing commercial interests presented testimony during the initial hearings on the ban. PISCES was represented by president Bo Cunningham; Pat Pace, owner of Pace Fish Company in Brownsville; and Houston chapter president Jim Tarr. Although private restaurant owners presented testimony in opposition to the bill, the powerful Texas Restaurant Association was not represented.

In his testimony Cunningham detailed some of the reasons why commercial fishermen and commercial fishing interests had lost faith in the ability of TPWD to consider them fairly in the management of coastal finfish. Responding to the question of why the commercials would not report their catches, Cunningham stated that it was "for the simple fact that every time that we have tried to cooperate with Parks and Wildlife they have used those figures against us...they don't turn in their statistics accurately."

Revealing the commercial industry's deep-seated animosity toward the Texas Parks and Wildlife Commission, he went on: "Until that time that we have a commission that isn't appointed by the governor, of ranchers, oil people and bankers—nobody that represents the commercial fishing industry—they have to go on the recommendations of men like Mr. Kemp....We'll fight TPWD regulations until the day we die. We're not going to have Parks and Wildlife regulate anything if we can help it."

Cunningham said SB 139 was not actually designed to protect red drum and spotted seatrout but rather to eliminate gill nets, "which Texas Parks and Wildlife has been trying to do for a long time."

Richard Frank's main point to the Natural Resources Committee was one of economics. Many sectors of the fishing industry in the United States were having, or would soon be having, critical financial problems, said Frank. In many cases, this would end in bankruptcies and reductions in the sizes of fleets, processing facilities and ancillary industries. He suggested that closure of the red drum and trout fisheries in Texas would have a significant adverse economic impact in the region, particularly because it would occur at a time when other fisheries, like shrimp, were already experiencing economic losses. Closing the finfishermen down would only exacerbate this situation, warned Frank.

If the legislators believed that further limitations were necessary, he suggested that they should consider less onerous limitations that would not cause an economic sector of the state to go bankrupt.

Field biologist Henry Hildebrand specialized in estuarine biology. Formerly a professor of biology at Texas A&I University (now Texas A&M at Kingsville), Hildebrand had studied coastal fisheries in the western Gulf of Mexico since the 1950s. He explained to the senators that fishery harvests, like agricultural harvests, fluctuate according to climatic conditions. Pointing to a chart that showed poor catches in the 1950s and record-high catches during the 1970s, he explained:

"These figures for the '50s are indicative of low populations and Mr. Kemp was saying then that if commercial fishing was not stopped, the catches would never go up....Yet the 1970s decade shows a record harvest....The reason for most of the fluctuations in fish yield is clearly related to the ever-changing environmental scene in South Texas. Mr. Kemp apparently doesn't believe in any climatic influence—at least he emphatically states that the ups and downs are due to overfishing."

Hildebrand had studied marine life in the Texan and Mexican Lagunas since 1950. In 1951, he and another biologist pioneered studies on the effect of rainfall on shrimp populations. During the hearing, he attempted to explain how just one environmental factor—rainfall—could influence the harvest of redfish.

The Texas coast is paralleled by a string of elongate barrier islands, Hildebrand explained. The waters between form a group of bay systems. Gulf waters enter the eight bays of Texas through passes and, once inside, come under the influence of rainfall and inflow from inland rivers. Abundant rainfall dilutes the seawater within the semi-enclosed bays, creating a haven for estuarine species like redfish and trout.

Nowhere is rainfall more important than in the Laguna Madre, which typically produced more than half of the entire state's commercially landed redfish.

Lying inshore of Padre Island, the Laguna is a particularly insulated habitat that runs nearly 120 miles, from Corpus Christi south to Brownsville. Not only is rainfall scarce, but there are no significant inland streams to feed this bay with fresh water. And the South Texas heat increases its rate of evaporation.

The Laguna is a curiosity that hydrologists call a hypersaline lagoon, a place where salinities can exceed those of sea water. There are four similar sites on earth: the Laguna Madre of Tamaulipas in Mexico; the Mar Chica, in Morocco; the Zaliv Kara Bogaz Gol, in the Caspian Sea; and the Sea of Azov in the Black Sea.

Commercial fishermen working the Laguna Madre had long noted that redfish catches increased following rainy spells and hurricanes, but declined during droughts such as had occurred during the 1950s. The reason, according to Hildebrand, was clear.

Juvenile redfish function best at salinity levels of about 25 parts per thousand. Seawater is about 35 ppt but, during dry spells, counts in the Laguna Madre sometimes reach 75 ppt. Without rain, the Texas coast—and especially the Laguna Madre—becomes not a haven for redfish but a hostile environment.

So they get out, and commercial landings decline.

Other researchers—including several on the state's payroll—had even more convincing data than Hildebrand's. In 1979, for example, hydrologists and biologists for the Texas Department of Water Resources quantified the relationship of freshwater inflows to fish populations. They found a 90 percent correlation between commercial redfish landings and freshwater inflow in the lower Laguna Madre. Yet no one called them to testify.

Because it relied on TPWD for information, the Legislature never learned that most biologists familiar with the controversy took Hildebrand's salinity thesis seriously—and believed that the proposed ban was unwarranted.

In closing discussion on the bill, Sen. Harris noted the discrepancies between the scientific data offered by those witnesses who opposed SB 139, and that offered by TPWD. The senators would just have to choose whom to believe, he said, while keeping in mind that "The Parks and Wildlife Department is our agency set up to advise us on these matters, and in this instance I find it very easy to believe them."

But the committee did not. Instead, it voted to refer the gamefish bill to a subcommittee for further study, which only lengthened the long road it had to travel before becoming law.

Cheers and applause erupted in the packed committee room when spectators realized that the "Redfish Bill" was not going to make it out of committee.

Fishermen left the hearing in a confident mood.

During the following Senate committee hearing of March 11, Sen. Bob Vale introduced a compromise bill that would allow fishermen to continue bringing in reds and specks but which also increased penalties for fishing infractions. Vale, a San Antonio attorney, said people who package and market the fish had told him that SB 139 would harm the seafood industry. "There are a lot of sports fishermen, but there are also a lot of consumers we have to look out for," he remarked.

The committee adopted Vale's substitute bill, which remained pending until the next Senate committee hearing, scheduled for April 8, nearly a month later.

While the Senate was taking its recess from hearings on proposed red drum legislation, the Environmental Affairs Committee of the House of Representatives—the equivalent to the Senate's Natural Resources Committee—took up the gamefish issue. On March 16, with the Senate version of the "Redfish Bill" still bottled up in committee, state Rep. Stan Schlueter introduced House Bill 1000. His bill was identical to SB 139, but with three amendments.

Rep. Hugo Berlanga, a Corpus Christi banker, offered one amendment that called for the removal of the "gamefish" designation from the bill. It would still be illegal to sell redfish and trout but, by not formally classifying them as gamefish, Berlanga's amendment indicated that the commercial ban was not necessarily permanent.

Another amendment to Schlueter's bill would continue to allow redfish and trout to be imported into Texas. (SB 139 prohibited *all* commerce in these fish within the state.)

These amendments were seen as a compromise between the bill's supporters and the Texas Restaurant Association.

In the past, the restaurant lobby had proven a formidable opponent to proposed fishing limitations. According to an article in *Practicing Texas Politics*, GCCA had taken note of this opposition:

> GCCA was instrumental in preparing bills to be used for bartering purposes in 1981. These barter bills would be pushed if leverage were needed to pass GCCA's bills. Several bills that would be costly to the restaurant business were introduced at the beginning of the 67th session. One bill proposed a truth-in-menu law for Texas. The lack of such a regulation allows restaurants to advertise fresh seatrout when, in fact, they might be serving once-frozen haddock or cod from New England. A truth-in-menu law would hurt many restaurants that claim to have, or allude to serving, freshly caught local fish. Another bill that threatened the restaurant business proposed eliminating tips as part of the minimum wage, thus forcing restaurant proprietors to pay the entire minimum wage while allowing employees to pocket their tips. Such a law could more than double the payroll of many restaurants.

The board of TRA had voted to oppose the original fishing and import ban, but once HB 1000 was amended to permit restaurants and fish markets to sell imported trout and redfish, its lobbyists thought prudence was the better course.

The group's membership was split on the issue, however. According to a 1983 *Texas Monthly* article on the gamefish controversy, "Traditionally redfish are the crown of coastal cookery, and in cities like Austin and Houston, restaurants have elevated them to delicacy status with dishes of fancy name: Redfish Fulton Beach, Redfish Bar

TEXAS SPOTTED SEATROUT
Historical commercial landings [a]

YEAR	POUNDS	YEAR	POUNDS
1887	941,000	1960	1,283,000
1888	872,000	1961	1,117,000
1889	1,077,000	1962	989,000
1890	1,120,000	1963	1,190,000
1897	1,012,000	1964	978,000
1902	1,119,000	1965	1,176,000
1908	1,055,000	1966	1,508,000
1918	1,613,000	1967	1,565,000
1923	1,524,000	1968	1,891,000
1927	1,700,000	1969	1,191,000
1928	1,160,000	1970	1,158,000
1929	1,178,000	1971	1,489,000
1930	1,043,000	1972	1,519,000
1931	1,084,000	1973	1,975,000
1932	976,000	1974	1,997,000
1934	2,462,000	1975	1,829,000
1936	1,836,000	1976	1,814,000
1937	2,109,000	1977	1,353,000
1938	2,083,000	1978	1,164,000
1939	1,485,000	1979	1,040,000
1940	755,000	1980	980,000
1945	1,720,000	1981	681,000 [b]
1948	593,000	1982	0
1949	630,000	1983	0
1950	584,000	1984	0
1951	434,000	1985	0
1952	479,000	1986	0
1953	585,000	1987	0
1954	670,000	1988	0
1955	843,000	1989	0
1956	835,000	1990	0
1957	899,000	1991	0
1958	1,158,000	1992	0
1959	1,109,000	1993	0

[a] *Includes some white trout*

[b] *Fishing curtailed September 1*

TEXAS RED DRUM

Historical commercial landings

YEAR	POUNDS	YEAR	POUNDS
1887	1,005,000	1960	705,000
1888	944,000	1961	617,000
1889	1,063,000	1962	699,000
1890	1,108,000	1963	685,000
1897	1,144,000	1964	447,000
1902	898,000	1965	533,000
1908	1,309,000	1966	797,000
1918	1,337,000	1967	768,000
1923	878,000	1968	925,000
1927	1,248,000	1969	1,085,000
1928	1,030,000	1970	1,586,000
1929	934,000	1971	1,991,000
1930	873,000	1972	1,468,000
1931	864,000	1973	1,678,000
1932	825,000	1974	1,921,000
1934	1,579,000	1975	2,120,000
1936	956,000	1976	2,029,000
1937	954,000	1977	951,000
1938	860,000	1978	861,000
1939	470,000	1979	690,000
1940	265,000	1980	1,114,000
1945	1,297,000	1981	613,000 [a]
1948	621,000	1982	0
1949	520,000	1983	0
1950	567,000	1984	0
1951	237,000	1985	0
1952	250,000	1986	0
1953	511,000	1987	0
1954	721,000	1988	0
1955	494,000	1989	0
1956	641,000	1990	0
1957	504,000	1991	0
1958	599,000	1992	0
1959	963,000	1993	0

[a] Fishing curtailed September 1

Catalan, Redfish al Basilico."

Even if importation of redfish were permitted, owners of many of these restaurants were concerned about the increase in price and the decrease in quality that they expected would accompany the importation of red drum and spotted seatrout from Louisiana, Florida or the Carolinas. Tom Gilliland, owner of Atlantis Restaurant in Austin and board member of the TRA, formed a new organization that supported the view that the basis for the ban was unfounded.

During the March 16 hearing, Gilliland testified on behalf of both the TRA and Save our Seafood in opposition to HB 1000 and SB 139, which he called the "Stinker Bill." He stated that the groups supported the Vale substitute for SB 139, which would allow fishing to continue but increase penalties and enforcement. Of all the bills pending, said Gilliland, both TRA and SOS preferred the complete moratorium offered by Deer Park Rep. Ed Watson.

Watson's HB 980 called for a total ban on the landing of redfish and speckled trout by *both* commercial and sport fishermen for a period of two years to let the allegedly declining species recover from the heavy fishing pressure. This measure was seen as one which supported conservation of the species on an equitable basis and would allow time "to collect and analyze data in depth so the correct legislation could be brought forward."

Watson's bill drew some support but was discouraged by a TPWD spokesman who testified that two years would not be long enough for the fish to "come back." The committee deferred to the new provisions of HB 1000, and killed Watson's bill on the spot.

After adding a third amendment that gave the Texas Parks and Wildlife Commission the authority to set seasons and bag limits for sport fishermen—who would continue to land redfish and speckled trout—the House Environmental Affairs Committee sent HB 1000 to a friendly five-member subcommittee.

During the March 16 hearing, most of the same people who had testified in the Senate also presented testimony in the House. PISCES, however, did not focus much lobbying effort in the House. With limited resources, the fishermen felt that their interests would be better served among the fewer members of the Senate.

Commercial representatives did use the hearing to call into question the data presented by Texas Parks and Wildlife.

To argue that redfish populations were tumbling, TPWD pointed to the decline in the commercial harvest, from 1975 through 1979.

Hildebrand and other critics of the state agency countered that such a short time-frame was insufficient to account for long-term cycles in fish populations.[11]

They also pointed out that one of the state's most productive redfish grounds—the Laguna Madre—had been declared off-limits to fishermen. And the Legislature in 1977 and then the Texas Parks and Wildlife Commission in 1980 had severely reduced the time that fishermen could work, and the amount of fish that they could land. These factors alone could account for the decline in landings, said Hildebrand.

Commercial representatives also challenged TPWD data that indicated that commercial fishermen alone were responsible for "overfishing."

Commercial landings data are gathered from the records of fishhouses, which purchase fish from the fishermen. Recreational landings—the number or poundage of fish brought ashore by sport fishermen for their personal use—are determined by a less direct method. In "creel" or "intercept surveys," sport fishermen are interviewed as they return from their trips. The results are then extrapolated to gain an estimate of the total number of fish landed by all sport fishermen.

The federal National Marine Fisheries Service assembles this data each year in most coastal states. With its 1975 commitment to develop sport fishing, Texas Parks and Wildlife instituted its own data collection system.[12]

Commercial representatives pointed out to members of the House committee that the figures being used by Texas Parks and Wildlife were almost completely opposite from those of NMFS: Those of the state agency showed that commercial fishermen were landing the majority of the redfish, while federal statistics indicated that recreational fishermen were bringing in the majority of the redfish.

Schlueter's amended HB 1000 easily passed through the Environmental Affairs Committee and was reported to the full House on April 8, when the bill was put to a no-roll voice count, which allowed representatives to vote off the record. The House overwhelmingly approved the bill. Though this approval was tentative—a formal vote leading to final passage of the bill was scheduled for the next day—the bill was clearly going to fly.

But the Senate's Natural Resources Committee also met on April 8. It killed Vale's substitute bill, which would have allowed fishing to continue. And, within an hour of its approval by the House voice vote, it took action on HB 1000. It resurrected SB 139, revamped it to mirror the amended HB 1000 and...tabled it immediately.

"It's dead," declared chairman Santiesteban, much to the delight of the commercial fishermen. Since his committee had tabled the Senate version of the bill which contained the exact language as the House version, "we could not bring it up again" if HB 1000 came to the committee, he said.

Instead, Senators Walter Mengden and Linden Williams of Houston, and Carl Parker of Port Arthur offered a resolution to address the conflicting figures regarding the recreational catch of red drum and spotted seatrout that had been presented in the House Environmental Affairs Committee. Senate Resolution 450 directed the Senate Natural Resources Committee to conduct a study on the state of the fisheries. The study was to determine the correct figures relating to the size of the red drum and seatrout populations in Texas coastal waters, whether the survival of the fish was threatened, and the reasons that the statistics from the TPWD differed significantly from those in federal government and independent reports. The committee passed SR 450 by unanimous vote. The study was to be completed and submitted to the Senate during the following legislative session, in 1983.

Interest group pressure on Senate Natural Resource Committee members had steadily escalated during the debate on redfish legislation, reaching a peak after this latest attempt to thwart passage of the Redfish Bill. In March, Sen. Walter Mengden received a telegram from fellow Houston Republican, James A. Baker, III.

After running the unsuccessful 1980 presidential campaign for longtime friend George Bush, corporate lawyer Baker had been appointed President Reagan's chief of staff. Like GCCA chief Walter Fondren, Baker likes to fish for redfish out of the small coastal village of Port O'Connor. His message to Sen. Mengden concerned redfish:

"I am sorry to hear that you are voting against the sport fishermen...Wadefishing is one of our state's great recreational resources and it is threatened by the nets. Please reconsider."

Mengden, who'd known Baker since high school, didn't reconsider.

41

"When my aide told me that we got a telegram from Jimmy, I thought, 'Boy they're really pullin' out all the stops on this one.'"

Later, seven of the 11-member Senate NRC received a message worded somewhat less delicately than that of the tactful Baker: "If you are so hell-bent on political suicide, we will oblige you by digging the hole and paying for the funeral," wrote Ralph Robbins, president of the Houston Sportsmen's Club. In his letter (excerpted in the April 22, 1981, *Houston Post*), Robbins threatened the senators that his club "will officially campaign against you in the next election and will solicit the support of all the state's sportsmen's clubs, conservation organizations and the sports-fishing industry, unless you change your stand against the trout and redfish conservation bill or at least vote to allow this bill to reach the Senate floor for a fair debate and an honest vote."

Robbins added, "If you continue in your attempt to destroy a quarter-century of our conservation work, we will take our message to the people and will take whatever steps necessary to insure that you never again serve in public office." In closing his 13-page letter, Robbins warned the recalcitrant senators, "This issue will be hung around your neck like a gill net around a redfish."

Declaring that his bill was not dead yet, Schlueter had HB 1000 formally passed by the House. The next step was to send it over to the Senate. Though Senate NRC chairman Santiesteban had declared the bill dead, Schlueter suggested that Santiesteban's committee could reverse the 6-5 vote by which it had tabled the Senate bill. Or, he suggested, Lt. Gov. William Hobby could keep the bill alive by avoiding the hostile NRC and referring the House version to another Senate committee, such as the Economic Development Committee. (One of the duties of the lieutenant governor is the assignment of bills to the appropriate committees.)

Reconsideration of the bill by Santiesteban's committee seemed unlikely, but Hobby refused to say to which committee he would send Schlueter's bill. Holding the fate of the bill in his hands, Hobby said only that he would refer it to committee the day after it arrived from the House.

On April 14, Hobby disappointed backers of HB 1000 by referring it to the Senate NRC. Lt. Gov. Hobby, who was said to be "under tremendous pressure from both sides" on the measure, explained that Natural Resources was "the committee where it ought to be."

The recreational proponents still held out hope that the committee would reconsider, saying that they thought at least two votes against it now were "soft" and likely to change.

But the committee ignored the bill and, at the request of Mengden, sent to the Senate floor the resolution calling for a study on the redfish problem.

The maneuver was perceived by the gamefish advocates as a way for the senators to "wiggle off the hook" by postponing a decision on their bill. But Senate Resolution 450 was necessary, Mengden told the Senate, because "the information we have so far has been incomplete and contradictory."

Mengden explained to the Senate that TPWD data indicated that in 1979 recreational fishermen landed 230,000 pounds of redfish. NMFS data, on the other hand, showed that the recreationals caught 2.12 million pounds.

"When you have a discrepancy to the power of 10, I'd say something is fishy," said Mengden, who pointed out that TPWD figures indicated that about 78 percent of all redfish were taken by the state's 635 licensed *commercial* redfishermen while NMFS figures suggested that nearly 75 percent of all redfish were caught by the state's 800,000 *sport* fishermen. (TPWD studies did indicate that commercials caught only a quarter of the trout landed by both user groups.)

"With these kinds of wide discrepancies, there is no way of knowing what to do," said Mengden. "But with a careful, unbiased 19-month study of redfish and trout, I am confident that we can get to the truth regarding the nature of the problem and thereby make some meaningful recommendations for the enactment of legislation in the next session."

In a *Houston Post* article, TPWD statistician Gary Matlock noted that the state and federal studies were not to be compared because the federal data were collected during the calendar year while the Texas study coincided with the state's fiscal year—September 1, 1978 to August 30, 1979. Differences in weather conditions, game laws, etc. during the period when there was no overlap were enough to invalidate any comparison between the two studies, said Matlock.

TPWD officials did not discourage Mengden's proposed study, however. Indeed, coastal fisheries chief Tom Moore welcomed it. "After all, some of the things that came out in the hearings made us look bad. The closer they look at us, the better I'll like it," said Moore.

The Senate gave SR 450 the nod in a tentative voice vote, but there was simply too much momentum behind the gamefish bill to allow it to die. Mengden would not get his study.

With both SB 139 and HB 1000 bottled up in the Senate NRC— where the hostile committee intended to keep them for the remainder of the session—Sen. Ike Harris, original sponsor of SB 139, petitioned Lt. Gov. Hobby to transfer the bills to the Senate Economic Development Committee. Because the proposed legislation involved the multimillion-dollar sport-fishing industry, it was of economic importance, he said.

Harris, who also happened to chair the Economic Development Committee, was said to have majority support of that committee for his bill.

Hobby agreed to make the change if a two-thirds majority of the senators approved.

"It was just stuck there, they couldn't budge it. It began to look like it was slippin' away from 'em, you know, that they'd have to go into the next session, which was two years away. Then, a very unusual thing happened," recalled Sen. Walter Mengden, now retired. Though an oilman himself, Mengden was one of the staunchest opponents of the gamefish bill, for which he was accused of "deserting his own kind."

"When Reagan ran against Ford, I was the highest ranking elected Republican official that supported him; in fact, I was the only one. That was against an incumbent president, but I'd been for Reagan all along. So everybody knew my position with Reagan.

"So we get this call, myself and another senator who was backing the fishermen. Somebody from the governor's office called us up and said the governor's plane was going up to Washington, D.C., on official state business. And there were some seats left over. 'How would you all like to go up, and while you're up there, say hello to President Reagan?'

"So we said, 'Well, that sounds great.'

"But before I left, I went to the senator who was leading the opposition against the gamefish bill and I said, 'Now you're not going to back out on this thing while I'm gone are you?'

"'Oh no,no,no, I'm sure not.'

"I told him, 'Now look, we've got enough votes—if there's no changing—that they can't bring this thing up until we get back. We counted the votes and they're solid, they're there.' We had checked because, you know, we figured that this would be a good time for them to bring this thing up, the minute we left. But we were assured by the guy who was leadin' the charge against it, 'They've already picked off everybody that they can pick off. Go ahead and go.'

"So the other senator and I and a few of the House members got on the governor's airplane and flew up there.

"Then, as we were coming back, we got a message on the airplane: The redfish bill had passed to the Economic Development Committee.

"With the two of us out of the way, all they had to do was get one guy to switch his vote."

On April 30, 1981, the 31-member Senate, in an action unprecedented in the history of the Texas Legislature, approved Harris' motion to withdraw SB 139 and HB 1000 from the Senate Natural Resources Committee and re-refer the bills to the Senate Economic Development Committee. The move passed by a vote of 19 yeas and 9 nays, a bare two-thirds.

By transferring the gamefish bills to the friendly EDC, HB 1000 was guaranteed a quick turnaround.

The question of allocating fishery resources on an economic basis had been reiterated since Bob Kemp first drew attention to the matter in his public statement of August, 1979. Additional statements made in the legislative hearings directed the need for the Legislature to have a full report on the economic consequences of a prohibitive decision.

Speaker of the House Bill Clayton had requested in March that Texas Parks and Wildlife prepare an economic impact statement. His request came under the purview of the Economic Impact Statement

Act of 1977, which gave the authority to the lieutenant governor or the speaker of the House of Representatives to request a state agency to "prepare an economic impact statement for any pending bill or joint resolution that directly affects that agency." Clayton's request marked the first time the speaker of the House had exercised this authority.

Texas Parks and Wildlife was to present its economic impact statement to the Economic Development Committee on May 11. But as the EDC hearing was about to proceed, San Antonio's Sen. Bob Vale postponed the "conservation" bill's becoming a "money" bill by "tagging" it. A 48-hour written notice is required before a bill can be heard, said Vale, a technicality that was overlooked in this case.

Tagging is a maneuver most often used in the final days of a legislative session as a last-ditch effort to kill a bill.

Irritated, committee chairman Harris immediately rescheduled the hearing on HB 1000 for May 13.

"For the first time, legislative committees were confronted by representatives of the tackle, boating, resort development and tourism industries—people who were ready to testify that speckled trout and redfish were worth more jobs and more millions of dollars as living sportfish than as cold fillets sold by the pound. *The sleeping giant called the sport fishing industry, which historically had never been able to get its act together on the Gulf Coast, was starting to stir.*"

So wrote *Field & Stream* shooting editor Bob Brister, describing the May 13 hearing in his recap of the gamefish fight, "Winning the War on Netters." In his outdoor column at the *Houston Chronicle* Brister boiled down the content and the outcome of the EDC hearing to two sentences: "The bottom line was that more than $800 million in income to the economy of Texas from tourism, tackle, boats, resort development etc., and 16,000 jobs would be endangered if the trout and redfish conservation bill did not pass. Legislators were stunned."

Testimony by the Texas Parks and Wildlife Department was based on an economic impact statement prepared by Gary Matlock. According to the statement, "Red drum and spotted seatrout are a minor component of the commercial fishing industry in Texas....it is projected these two species comprise approximately 2 percent of the weight and one percent of the value of all commercially landed seafood in Texas."[13]

If the bill's passage caused the unemployment of all 887 licensed commercial saltwater finfishermen and 80 fish dealers living in 18 coastal counties, the statement projected that the unemployment rate for that area would increase from 5.39 to 5.44 percent, only .05 percent.

The statement projected a loss of $11.8 million in sales of redfish and trout for 1982 and 1983 if the Legislature passed HB 1000.

On the other hand, if HB 1000 were not passed, the report projected an $819 million loss to the Texas economy for the same two-year period. According to the statement:

"Red drum and spotted seatrout make up about 52 percent of the sport finfish fishermen's catch and the availability of these fish has declined dramatically in recent years. In turn, the number of hours spent fishing by sport fishermen has decreased by approximately 35 percent since 1974. As availability of these fish continues to decline because of overharvest, the expenditures of sport fishermen can be expected to decline."

A Texas Department of Water Resources study indicated that saltwater sport fishing was worth $709 million in fiscal year 1979.

Since about 50 percent of the state's 800,000 saltwater anglers preferred to catch redfish and trout, the TPWD study projected that the economic value to the state contributed by these 400,000 sport fishermen would be $354.5 million in 1980, and "assuming a 10 percent annual inflation rate," $390 million in 1982 and $429 million in 1983. Therefore, if the Legislature forced these 400,000 recreational fishermen to share the species with the commercials for two more years, they would immediately stop fishing—or so the TPWD inferred—and the state's economy would lose $819 million.

The $11.8 million economic loss resulting from the prohibition of sale of these species would therefore be "far offset by the retention of sport fishermen catching red drum and spotted seatrout."

Only one member of the Economic Development Committee also served on the Natural Resources Committee. This was Sen. John Wilson, a LaGrange rancher and businessman. However, he was absent from the hearing on May 13. Consequently, all of the committee members except Harris were hearing testimony on the issue for the first time.

After just an hour-and-a-half of debate, the nine-member committee tabled SB 139 and approved HB 1000 with a vote of 8-0. On the following day, May 14, it went to the full Senate.

But when it did, Walter Mengden was there. The Houston senator offered an amendment to HB 1000 that would place a two-year moratorium on *all* fishing until sufficient facts could be determined. His plea to the Senate was one for conservation and equality:

"Equality under the law seems to have taken a backward step at this stage and we should have an equal, uniform law that applies to everybody to save this very valuable natural resource that is so important to all of us in Texas."

The Senate killed Mengden's amendment by a vote of 23 yeas and 7 nays.

To soften opposition by the commercial fishing and restaurant interests, Sen. Harris—EDC chairman and sponsor of SB 139— offered a compromise amendment that eliminated the *permanent* prohibition on commercial fishing. The Texas Parks and Wildlife Commission would gain the authority to regulate, by proclamation, "the catching, possession, transportation, sale, and purchase for commercial purposes in this state of redfish and speckled seatrout," on January 1, 1983. Harris' amendment permitted the commission to reopen commercial fishing for redfish and trout after that date, if the department determined that such fishing would not damage the fish population.

In addition to this provision, HB 1000, in its final form, eliminated the verbal designation of gamefish. It provided for the sale of redfish and spotted seatrout that were raised on fish farms, and allowed the importation of the fish from out of state.

The Senate passed the amended bill by a two-thirds vote and returned it to the House on May 19. After the House confirmed the amended version, it sent it to Gov. Clements.

On the same afternoon, Clements signed into law the "two-year" ban on the sale of Texas-caught redfish and speckled trout.

Later, a reporter asked Clements if the gamefish bill he had signed into law wouldn't deprive Texans of fresh seafood. The governor responded that if *he* wanted to eat redfish, he'd fly to New Orleans.

"And what about those Texans who couldn't afford to make the trip?" the reporter asked.

Clements answered, "Let 'em eat catfish."

Commercial fishermen were granted a grace period from May 19, when HB 1000 was passed, until September 1, when the bill took effect. Fishhouses bought all the Texas-caught red drum they could to stockpile for the anticipated shortage. In the first two days, the price of red drum and seatrout increased approximately 20 percent in some areas. According to Brownsville seafood dealer Pat Pace, the highest price paid for red drum prior to the ban was 90 cents a pound. By August, fishermen were receiving $1.35.

The price increases and the prospect of having to deal with various importers caused commercial interests to make one last effort to stop the ban. PISCES representative Pat Pace and George Solis, owner of Gulf Queen Seafoods in Houston, filed a lawsuit against TPWD and Texas Parks and Wildlife Supervisor Robert Miles. Plaintiffs named in the suit included Charles C. Cobb, a commercial finfisherman from Port Mansfield who represented 3,000 fishermen and more than 600 licensed redfishermen.

They filed the suit in Brownsville before U.S. District Court Judge James DeAnda on August 17, 1981. Claiming that the recently enacted law was unfair to them and would force them out of business, the commercial interests sued for an injunction against its enforcement.

They hired Austin attorney Shannon Ratliff to represent them; Dr. John Stockton, professor emeritus of statistics and former director of the University of Texas Bureau of Business Research, to review the economic impact statement prepared by Texas Parks and Wildlife; and Harvey Bullis, a biologist formerly with the old federal Bureau of Fisheries and, later, the National Marine Fisheries Service.

During the September 14 hearing, Ratliff attempted to show that TPWD officials did not provide legislators with accurate information concerning the numbers of red drum and spotted seatrout. Bullis backed up the claim by stating that the numbers of the species might actually have increased in Gulf waters over the past few years.

Stockton, the dean of statistical methodology in Texas, had a field day with the TPWD economic impact statement, testifying that the figures given to the Legislature on the ban's economic impact were "misleading, unsupported, and not verified." During the prior debate in the Legislature, commercial representatives had been unprepared to counter the economic arguments made by Texas Parks and Wildlife. When, for instance, Economic Development Committee members had questioned Pace about the state's economic impact statement, he responded that the hearing was the first time he had heard of it. Commercial interests were ready for the judicial hearings, however.

Stockton cited the department's own reports to counter claims made in its economic impact statement that sport fishermen were spending less time fishing—and less money—due to the decline in resources. In the years between 1977 and 1980, said Stockton, the number of saltwater sport fishermen increased by 33 percent. From 1975 to 1980, the number of short-term sport-fishing licenses—those usually purchased by tourist anglers—more than doubled, from 30,000 to 71,000. And from 1975 to 1980, as TPWD was reporting a decline in total sport catch volume, and the Boating Trades Association of Texas complained of lagging sales, recreational boat licenses in the coastal counties increased from nearly 133,000 to more than 147,000.

Stockton contested virtually every premise of the TPWD economic impact statement, from the purported economic value of the recreational industry to the reliability of the TPWD fishing data, which he showed had an average margin of error of 50 percent, "way too much for confidence." His review concluded:

"No professional economist, experienced in assessing economic impacts, would either rely on the 'data' presented or make the clearly specious assumptions made in the Department of Parks and Wildlife's 'Economic Impact Statement.' Any policy or legislative action based on such a 'Statement' is similarly without foundation and substance."

The federal court did not agree, however. One month later, on October 15, 1981, Judge DeAnda handed down his decision on the case. He denied the request for an injunction, stating that it was up to the Legislature and not the courts to decide what species to "protect."

In November, the fishermen formally notified Judge DeAnda that they would not pursue an appeal in the case.

Unless the Legislature acted during the 1983 session, the ban on commerce in redfish and trout would remain in force at the discretion of the Texas Parks and Wildlife Commission.

Prior to the session, GCCA distributed $140,000 to 115 of the 150 House members and 22 of the 31 senators—enough to command the attention of a two-thirds majority in the House and Senate. PISCES contributed $4,400.

Not surprisingly, legislators failed to rescind the ban on commerce in Texas redfish and trout. Instead they began to consider a ban on importing the two species. The majority of the fish being imported into Texas originated in Mexico and Louisiana.

TEXAS GAMEFISH BLUES

I n 1934, the Texas House of Representatives appointed five of its members to the Legislative Committee on Salt Water Fisheries and Marine Taxation, which was assigned the task of studying "all questions pertaining to our commercial fisheries." The group boarded a boat and traveled the length of the Texas coast, visiting all of the state's bays, and holding public hearings in each coastal village, town and city. The following is an excerpt from the committee's report to the 1935 Legislature:

The chief difficulty seems to be that a war exists between the commercial fisherman and the sports fisherman, and either side is willing to make almost any statement in order to show that their enemy is a villain and a scoundrel. The commercial fisherman makes humorous jibes at the hoggish and selfish attitude displayed by many so-called "sportsmen," who seem to believe that fancy rubber boots, creel, and a rod and reel are all that it takes to make a sportsman out of a man, and they are not without some basis of criticism.

The committee feels proud to consider themselves sportsmen. We believe in fair play; we believe in not only giving the fish, the birds, and our wild animals a chance, but we believe in giving our fellow man a chance, and we believe that commercial fishing in the littoral coastal waters of the State of

Texas is absolutely necessary for the welfare and perpetuation of our Texas fisheries and for the inland consumers of sea foods which necessarily depend upon the industry.

A lot has changed in the years since that legislative committee took its leisurely, fact-finding cruise along the Texas coast. The state's government no longer believes in giving its "fellow man,"—the commercial fisherman—a chance; and it no longer believes that commercial fishing in the state's coastal waters is necessary, either for the perpetuation of its fisheries, or for supplying inland consumers with seafood.

Not long after the Texas Legislature banned the commercial harvest of redfish and spotted seatrout, it banned all nets in the state's tidal waters, effectively curtailing finfishing along the Texas coastline. The wild fish would be used as bait to lure a commercialized tourist fishery.

A 1990 Sea Grant press release reported on the success of the state's marketing campaign to promote coastal tourism: "More than 200,000 of them converge in the Rio Grande Valley each year. Several thousand more congregate in the Coastal Bend region and still more dot the coast up to Galveston and other areas. They are Winter Texans—folks who travel from all over the country to Texas every year so they can escape the cold weather and enjoy the winter months in warmth and fun."

According to a spokesman for the Texas Department of Commerce, "There's some opportunity down here for further expansion but it is going to have to come with development."

In addition to the $200,000 earmarked for its Winter Texan marketing campaign in Midwest lake states, Texas' annual tourism advertising budget exceeds $5 million. One television commercial claims, "We speak a different language down here. Y'all come."

TEXAS GAMEFISH BLUES

In October 1989, I went. My assignment was to seek out the Texas finfishermen and see how they were coping under this new regime.

I ambled down the coast from Sabine Pass to Corpus Christi and, true to the ad's claims, I did find a different language being spoken. But it wasn't among the oil refineries and chemical plants that help make Texas, according to the U.S. Environmental Protection Agency, the most polluted state in America. And it wasn't among the "Winter Texans," the red-faced Midwesterners in their trailer parks and beachfront condominiums.

I found a different language among the quiet fishing villages of Palacios and Seadrift, Smith Point and Sargent, the mouth of the San Bernard River and the West End of Galveston Island. And the men who were speaking it were mad as hell.

"Here again we've got a scenario of a few rich people that can basically dictate through their power and clout what happens to the politics and to the people of Texas," complained Bill Templeton, a Sargent-based shrimper and finfisherman, as he recounted the 1981 gamefish fight. "And I don't know what can be done about it.

"There's just no way that dummies such as myself can go up there and fight people that have been trained all their life in the political arena. They get the best lobbyists, and these people know who to buy, how to buy, when to buy and how to make things move. We go up there with no money and we're the good old boys. We're honest, we've got the integrity, but when the final rattle comes out...money talks."

The money spoke eloquently in 1981. In the face of overwhelming odds, the Texas fishermen, like the defenders of the Alamo, fought tenaciously. And met with the same success.

The loss of their keystone species immediately devastated most full-time finfishermen; other Texas fishermen soon felt the impact, as well. Many shrimpers, for instance, fished part-time, during the winter months. "We used to shrimp six months out of the year and fish six months," said Templeton.

"That's how we used to make our livin'," added Ted Schweinle, from down the San Bernard River. "When the shrimpin'd slow down, we'd fish. We'd shrimp in the season and fish in the winter. Now we shrimp in the season and take an unpaid vacation the rest of the time. It makes it hard, especially after a bad season."

Oystermen who worked the public reefs during the winter also felt the pressure as out-of-work finfishermen rigged out for that fishery. Oyster dredge license sales more than doubled, from 52 in 1980 to 109 in 1981. The increase was even more dramatic in the aftermath of Texas' outlawing of all nets in 1988. In 1987, fishermen licensed 185 dredges; in 1988, 784, and in 1989, 941.

Some netters, however, continued to target redfish and trout in spite of the ban. "We had to do something, you know," explained a young fisherman. "Another guy and I, we were haulin' the fish about 50 miles from here and sellin' 'em. We'd watch 'em weigh the fish and then we'd be gone. Every two days we were pickin' up anywhere from 2,000 to 2,800 pounds. Mostly reds but some trout at times."

Rustlin' redfish was serious business, though. "I've got a stack of violations," he admitted.

Another fisherman explained the situation immediately after the closure: "When they closed it down, you could still make good money bootleggin' because these restaurants and fishhouses were in a state of shock. They had a lot of money invested and they had to have fish. They'd buy bootleg fish then. But then they came out with these different kinds of fish."

Although fishermen did shift their efforts to other species of fish,

William Auzston: "It's our world against their world and we have to do without. Now we have to live in poverty so they can have fun."

they were already invested to the hilt in gear that the gamefish bill rendered obsolete. "I heard tell that in the Great Lakes, when they shut down the fishin', they bought 'em out so they could go and do somethin' else," said Galveston fisherman William Auzston. "But here, when I was shoved out, I had over $10,000 worth of equipment that's now over there in that garden goin' to hell. I never got one dollar to help me along. And that's unfair. But it's our world against their world and we have to do without. Now we have to live in poverty so they can have fun."

Although dealers soon made other species of fish available, Texans still like their redfish and trout. "Specks and reds were always the main sellers on the Texas coast," claimed Tony Milina, who runs a fish market in the Galveston area. "And today people still walk into my place and ask, 'Do you have trout or redfish?' 'No ma'am,' I say, and they turn around and walk right out the door. We lose over half our customers because they're lookin' strictly for trout or redfish.

"And if we do have it," added Milina, "it's not the best quality because it has to come from a long way."

It's not surprising that fish markets, denied a steady supply of fresh fish, have also been hit hard by the state's change in policy. According to TPWD, the sale of retail fish dealer licenses fell from 6,696 in 1979 to 3,800 in 1989, suggesting a loss of nearly 3,000 retailers—more than 40 percent—within just 10 years.

Gamefish proponents in 1981 weakened opposition to their bill by amending it to allow Texas fish dealers to import trout and redfish from neighboring states and Latin American countries. A bill passed in the 1989 Legislature, however, prohibited all importation of wild-caught redfish. According to Gary Matlock, director of fisheries, TPWD, "After December 31, 1990, no redfish other than those raised in fish farms may be sold in Texas." Wild-caught trout still may be imported.

This law makes it more difficult to "bootleg" redfish caught in Texas waters. It also provides the fish farmers with total control of the intrastate market for this species. Outlawing the importation of redfish also helps kill the demand for wild-caught fish harvested legally in other states, such as Louisiana.

From 1981 until 1988, resourceful Texas finfishermen redirected their efforts to other species of fish including flounder, alligator gar, black drum, sheepshead and shark. But, in 1988, when the Texas Parks and Wildlife Commission outlawed the use of all nets, it was no longer possible to earn a livelihood as a coastal fisherman. It was over.

During the summer of 1988, the Texas Parks and Wildlife

Commission held a statewide round of public hearings on its proposal to ban the use of nets. At the same time, the commissioners aired another proposal—cutting the sport fishermen's bag limit from five redfish to two.

TPWD fisheries director Gary Matlock told the commission that only about 10 percent of the redfish were growing old enough to spawn, which he attributed to a combination of increased recreational fishing pressure, illegal netting, the 1987 red tide, the 1983 freeze and incidental catches of redfish in the nets of commercial fishermen who were legally harvesting other species. Matlock recommended that the commission adopt the new restrictions in order to avert a "collapse" of the species in Texas.

As the hearings progressed, sport fishermen expressed a general consensus on the proposed restrictions: They were pleased at the prospect of net-free waters, but questioned the need to limit their own harvest.

"Nobody is arguing that they want to get rid of the nets," wrote outdoor columnist Mike Leggett in a May 29, 1988, *Austin American-Statesman* article about the commission's proposals. "That's how GCCA came to be in the first place. However, GCCA's executive committee met in emergency session and declared that TPWD was placing 'the total burden of rebuilding finfish populations on the recreational fishery, after allowing for a continuing illegal commercial harvest.'"

Sport fishermen's references to the "illegal harvest" stemmed from Texas Parks and Wildlife's claims—which were well publicized throughout the summer in outdoor columns and angling-club literature—that nearly 40 percent of the redfish taken each year were being lost to illegal netting. Not surprisingly, sport fishermen asked, "Why should we be asked to pay the price for the state's inability to enforce laws against illegal netting? Get rid of the nets and then let's talk."

Others, however, began to ask what was wrong with an enforcement division that allowed illegal netters to take 40 percent of the redfish harvest. That's when TPWD Law Enforcement Director Chester Burdett spoke up, pointing out that Matlock's 37 percent netting-loss figure actually represented *all* redfish taken illegally. In addition to those redfish taken as bycatch in nets set legally, illegal nets and in shrimp trawls, the figure included those under- and over-sized fish kept by anglers as well as those fish anglers retained in excess of their daily bag limit.

"We did not make that clear in the presentation for simplification purposes. We should have made that distinction," said Matlock, as quoted in a July 17 article by Leggett.[1]

Immediately before the July 21 commission meeting in Austin, when commissioners were to vote on the department's recommendations, TPWD undercover agents sprang a trap that they had set by establishing phony fish businesses where they bought illegal redfish and trout from commercial fishermen and offered the fish for resale to restaurants and fishhouses around the state. The sting operation netted a number of businesses; charges were filed in Houston, Dallas, San Antonio, Corpus Christi, Port Aransas, Seadrift and Austin.

It was a cinch that the commissioners were going to take out the nets; but cutting the sportsmen was another matter. Nearly 3,000 had testified during the round of hearings; what they said was that they wanted to keep retaining five redfish.

In 1981, when commercial fishermen, consumers and approximately 400,000 saltwater sport fishermen shared the resource, anglers were permitted to retain 10 redfish per day. Those who had lobbied for the 1981 gamefish law were convinced that the netters were landing the lion's share of redfish. Therefore, they reasoned, shutting down the commercials should allow redfish populations to boom, radically improving the quality of their sport. Dressed in his "Save the Redfish" T-shirt, even the most amateurish of "sports" anxiously anticipated the day when he would be able to fill his ice chest with the wary redfish.

But, following a December 1983 freeze, the Texas Parks and Wildlife Commission slashed sportsmen's bag limits in half, from 10 to five. (Freezes severe enough to cause fish kills are regular occurrences on the Gulf Coast, with at least one, frequently two, recorded each decade of this century.)

By 1988, commercial fishermen, guides, marina operators and anglers were reporting record numbers of redfish in bays up and down the coast.

In Leggett's May 29, 1988, article, Alan Allen, executive director of Sportsmen's Clubs of Texas, said a number of board members had serious doubts about Matlock's statements that fishing on the coast was declining and that numbers of redfish weren't greatly improved since the 1983 freeze and the banning of commercial redfishing in 1981. "We have a number of people on the board who are saltwater fishermen," Allen said, "and they find it very hard to believe that it's not better than it's been in a long time." Allen also noted that biologists' reports and news emanating from TPWD had seemed to indicate that fishing was improving all along. "Now they're saying that the numbers have declined to where it's almost an emergency situation to save the redfish," Allen said. "That's difficult to believe."

Matlock replied that the anglers' perception of an abundance of fish was an illusion, created by the moves taken after the freeze of 1983-84. No more redfish were getting free to spawn and the numbers seemed to be going down, said Matlock, who refused to back off his recommendation that the recreational harvest be reduced.

At their July 21 meeting, Texas Parks and Wildlife commissioners compromised on the issue of how many redfish the state's 566,000 licensed saltwater anglers would be permitted to retain: Sport fishermen could keep three redfish rather than the proposed two, voted the commission, but the fish had to conform to a size limit of between 20 to 28 inches, more restrictive than the former slot of 18 to 30 inches.

The commission also voted to ban the use of nets by commercial finfishermen.

Following the ban on nets, fishermen could still harvest finfish with trotlines but, said Galveston fisherman Billy Praker, "You've got to have a circle hook with a turned-in point and it's got to have at least a half-inch opening. And your trotlines have to be underwater and you've got to pick them up from one o'clock Friday afternoon until one o'clock Sunday. You can't make it like that."

G.P. McCreless of Southern Texas Seafood, Corpus Christi, thought he had found a way to make it. After the net ban in 1988, McCreless put hundreds of fishermen to work harvesting mullet with 10-foot cast nets. "We were buying mullet from dealers from Brownsville to Galveston," said McCreless, "and sending the roe overseas. For our first year we were very successful."

During that first season, McCreless cut the valuable roe from the fish and sold the rest of the fish as crab bait for pennies a pound. Afterward, he worked with Texas A&M to determine the shelf-life of mullet fillets which, he learned, could be sold to hospitals and penal institutions for $1 per pound. The remainder of the carcass would be utilized for fertilizer. "We did a lot of footwork between '88 and

'89," said McCreless, who was anticipating an even greater season in 1989.

Then, in early autumn, just a few weeks before the mullet got right, the bad news came in: There was a law on the books that restricted the use of cast nets to catching bait only.

"They were catching edible fish illegally in 1988," Matlock said. "If people weren't cited, it's because we weren't aware it was going on. So, for 1989, we made people aware that it is illegal."

"We really intended to make money in '89," lamented McCreless, who estimated his loss at $100,000 to $150,000 for the six-week season. "And the fishermen hoped to make their Christmas money."

Not only are Texas fishermen finding it increasingly difficult to earn a living but they complain of harassment which they say became widespread when a general anti-commercial fishing sentiment began to pervade the state's wildlife and fisheries agency in the late 1970s. One shrimper cited an unauthorized boarding of his shrimp boat as an example: "I'm runnin' along there, the season was shut down and I'm crossin' Galveston Bay, goin' home. I've got my feet propped up, it's Sunday afternoon and I'm drivin' the boat and watchin' the football game.

"Next thing, my little dog starts raisin' Cain and here's a game warden standin' at the door! I told him, 'Man, what are you doin' on my boat? At least come up front and let me know you want to board me.' He got on my boat without ever lettin' me know he was there.

"It's a sad day when they can do that. And they do that here. Over in Lou'siana, the wardens are pretty good—they'll hail you before they try to come aboard. But these people here in Texas, well, they don't act like professional lawmen. They act like a bunch o' kids. It's a sad day in Texas that we have to put up with this."

James "JB" Milina, 30, a Galveston finfisherman, described a recent law that prohibits the possession of a net within 500 yards of "an area where that gear is illegal," i.e. the water.

"If you live within 500 yards of the water, you better not have a net in the yard," warned Milina. "They said they aren't goin' to enforce that—they won't come in your house and arrest you for ownin' a net, but they can if they want.

"When we go to Louisiana to fish we take Route 87, and it runs along the beach. The game warden told us that we better not stop. He said we can stop at a store or a gas station but if we pull alongside the road by the beach and he sees us, he's gonna take our nets right there."

Since the 1988 ban on all nets, more Texas fishermen are traveling to Louisiana to fish. And Bayou State fishermen, who are working under restrictive quotas, don't appreciate the new competition. This additional hardship on Louisiana's finfishermen is but one more aftershock of the Texas ban on inshore commercial finfishing.

William Auzston, 58, has fished all his life. "And," said Auzston, "my daddy fished all his life and my grandpa came from the old country when he was 30 and he fished all his life. When he fished over here they had to keep the fish in live boxes until they took them to town in wagons.

"When we used to haul seine on the beach we were a real tourist attraction. We'd pull the seine in and you'd be surprised at how many people from up around Illinois, Missouri, even Michigan would come around. Boy, they enjoyed seein' them netters pullin' fish in. They'd wanna help pull the net, they'd stay with you and talk for hours.

"Back in those days people were friendly with you. If they saw fresh fish comin' in they knew they were gonna eat fresh fish. But then there just got to be too many hard-blooded sports fishermen that wanted it all for themselves.

"And when it got to the point that they wanted to start closin' the beach I told all these people, 'Man, you better write your congressman or you ain't gonna see this no more. You ain't gonna get any more fresh fish.' 'Why?' they'd ask and I'd have to explain it to them and they'd say, 'Well, I just don't think I'll come to this state anymore. Next time, we'll just bypass Texas.'"

After just a week of hanging out with the bitter and disenfranchised finfishermen of coastal Texas, I myself didn't feel too comfortable there. When I reached Corpus and figured I had my story, I pointed my little rental car East and stomped it. At about midnight, when I finally crossed the border into warm Louisiana, I couldn't help sighing in relief.

BILLY PRAKER

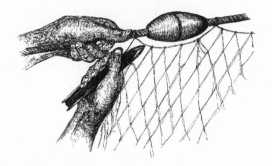

Spirited Galveston fisherman Billy Praker, 41, speaks for many Texas fishermen: "I've fished for 20 years, and I never took a paycheck from a man."

When the state took redfish and trout from him, Praker didn't ask, "Now what do I do?" He asked instead, "Now what do I catch?"

Praker built himself a 60-foot shrimp boat and named it Revenge. "I named it Revenge because Texas Parks and Wildlife put me out of business catchin' trout and redfish so I said I'll just get me a boat and catch shrimp—I'd get revenge on those boogers."

Billy also continued to finfish in Texas, which often proved more profitable than shrimping. Since 1988, however, he's been forced to fish in neighboring Louisiana. "But I'm still fishin'," said Praker, during our 1989 interview. "I'm gonna fish."

Here, Billy Praker describes the gamefish fight of 1981 and the ensuing trials of earning his livelihood in Texas:

Back in 1981, we had people from Corpus Christi, Brownsville, Laguna Madre—all over—and we had that room loaded up there in the top floor in Austin for the vote. And there were very few of the guys there with the suitcases. But the suitcases were filled with the right stuff. I'm tellin' you, we went up there with the facts, but they went with the money.

And when I came home, I had about $4,000 or $5,000 worth of nets that were worthless. The state wouldn't reimburse me any money or even consider my loss. I got caught with my pants down, with a lot of stuff I couldn't use. Which wasn't fair to me, you know.

They took away the three-inch mesh and said you couldn't use anything less than six-inch.[1] Man, I complained about that. "Are you crazy?" I said. "I'm gonna starve to death with six-inch!" But it turned out to be a blessing in disguise. You wouldn't catch the trout, and the redfish you had to throw back, but I could catch a lot of other fish. I made money with that six-inch.

See, every time you take away one fish, that increases the value of the others. They started callin' sheephead "black snapper," and we were gettin' 50 cents a pound for it. When reds and trout were open you wouldn't see me bring in a sheephead for 10 or 15 cents. My best price for black drum when redfish and trout were still open was 25 cents. But after, we were gettin' $1.25. That took away the pain—we were still makin' good money.

But last year, they took away *all* the nets. They said we were catchin' too many redfish. And I had just built up a helluva trade in sharks. I was filletin' 'em and sellin' 'em to the restaurants for $2 a pound. Man, I never thought I'd jump overboard to save a five-foot shark, but that fish got to be worth $75!

One night I brought in a thousand pounds of devil rays. I figured I'd sell 'em for crab bait for about a nickel, but I made a new connection with the Vietnamese and sold 'em for 30 cents a pound. Hell, I had a market for devil rays!

There you are, I mean they'd buy anything. Jackfish, mackerel, garfish. Garfish is a good seller now—you can get $1 a pound for gar

Billy Praker

and they're all over the place. And flounder? I fished flounder for six or seven years. We'd use six-inch mesh, in the fall when they were fallin' out of the bays. We were makin' $300 to $400 a night. But that's all gone now.

I could sell any kind of fish—people want to eat fish. But you've got to have the equipment to catch 'em. And now we don't have it and I doubt if we'll get it back. The redfish closure was only supposed to be for two years and it'll soon be 10. We're down to nothin' here in Texas. Teetotallin' nothin'. And there's no reason for it to be. It's just greed.

A long time ago, I used to come in with a thousand pounds of fish. If the sports would see me they'd say I was a damned hog or greedy but, like I'd tell 'em, "Come look at my house. You don't see a fish in my house." They'd act like I was hoardin' 'em, fillin' my yard or stuffin' my mattress with trout and redfish. But they weren't for me, they were for people to eat!

Hell, I don't wanna get rich, I just want to do my job—pay my bills. My dad was a commercial fisherman, I'm a commercial fisherman and my son, he quit school to help me fish. Now they put us all out of business. My daddy's 68, fished all his life and now he's paintin' houses. And my boy's 19. What's he gonna do?

Money ain't everything, heck. The idea is, it's what you want to do. I like fishin' but I like to be able to do it when I want to. Right now politics is eatin' you up with everything you want to do.

I was in Vietnam in '68 and '69 and it was rough. But I guarantee you, it's harder fightin' for your livelihood over here in Texas than it was in Vietnam. I was in the 82nd Airborne and that was like Disneyland compared to fightin' the politics and laws over here. You ain't got a chance.

And, on top of everything else, they got to harass you. When they catch a commercial fisherman with over the limit or the wrong net or something, they take you straight to jail. But you ain't never seen a sport fisherman go to jail. How many rods and reels you seen burnt in the state of Texas? None. But nets? You seen a lot burn. Take a little "plug head" with some undersized trout, you never seen him with his hands handcuffed behind his back. But catch me with a little trout and I'm handcuffed in the back of that car and goin' to jail.

Last year I had 300 pounds of sheephead and about 175 pounds of drum. And the game warden was right there to check my fish. I had to lend him my ruler—my son had just used it to measure the fish. This is 28° weather, it's blowin' and freezin'. But we had one sheephead that was 11 1/2 inches—they're supposed to be 12. So he wrote me a ticket, and took the damned thing for evidence!

Then I got a letter from the judge fining me $130 for that one sheephead. "Damn," I thought, "I'm only gettin' 50 cents a pound. A one-pound fish oughta be worth 50 cents, why should I pay $130?"

So I went to court on it. I didn't have no lawyer, I represented myself.

The judge called us both up there—the Parks and Wildlife man and me—and he asked, "Now what seems to be the problem?" The game warden said, "I saw Mr. Praker comin' in to the ramp, and I saw that he had a considerable amount of fish and I measured them and I noticed that one fish was too little."

Then I told my side, that it was freezin' and blowin' and that we had 300 pounds of sheephead and about 175 pounds of drum. I even showed the judge the fish ticket. And I said the game warden found one sheephead a half-inch too little. And the judge said to the warden, "Do you mean to tell me this man had over 400 pounds of fish on his boat and out of all that, one fish was one-half inch too small?"

The game warden stood up real proud and said, "Yes sir."

And the judge told the game warden, "Don't you ever come in here with somethin' like that again!"

But that just shows you what you have to put up with. Like the other day, I was hangin' this net to take to Lou'siana. And this game warden came over and he was accusin' me of usin' the net to outlaw with over here. I showed him my Lou'siana license but it didn't matter—he was just hasslin' me.

I've been goin' to Lou'siana for about four years now, around Sabine Lake, Johnson Bayou. We fish trout and flounder. When I started goin' over there, a lot of those guys in Lou'siana said, "There's no way they're gonna take our redfish away from us." I said, "It's comin' in the future for you guys too," and they said, "Ain't no way, they can't do that." But the men from the GCCA went over there, and you know what? They did it!

PART II

Conservation of fishes in both Texas and Louisiana has generally followed the pattern set elsewhere, moving with the interests of the groups with the most political power ....Therefore, in Texas the commercial fisherman has gradually been squeezed out in all but a few areas, with the only large catches in recent decades occurring during World War II, when food was needed and recreational fishing was restricted....The rationalization for choosing sports fishing over commercial fishing has always been economic, but the economic theory has not taken into account all costs (to name one, increased pollution with increased tourism), and it remains to be seen if it really will win over the long term, especially since sports fishing, as great as its benefits are, is less a necessity and can only exist in an economy providing many luxuries.

In Louisiana the situation has been much less pronounced, probably because of a lack of tourism, a more depressed economy, and the difficulty of access to coastal waters. However, as sports fishing increases, so do the conflicts, and Louisiana is rapidly following in Texas' footsteps.

—H. Dickson Hoese & Richard H. Moore,
"Fishes of the Gulf of Mexico, Texas,
Louisiana and Adjacent Waters," 1977

REDFISH: FISHING WITH EDVILLE "PAGAIE" CHERAMIE

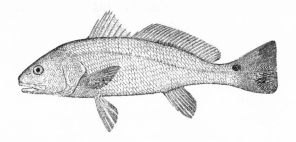

Edville "Pagaie" Cheramie was born and raised in Pointe au Saucisse, the end-of-the-road community in Golden Meadow, Louisiana, where the big Cheramies come from. The knife-carrying, close-to-the-land Cheramies who, in their Cheramie-built boats, go where they please in the marsh that grows close by their Cheramie-built houses. Natural hunters, trappers and fishermen, most of the Cheramie clan from the Pointe are also natural woodworkers.

With his bear paw hands Pagaie (pronounced pa'-guy, French for paddle) builds boats the old way. The Cajun way. Unable to read, he works without plans and doesn't even bother to keep labor-saving patterns. Untainted by so much as one day of schooling, Pagaie relies on his experience, talent and imagination.

"I see the boat in front of my eyes before I go to sleep." The next morning, sculpting freely with a sharp axe, he puts it together. Whether yacht, oyster boat or high-speed, shallow-running *chaland*, each boat he turns out is one of a kind.

Between working the wood and the water, Pagaie made a good living for his family. Whether it was to hunt deer or wild pigs to eat; or alligators, oysters, shrimp or fish to sell, he could do it. But he likes best the challenge and the thrill of catching fish.

Now in his 60s, Pagaie fished for redfish all his life—and never saved a penny. Living day by day, he knew that he could always find enough of these elusive fish to take care of business, be it January or July.

But Pagaie can smell a school of redfish from 100 yards; he can herd them like cattle; and by intently peering into the shallow water, he spots "mud boils"—the muddy clouds that the fish stir up with their tails as they take off ahead of the approaching boat. The size and shape of the boils tell him whether it's redfish up ahead or just mullet or sheepshead.

The inshoreman has to be versatile in order to succeed, but, as Pagaie summed up his lifetime of living off the marsh, "Redfish is da beans."

"Get ready, Nu!" shouted Pagaie as we quietly idled into yet another "duck pond." This was the tenth one we'd checked out that day, and we still hadn't wet the net. "This used to be a good pond, yeah," repeated Pagaie, as we entered each one but, thanks to subsidence, they'd all sunk beyond productivity to craterlike holes, devoid of plant life, their bottoms covered with a fluffy and sterile muck.

But this one, high up in the marsh and with a clean firm bottom, was just what we had been looking for.

As I stepped aft, toward the net stacked on the boat's table-like fantail, I kept watch over my shoulder, scanning the water's surface ahead for some sign of fish. Redfish.

On that still July afternoon the pond's surface was smooth as a pool of mercury. A single red—outsized in the foot-deep water—would push a torpedo-like wave that only a city boy could miss.

At the distant end of the football-field-sized pond, the shoreline

Edville "Pagaie" Cheramie: He can smell a school of redfish from 100 yards away.

Looking for signs of redfish

Some redfishermen power their homemade craft with automobile engines. A V-6 Buick propels this 18-foot *chaland*.

Simple and rugged, this Cajun "putt-putt" is powered by a hand-cranked 16 hp Briggs & Stratton air-cooled engine.

dissolved into islets of *Spartina*, the tall grass that *is* the marsh. And wading about the clumps of grass, an egret.

After fishing together for more than a year, there was no need to say a word; we both recognized the signs: The shy redfish demand serenity—they'll always retreat as far as possible from a well-traveled bayou or canal. And in that distant end, each of those islets of vegetation was a miniature reef harboring a smorgasbord of minnows, baby crabs and shrimp.

The bird was icing on the cake. It wouldn't be wasting its time there if there weren't some little fish to eat. Waiting, ice still, for a minnow to stray within striking range of its snakelike neck, the bird wouldn't be disturbed by a loose school of big fish, resting in the ankle-deep water.

The reds would be sculling gently, like fat bass, just enough to keep them off the bottom. Each more than two feet long, they'd be three, four, maybe five years old. In the upcoming autumn, many of these fish would depart their marshland home, drawn toward the beaches to join the huge schools of big breeders coming in from the Gulf to spawn.

Before they left, it was our job to get some into the boat and take them to town.

Our tools were simple: a boat and a net. The little boat, Pagaie and I had built together. We made it solely to fish the reds and, with a perfectly flat bottom and a weedless propeller turned by a V-6 that we pulled from a wrecked Buick LeSabre, it was ideally suited to the task. The gill net coiled neatly on the stern was a lattice of diamond-shaped meshes, each of which stretched to 5 1/2 inches. The large mesh wouldn't stop a fish unless it weighed close to five pounds; anything smaller would swim right through it, which suited us just fine.

"*Mais* you gotta be stupid to catch 'em when they're only worth three dollars," Pagaie would say, "when next year they'll be worth seven."

As Pagaie idled along the shoreline, looking for signs of redfish, I picked up the "let-go," the sash weight tied to the end of the net. Holding it carefully so as not to knock the boat and spook the fish, I was ready.

Standing in the stern with the small weight in my hand made me think of Gordon Serigny, whose family had worked the marsh for four generations.

A wiry Frenchman in his early 30s, Gordon had once told me that, formerly, bayou fishermen did not set their nets by throwing an attached weight onto the shore; instead, the deckhand leaped overboard at every set, scrambling ashore to plant a staff in the muddy bank.

"In the wintertime I used to have to jump overboard and, man, it was freezing. I'd have to make sure the end of the net stayed on the bank and that it was touching the bottom where it came out, because the redfish wouldn't hit that trammel net, they'd follow the net all around, looking for a place to get out. They'd follow the bank and if there was a little place where the net was off the bottom, they'd all pass there, and my daddy *hated* that!

"I'd climb back in the boat and, after we'd get the net up, I'd take off all my clothes and stand over that putt-putt, trying to get warm. I'd be shivering, turning blue and praying my daddy wouldn't see any more redfish. But he always did and, man, he'd have to chase me with a stick to make me jump again."

It was the deckhand's job to keep his end of the net from being pulled from the bank while his partner slowly towed the opposite end toward him with the boat. As the net was drawn down it swept through the encircled fish, forcing them into the three-walled trammel net.

Traditional redfishermen fished in this manner until the early 1970s, when several Florida finfishermen relocated to Louisiana. Recreational interests had grossly overdeveloped many coastal areas in that exploding state, destroying habitat for both fish and fishermen; as the fish declined, sport fishermen multiplied. The deadly combination forced members of several old Florida fishing families to seek refuge in Louisiana.

Superb finfishermen, their net of choice was one that did not present as formidable a barrier to the fish as did the trammel net. With its fine twine and large meshes, the gill net didn't necessarily need to be dragged because the fish were more inclined to hit it. And since it didn't need to be dragged, the gill net didn't need to be pinned to the shore; it was enough to fasten a small weight to the end and, when the fish were sighted, heave this "let-go" toward the shore.

The *tramailleurs* eventually adopted the gill net, but old habits die hard. For the tradition-bound and chauvinistic coastal Cajuns, simply lobbing a weight onto the bank instead of gamely leaping overboard, staff in hand, seemed, at first, decadent.

"*N'est pas bon*. That ain't no good," they said, resisting even this modest innovation.

It's hardly surprising that some of the last vestiges of the traditional culture are preserved among the simple finfishermen like the Serignys, trying so hard to maintain their independent way of life.

"Hey! Wake up," exclaimed Pagaie, jerking his head toward the wake of a big fish, right off the bow. It streaked directly for the bank and then doubled back in a hard 180. "Sheephead!"

Then a muddy swirl the size of a pie plate erupted by the boat and quickly six more popped up, one after another, in a line, as evenly spaced as the corks on our net. It had to be a fish beating its tail against the bottom as it got out of our way. "Flounder!"

But still no red. Until we were about 60 yards from the grassy end and there was one by the bank, right ahead of us, cruising lazily, like a shark.

"*Poisson rouge*!" Pagaie whispered.

As it passed a tiny cut in the bank, another glided out to join it. As the two syrupy wakes followed the shoreline, another pair emerged from a little nook to make a school of four. Pagaie slipped the clutch into neutral to avoid overrunning them but still used the coasting boat to gently herd them ahead.

When they reached the grassy end, the fish settled down, telling us what we'd suspected all along.

"That end's gotta be full," whispered Pagaie, engaging the clutch. "Let 'er go, let 'er go." As he turned the boat hard to cross the pond I heaved the let-go well up into the grass and the net began to pay out, leaving a trail of corks floating behind us. As we sealed off their only exit, we couldn't help grinning at each other. Today we'd get our revenge, for all the times they'd given us the slip.

Young redfish enter the marsh as larvae or fingerlings. Once they've staked out a territory, they learn every blade of grass. Rarely do they let themselves get boxed in. But we couldn't see any cuts into the marsh behind them. The only way out was the same little bayou we came in on...behind us.

Seeming to know they were trapped, the fish squatted down in the mud, chancing it that the little boat would turn around and leave before they had to show themselves.

But as the net started to slip into the water they felt it from 50 yards away and knew that it was not good news. A male drummed sharply, "boom, boom," and, suddenly, a kitchen-sized area of water simply raised up.

"Here they come! Here they come!"

There was no missing them then, as the 20 or 30 big reds pushed through the shallow water that crested over their backs in V-shaped waves. Coming together in tight formation, they were still in no big hurry; they'd check out the situation before doing anything rash.

But with all this activity, the egret could no longer concentrate on its fishing. Leaping into the air, its great wings flashed a shadow over the already skittish fish. In reflex, they launched toward the net in a single pulse.

"Too fast, too fast!" hissed Pagaie, as the stampeding fish picked up speed. Helpless, we could only pray that they would slow down, and spread out.

And then the boat abruptly lurched upward as it ran over an ancient cypress log lying just beneath the surface. As the barnacles and the oyster shells scraped along the bottom, the fish charged. With the boat hung up, the prop rapped the log like a machine gun, panicking the fish which accelerated with each rap until they were half out of the water, humping like porpoises straight for the net.

"*Merde, merde...shit de merde!*" I heard Pagaie moan behind me, as we both watched the tight knot of powerful fish—each nearly a yard long and the hard-bodied veteran of a hundred assaults by cormorants, mergansers, bigger fish and the lithe otter—prepare to ram our net.

"They're gonna blow it. They're gonna blow it for sure!" warned Pagaie, who knew that when too many reds traveling too fast in too tight a bunch hit the little flap of net standing in this shallow water, they were going to just flatten it.

Sure enough, when they slammed it with their big heads some of the fish actually vaulted end for end over the net, coming down across the corkline. At the same time the rest of the school plowed out over top, splashing muddy water into the air. And then...nothing.

On the safe side now, the reds slowed down, regrouped and nonchalantly paddled for the little bayou, seeming to wave "bye-bye" with their broad tails.

"Bastards!"

In wide-eyed disbelief, and still hung up on the log, we could only look back up the net—over 200 yards long and completely empty. Not a splash. In the silence, I let out a dejected sigh and glanced over at Pagaie. He looked back at me, dropped one eyelid like a little stage curtain, and we both started laughing.

LOUISIANA REDFISH FIGHT I

S enate Bill 829, enacted in 1988, made redfish a gamefish for the next three years in Louisiana. After a preliminary draft had easily passed the Senate, Sen. Fritz Windhorst jokingly asked fellow New Orleans Sen. Ben Bagert, author of the bill, if he thought St. Peter would approve.

Bagert answered, "St. Peter answers to the big man and the big man said we should be good stewards of our resources."

"So," said Windhorst, "we're doing the Lord's work." Bagert, who was dressed totally in white for the occasion, just smiled.

Several months before, during a late night strategy session among seafood dealers, Ted Loupe, of Gulf Tide Seafood in Leeville, had stated that "St. Peter didn't just go fishin' on Saturday. He never won a gold cup. St. Peter used a net, and he fished to make a living."

It's natural that St. Peter would be called up during the recent struggle over redfish in Catholic-dominated South Louisiana. The way things turned out, it's also lucky he switched to netting for men because, as a fisherman, the good saint would now be having a heck of a time makin' a livin'.

Republican Sen. Bagert originally introduced SB 829 to the Senate

Natural Resources Committee on June 2, 1988, with the intent of making both redfish and speckled trout gamefish indefinitely.

After more than a month, during which the "bill that wouldn't die" was debated, killed, resurrected, amended and redebated, it emerged in its final form, which was signed into law on July 11 by Gov. Charles "Buddy" Roemer. With the governor's signature, the controversial piece of legislation became Act No. 889, the "Redfish Bill."

The act contained several significant provisions. It reduced the recreational fisherman's daily limit from 50 redfish or speckled trout to five redfish and 25 trout; it raised the annual commercial quota on speckled trout by 25 percent, from one million to one-and-a-quarter million pounds; and it included the definition of a strike net, identifying and differentiating this fishery for the first time from that based on fixed gear.

Though of some benefit to the commercial fishing industry, these concessions were far outweighed by the damaging provision that designated redfish as a gamefish for the next three years. Commercial redfishing had been closed earlier in the year, when fishermen filled their first-ever quota, and was to have resumed under a new quota on September 1, 1988. Under this "sunset gamefish" provision, however, the fishery was to remain closed until September 1, 1991.

But three years was a little too far down the pike for someone like Yvonne Friere, whose husband, son and two sons-in-law are fishermen in the Hopedale area. Like many fishing families, the Friere's always got by, she said, by trawling for shrimp in the summer and trammel netting for redfish during the winter.

Friere expressed anxiety as to how her family would make it through the winter without redfish. "There's a mullet run but it only lasts about six weeks, until the end of December, and trawling season doesn't start 'till May," she said. "You used to be able to trap, but the high tides from the storms either drowned all the animals or ran them off, and fur's not worth anything anyway. I just don't know how we'll do it."

The closure on redfish not only crippled independent coastal fishermen, but dealers were hard hit as well. Terry LeBlanc of Chauvin had run his fishhouse, Terry and Brenda's Seafood, for seven years. During the peak of the redfish season, he employed up to 15 people. The closure forced LeBlanc to shut down his business.

"We were based on marshland fisheries," he said. "In the marsh, if you can't fish reds, you can't fish nothin' else. You use the same mesh size for redfish that you use for market drum, flounder and garfish. They want you to try to make a living with your bycatch but you catch too many reds. Right now, there's almost no commercial fishing on the Terrebonne Parish marsh."

Just a short time before, the redfish industry was booming. But thanks to the recent legislation, fishermen and dealers found themselves uncertain of their futures, under siege by creditors or bankrupt. What happened?

The moment Louisiana redfishing ended is clear-cut—January 15, 1988, the last day fishermen fished under a 1987 quota of 1.7 million pounds. The beginning is less easy to determine.

Commercial landing figures have been recorded annually since 1887, but fishermen harvested redfish and transported them to inland consumers long before that date. Fishing reds for the market is ingrained into the occupational folklore of the coastal cultures of Louisiana.

Cajun trammel netter Houston Serigny of Leeville recalls the days when, nearly 50 years ago, he and his father netted redfish, the elder

LOUISIANA RED DRUM
Historical commercial landings

YEAR	POUNDS	YEAR	POUNDS
1887	289,000	1960	428,000
1888	288,000	1961	666,000
1889	314,000	1962	567,000
1890	339,000	1963	466,000
1897	465,000	1964	312,000
1902	442,000	1965	471,000
1908	716,000	1966	532,000
1918	566,000	1967	654,000
1923	665,000	1968	741,000
1927	556,000	1969	782,000
1928	434,000	1970	789,000
1929	445,000	1971	724,000
1930	335,000	1972	889,000
1931	369,000	1973	1,184,000
1932	282,000	1974	1,436,000
1934	492,000	1975	1,362,000
1936	347,000	1976	2,212,000
1937	450,000	1977	1,435,000
1938	522,000	1978	1,219,000
1939	694,000	1979	1,057,000
1940	183,000	1980	725,000
1945	596,000	1981	899,000
1948	254,000	1982	1,455,000
1949	480,000	1983	1,939,000
1950	455,000	1984	2,608,000
1951	384,000	1985	2,934,000
1952	328,000	1986	7,818,000
1953	273,000	1987	4,571,000
1954	271,000	1988	245,000 [a]
1955	344,000	1989	0
1956	407,000	1990	0
1957	353,000	1991	0
1958	488,000	1992	0
1959	488,000	1993	0

[a] *Fishing curtailed January 15*

setting the net with oars. The *tramailleurs* earned eight or nine cents a pound for their fish, which were trucked 100 miles to the French Market in New Orleans.

Traditionally, Serigny and other inshore netters harvested only the commercially valuable juvenile fish, ranging from about two to 12 pounds. Dealers shipped the young redfish to retail markets and restaurants in New Orleans and around the state; many were also trucked to neighboring states, particularly Texas, after its Legislature banned the commercial harvest.

Fish larger than 12 pounds—"bull reds"—had always been considered too strong-tasting and coarse-textured to have any significant commercial value. Biologically, however, these adult fish are the most valuable since they're the ones that breed.

Every autumn, the bulls, which can get up to 50 pounds and may live for 40 years, spawn in the offshore waters, usually near the mouths of the passes. Tidal currents carry the spawn inshore to the fertile marshes, where the fish rapidly grow. When these fish are about five years old and weigh 12 to 15 pounds, they fall out of the marsh during the fall and winter to join the offshore brood stock.

The species' life cycle, combined with the market structure, formed the basis for a perfect system—a perpetually renewable fishery that sons and grandsons of today's inshore fishermen could look forward to with hope.

But now, Serigny, whose only son is a fisherman, says discouragedly, "I don't see no future where the people can make a living."

The beginning of the decline of the wild redfish industry might be traced to the late 1970s when a growing fleet of purse seiners began to eyeball the huge stocks of bull reds. Gulfwide, the virgin schools of fish were reminiscent of the sprawling herds of bison on the unfenced Great Plains.

Jane Black, who was co-owner with husband Lonnie of J&L Seafood in Leeville, says there were at least 20 companies on the Gulf Coast trying to figure out how to sell bull redfish to the American public. "They were freezing it, they were steaking it, they were even making sausage out of it," she said.

"They were trying real hard, and when they finally came up with the blackening process, everything went crazy. I imagine they came up with the heavy-duty seasoning to cover the taste and the fact that the flesh of big redfish oxidizes when it's frozen—it turns dark."

Runaway demand for the essential ingredient in famed New Orleans chef Paul Prudhomme's blackened redfish recipe made bull reds worth big money almost overnight. A small fleet of purse seiners, mostly from out of state, worked the fish amid growing controversy until the fishery was shut down in federal waters late in 1986.

The federal shutdown crippled the redfish industry gulfwide and initiated the collapse of the market for the large fish. Before the closure, however, purse seiners were involved in two highly publicized incidents in Louisiana that helped precipitate the rapid demise of the state's entire industry.

In late April 1986, Louisiana authorities seized a purse seiner with 90,000 pounds of bull redfish aboard. Purse seining for reds within the state's waters was already illegal. Although the boat was only about 1,000 yards inside the three-mile state/federal boundary, the incident attracted extensive media coverage, arousing the interest of the public that was piqued as much by the sheer volume of the catch as by the violation itself.

Purse seining of the huge red-orange schools of surfacing fish made such excellent visuals that television crews made frequent return trips to the grounds, keeping the increasingly controversial fishery before the public eye.

Then, just a few weeks after the first incident, a purse seiner, reportedly working for a seafood company outside Louisiana, dumped thousands of pounds of dead bull reds. "Some boys struck more fish than they could handle," said Fred Black who was, himself, operating a pair of purse seiners out of Hopedale. "They had oyster boats, shrimp boats—anything—running out there. They were giving half the fish away just for hauling them in," said Black.

After a large school of fish is captured in a purse seine, the net is constricted or "pursed" alongside the vessel where the fish are scooped aboard. Closely confined and unable to swim, the fish can suffocate and, in the warm waters of the Gulf, rapidly spoil. Explaining that most of the participants in this brand- new fishery had to learn the hard way how to nip off manageable portions of the great schools of redfish, and how to handle them once they got them onboard, Black added, "They should have turned those fish loose before they died."

The wind and current carried the eight-mile line of dead reds into state waters in Breton Sound, east of the Mississippi River. Television and newspapers wasted no time reporting the kill, and the image of the entire redfish industry in Louisiana took a real nosedive.

In the wake of these incidents, amid public outcry, the state Legislature easily passed two bills in the summer of 1986 to further restrict purse seining. Act 611 prohibited the possession of a purse seine and redfish on the same boat in Louisiana waters. That measure precluded the landing of redfish caught in federal waters. Act 387 prohibited the use of purse seines for taking any fish except menhaden in Louisiana territorial waters. (About one billion pounds of menhaden are harvested each year in Louisiana waters by large purse seiners owned by corporations like Zapata-Haynie. The small, oily

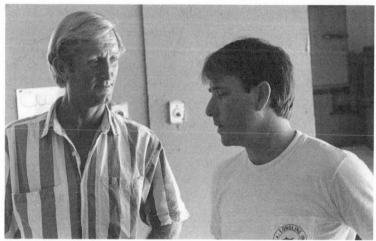

Frank McCain (left) was one of the many inshore netters who were apprehensive about the offshore harvest of bull redfish.

baitfish has many industrial uses including the manufacture of paints, fertilizers and livestock feed.)

Before the ban, purse seining of bull reds in Louisiana had become a divisive issue among the state's commercial fishermen. "This bull red crap's got to stop," complained Frank McCain, a coastal netter who earned his living from redfish and spotted seatrout. "They're killing our livelihood," said McCain, who would fish for several years to catch the 100,000 pounds of redfish that a purse seiner could take in a single set.

Harlon Pearce, a New Orleans wholesaler, was supplying the purse-seined reds to out-of-state markets. Pearce was also tanning the skins of the large fish into a fine-textured leather and envisioned a local industry based on that product. "In order to develop a market, you have to have a continual supply of product and in a volume that only purse seiners can supply," explained Pearce. "A purse-seine fishery is easily controllable because there are so few boats in it."

In theory Pearce was right; with a limit on the number of vessels and an observer aboard each one, the purse-seine fishery might have become as integral to the red drum fishery as the recreational fishermen and inshore netters. But at that early stage in the game the available biological data was inadequate for calculating a sustainable level of harvest. Data on the species was so scant that, in 1980, when two purse-seine fishermen testified before the Gulf of Mexico Fishery Management Council[1] that, if they had the market, they could harvest one million pounds of red drum a year from the Gulf, some council members argued that there were *no* red drum in the Gulf's offshore waters.

Ironically, the best way to gather this data was to allow the fishery to continue but, as momentum built against the purse seiners, this option faded. Both the recreational industry and the inshore netters had too much to lose if the purse seiners overfished the brood stock off Louisiana.

Ben Knous, inshore netter and spokesman for the Galliano-based Organization of Louisiana Fishermen, agreed in principle with Pearce. "You don't need all the bulls," said Knous. "After they get so old, the reproductive rate is not all that high. Stocks die off with nobody using them. Although I, personally, think purse seiners are an elite bunch and consider their gear unfair to the nearly 2,000 inshore fishermen, they are part of the industry, and any time you lose a part of the industry, you're weaker."

Knous claimed that most inshore fishermen were against the purse seiners from the start. "We didn't want 'em," he said, "we knew we were headed for trouble. You can't handle that volume of fish without destroying some. And once it started, we knew that when they got rid of the purse seiners, they'd come for us."

In spite of this knowledge, some of the traditional fishermen, including Knous' group, banded together to help convince the Legislature to ban purse seining. They also had to convince members of a recently formed coalition, which had promised a strong, unified voice for the entire industry, to turn against the purse seiners, who were also in the group. Infighting between the purse seiners and the small inshore operators may have contributed to the eventual disbanding of this effective coalition.

In an unprecedented move, some inshoremen even sided with GCCA as that group fought to stop the purse seiners. (The bizarre alliance didn't last long—the following year GCCA sponsored legislation that would have eliminated all nets from inshore waters.)

GCCA, however, didn't need a lot of help from the fishermen. The group's overt opposition to the unpopular purse seiners attracted sport-fishing members to state chapters across the Gulf Coast; as its membership swelled so did the group's funds and clout, which helped attract yet more members.

Up went the billboards. A huge skeletal redfish, accompanied with the plea, "GOING, GOING,...GCCA, JOIN BEFORE IT'S TOO LATE!" stirred the public's emotions with its suggestion that the species was threatened with extinction.

Rumors about the group's tactics ran rampant during the preparation of the Commerce Department's federal management plan for redfish. It was alleged that Walter Fondren, president of the Coastal Conservation Association,[2] had flown U.S. Secretary of Commerce Malcolm Baldrige[3] to the Christmas Islands for a fishing trip, and that Winthrop P. Rockefeller had raised more than a million dollars in a single evening for the recreational lobby.

"Some of this was complete fabrication, and most was wildly

Working from the boat's fantail, an inshoreman clears a red from a 5-inch nylon gill net.

exaggerated," said CCA executive director Randy Bright in a 1987 *Seafood Business* article. Bright conceded that pressure was put on Baldrige by the recreational lobby, but he insisted that the action was totally justified, given the circumstances. The "circumstances" were that no one knew how many redfish were in the Gulf of Mexico.

Normally, it takes a few years to build a data base on a new fishery that is adequate to design a sustainable fishery management plan. Under intensifying political pressure, however, government officials could not allow the purse seine fishery to continue for that long without restriction. Secretary Baldrige, in a precedent-setting action, invoked a never-before-used provision of the Magnuson Act[4] that empowered the secretary of commerce to put an interim management plan in place in the absence of such a plan by the responsible fishery management council. Since the Gulf of Mexico Fishery Management Council hadn't had time to collect information about redfish populations and breeding on which permanent regulations could be based, Baldrige installed his own plan.

In 1986, he issued a pair of 90-day emergency rules. During the first, which took effect June 25, the purse seiners were allowed to bring in a quota of one million pounds, which horrified those who felt the fishery should be shut down entirely.

"I take full credit, or blame, for the recommendation that the quota for the first 90-day emergency period be one million pounds," said Jack Brawner, Southeast regional director of the National Marine Fisheries Service, in a 1987 interview with *National Fisherman*. "I made that recommendation with full knowledge of the emotional climate....If I had been making the decision, I would have allowed another one million pounds to be harvested the second 90 days."

Brawner viewed his stand as "super-conservative," noting that in the first six months of 1986, the purse seiners had harvested more than six million pounds of reds from the federal zone. If they had been allowed to continue unchecked, he noted, they probably would have harvested up to 14 million more pounds by the end of the year.

"So from the perspective of the resource," said Brawner, "my recommendation had the effect of cutting back a potential additional harvest of 14 million pounds to one million pounds."

Brawner said that he based his decision on biological evidence that suggested there were "enormous quantities of red drum" in the Gulf. And on scientific advice that the Gulf's spawning redfish stocks could be reduced to 20 percent to 40 percent of the standing population without affecting the welfare of that resource.

The purse seiners landed their million-pound quota in just over three weeks. Baldrige closed the offshore red drum fishery for the remainder of the first 90-day period, until September 23, when he had the option of leaving the fishery closed or setting another 90-day quota.

He left it closed—the second 90-day emergency rule called for a zero quota, and was followed by the shutdown of the commercial harvest of redfish in federal waters.

The purse seiners either steamed back to their home ports of Florida, Alabama or Mississippi, switched to other species of fish or went to Mexico where some continued to fish the bulls, exporting the fish to the United States where the demand for blackened redfish seemed insatiable.

As the purse seiners sailed off into the sunset, GCCA took the credit for singlehandedly putting a stop to the unpopular bull red fishery. GCCA had expanded into Louisiana from Texas in 1983; in just three years, the Louisiana chapter had risen to prominence as the white-hatted protector of the state's marine resources.

Though happy to see the purse seiners leave, the leaders among the inshore fishermen sensed that they were out on a limb. They knew that, as the purse seiners left, they would take their money with them—money that would come in handy in the allocation fights that everyone knew were coming. Inshore netter Knous' prophetic words came true—politically, the industry was weakened.

According to Matt Raigan, spotter pilot for the purse seiners, there were only eight vessels working redfish off the Louisiana coast. It was the Texas trout massacre all over again. While GCCA smelled like a rose, the micro-fleet of purse seiners left behind a stink that clung to the traditional redfishermen like that of rotten shrimp.

Political fights are determined by influencing public opinion, which takes money and skill in public relations. As the upcoming battles over Louisiana's inshore redfish approached, the battle for the public's mind was already won by the well-organized and politically astute GCCA.

To the public, with no identification with, or even awareness of, the traditional inshore fishery, all redfishermen were greedy opportunists in 75-foot vessels. As events unfolded over the next two years, the inshoremen would win no new friends.

The purse seiners had supplied redfish in sufficient volume to establish a national, even international, market. When they were put out of business, the only source for the product was inside waters. As the price of redfish skyrocketed, the ranks of the traditional fishermen were complemented by new recruits out to make a quick buck.

Retirees, high-school kids, weekenders and oilfield workers on week-on, week-off shifts staked nets throughout the marsh. Professionals often found themselves standing in line at their regular fishhouse while recreational fishermen, with their newly purchased commercial licenses in hand, sold their catches.

At the same time the net fishery was rapidly expanding, over 200,000 licensed recreational anglers were still permitted to catch 50 redfish per day, and to have two days' limits in their possession. In 1987, local "sportsmen" purchased 588 recreational gill net licenses, 167 recreational trammel net licenses and 117 recreational seine licenses.

It was a gold rush, a free-for-all. For the old-time professionals, it would get even worse.

During the 1970s, the Arab states embargoed the export of their oil, driving the price sky-high. When the Arabs fell out among themselves in 1982, oil prices spiraled downward from $40 a barrel to a low of $10 in 1986. As the oil industry bottomed out, a multitude of unemployed oil workers took to the water to try to pay their bills. The army of newcomers to the fishery created a highly visible presence in the marsh yet few were committed enough to the industry to join the organizations that represent fishermen during debates over legislation.

As the number of nets in the marsh proliferated, the hard-core cadre of professional fishermen saw their profits diminished, which further lessened their ability to lend support to their own advocacy groups. And in the near future, those groups would need all the help they could get.

Historically, fishery management in Louisiana had been a policy of *laissez faire*. With vast resources and relatively few fishermen, efforts had been directed more toward developing fisheries than regulating them. Redfish changed all that.

The "redfish crisis" focused the attention of federal, state and academic biologists upon the species. As the data began to come in, concern shifted from the bull redfish in the Gulf to the juvenile fish in the marsh. Just as in medicine, where attention drawn to an acute injury like a bruised rib can lead to the discovery of a more malignant condition like lung cancer, so the scrutiny prompted by the dramatic offshore purse-seine fishery revealed a more insidious problem in the inside waters.

As the purse-seine fishermen captured bull reds, biologists studied the fish in a variety of ways. For instance, they removed pearl-like "otoliths" from their heads. By dissecting the otoliths and counting the number of rings—much like the annual rings in a tree trunk—the age of each fish could be determined. By aging and measuring large quantities of red drum, biologists were able to determine their growth rates, and estimate the relative size of each year-class of fish produced over the past 40 years.

The results of their sampling revealed that the offshore schools of red drum contained fewer young fish than they expected. Biologists were shocked to learn that the number of reds that were surviving long enough to escape the marsh and join the offshore brood stock had become dangerously low. Only two out of 100 redfish that did not die from causes other than fishing were making it out of the marsh in 1986, said some biologists, who recommended taking action to get the escapement rate up to 20 percent. Otherwise, they feared, the older generations of fish would die off without being replaced, leading—in the future—to a "collapse" in the population of the species.

The federal government began to pressure the Gulf states to do something to address the problem.

In July 1987, the Louisiana Legislature passed a comprehensive management plan. The plan was forged as a compromise between recreational fishermen, led by GCCA, who sought a total ban on net fishing in the state, and commercial interests who needed to keep fishing. Louisiana Department of Wildlife and Fisheries (LDWF) biologists supplied data and their own recommendations while committee members in the Senate and House mediated. By the time the smoke cleared, both user groups were forced to make some sacrifices.

First-ever minimum size limits were put on the anglers. Recreationals now had to return to the water any redfish smaller than 14 inches. In 1988 the minimum would increase to 15 inches and to 16 inches in 1989. The sportsmen retained their daily limit of 50 redfish, which vexed commercials since it had been determined that the recreational harvest, from 1980 through 1986, averaged at least 70 percent of the total redfish pulled from Louisiana waters. Still, the minimum size limits were projected to reduce the sportsmen's take by nearly 50 percent.

Other legislation raised minimum size limits for commercials to 18 inches and put them under a first-ever quota of 1.7 million pounds. This figure represented the commercials' 10-year harvest average, with the highest and lowest years thrown out.

The quota was trouble from the beginning for the industry. Not only did it end redfishing midseason, but it crippled the dealers as well.

Besides considerably reducing the harvest over the previous year, an omission in the wording of the bill led to a controversy that further galvanized recreationals against the redfish industry.

Early drafts of House Bill 692, to become Act 381, the quota bill, commenced unambiguously: "An annual quota for 1987 for the commercial harvest...." Later drafts, including the final—the only one that counts—commenced vaguely with, "An annual quota for the commercial harvest...."

According to Sen. Bagert, who had the bill drawn up, "I relied on a lawyer to work on this bill. I wasn't aware until the end, of the omission."

Without the words, "for 1987," in the bill, it was unclear exactly what the time frame for the annual quota was intended to be. Was it January 1, 1987 to December 31, 1987? Or did it begin September 1, 1987 (when the bill went into effect) and run until the following September?

Fishermen assumed that the tally for the quota could not commence until September 1. Sen. Leonard Chabert, then chairman of the Senate Natural Resources Committee, declared, "There is no way this bill can be retroactive," meaning the count could not be started on January 1, nine months before the bill became law.

Biologists had intended just 1.7 million pounds of reds to be taken in all of 1987, however, and LDWF officials told fishermen and seafood dealers that the tally for the quota would almost certainly commence retroactively to January. Since the quota had already been exceeded by September 1, fishermen braced themselves for a shutdown.

The seven-member Wildlife and Fisheries Commission was to convene on September 4 to decide when to impose the new quota law. Two days before, it held a public hearing.

Commercial fishermen, along with wholesalers and retailers, stormed the meeting to protest a retroactive tally and an immediate shutdown. Representatives from GCCA and other recreationally oriented groups declared that the intent of the law was to make the quota commence on January 1, 1987. They urged the commission to make the limits retroactive.

It was a no-win situation for the commission—either way it went, it was bound to catch flak and plenty of it. When the commissioners reconvened two days later, they stated that the quota law could not be retroactive and that the tally on the 1.7 million pounds began on September 1.

Commercial fishermen were ecstatic and went back to netting. Recreational interests were peeved, however. The outdoor press was indignant at the commission's decision and portrayed it as biased toward the commercials. But their chagrin was nothing compared to what would happen later.

When the commission finally did shut down the commercials, it shut down the sport fishermen as well.

By early January 1988, a little over four months after the count had begun, fishermen filled their quota. On January 7, the commission met to carry out what the law required—closing down the commercial fishery until September 1, when the next quota was scheduled to begin.

Commercials, who just couldn't adjust to the reality that they were, for the first time ever, being shut down, again showed up at the commission meeting in force. In frustration, they lashed out at the recreationals.

"If I can't fish, no one can fish," grumbled New Orleans seafood patriarch Preston Battistella.

"If it comes down to a quota, divide it among all the people," requested Henry Truelove, president of Charenton-based Louisiana Fishermen for Fair Laws, "and when we reach it, let's all quit fishing."

But the quota had been put on the commercials, not the recreationals. The commission's function was to carry out the law, not make new ones. Yet, it surprised everyone and did shut down the recreational fishery until June 1, 1988, by which time the Legislature would reconvene and could act toward reducing the excessive recreational daily limit of 50 fish.

Closing the recreational fishery, however, was not on the agenda published for the January meeting. Louisiana state laws require that public notice be given to allow concerned citizens input before laws are changed.

Members of the recreational lobby, now facing a closure themselves, threatened to press suit. A week later, the attorney general forced the commission to rescind its action because of the procedural error. The recreational fishery was reopened.

On February 4, the commission held another hearing to discuss a ban on the recreational harvest of redfish. This time the proposed ban was on the agenda. Commercials again made it known that they wanted the sport fishery closed. Mark Hilzim, executive director of Louisiana GCCA, implored the commission to keep the recreational fishery open and let the Legislature reduce sportsmen's bag limits. (The commission had authority only to close the fishery; it could not change bag limits or seasons.)

Dr. Richard Condrey, LSU biologist and chairman of the Red Drum Stock Assessment Group of the Gulf of Mexico Fishery Management Council, had told the commission the month before that a short-term closure would be insignificant toward achieving the council's escapement goal, which had recently been increased to 30 percent. Condrey repeated this message at a series of GCCA-sponsored "sportsmen's forums." But during the February hearing, he reversed his position and recommended that the commission close the harvest to both commercial and recreational fishermen "until such time as the Legislature or the commission can implement management measures that are in line with current restrictions in other Gulf states.

"I had testified that I did not see the benefit of a short-term closure," Condrey told the commission. "I am now backing away from that position. If you're going to take a stand, close the whole fishery down until you or the Legislature can develop a management plan to achieve 30 percent escapement."

According to Dr. Condrey, there was still no scientific need to shut down the recreationals, but he reversed his position for political reasons in order to show good faith to the federal government. Condrey feared the feds might scrap their entire management plan and even go so far as to reopen the bull red fishery if states did not make diligent efforts to limit the harvest of inshore redfish.

Gerald Adkins, then head of the Finfish Section, LDWF, also reversed his position from the January meeting, where he had stated that there would be no biological advantage to a short-term recreational shutdown. In February, he too recommended to the commission that if it couldn't reduce the possession limits, then it should shut down the fishery.

After listening to the public comment, the commission voted 5-2 to shut down the anglers until June 1.

Commercial fishermen, who made up the majority of the packed house of 1,500 to 2,000, cheered the decision. They'd already been cut out of the fishery and felt that it was fair to shut down the anglers. The recreational lobby complained bitterly that the commission had yielded to pressure from commercial interests.

Joe Palmisano Jr., then chairman of the commission, said, however, "I don't care about user groups—I'm interested in saving the redfish. We shut down the recreational fishery because, in December 1987, we were requested by the National Marine Fisheries Service to do so.

"The commission did not have the authority to reduce the recreational limit. We could only curtail the recreational harvest until the Legislature could reconvene and take action toward increasing escapement to the recommended 30 percent, which the 1988 Legislature did accomplish."

That two leading biologists recommended the shutdown, albeit for political reasons rather than for biological considerations, was scarcely acknowledged in the outdoor press; neither was the commission-directed recommendation for a sports closure by NMFS. Rather, the press immediately attacked the commercial industry and questioned the integrity of the commission.

The New Orleans *Times-Picayune's* outdoor columnist Bob Marshall wrote: "The commercial fishermen's insistence that sport fishermen stop had nothing to do with a concern for the resource. It was sour grapes, a vindictive move born of a feeling that their quota was the result of political pressure from sport fishermen who are out to make the species gamefish and close commercial fishing forever."

Regarding the commission, Marshall stated, "The fact is, the decision to close the sport fishery was motivated by a desire to appease an angry group of constituents."

GCCA's Mark Hilzim was quoted as saying that it seemed commission members wanted to punish sportsmen for demanding commercial cutbacks in the first place. "The Legislature gave both groups a piece of the pie," said Hilzim. "The commercials ate 2 1/2 pies, and now they're angry that we have a slice left. This was sour grapes, that's all."

"Two-and-a-half pies" refers to the oft-repeated point that commercials had been allowed to catch their 1.7 million pound quota twice, plus the amount they caught during the lag time in reporting.

According to NMFS, the commercials' 2 1/2 pies in 1987 were equivalent to 1,142,794 fish or 40 percent of the total annual harvest. The recreationals' "slice" equaled 60 percent—1,705,024 redfish. This did not make headlines.

Still, the commercials' taking "2 1/2 pies" and their alleged participation in the recreational closure was more than many previously neutral anglers could take.

The Louisiana Wildlife Federation was the first organization to put into writing a resolution to make redfish a gamefish. LWF is a state affiliate of the National Wildlife Federation, a prestigious conservation group headquartered in Washington, D.C. The 9,000-member LWF includes about 5,000 sportsmen enrolled through 45 rod-and-gun clubs; the other 4,000 members join directly and, in addition to sportsmen, include many who enjoy "non-consumptive" outdoor activities such as birdwatching, hiking or canoeing.

According to Randy Lanctot, youthful executive director of the LWF, the membership did not feel that the commission had acted objectively. "That's what got the sportsmen so fired up—the commission provoked them. The sports felt that they got the shaft, and they were mad. If they had felt that the commission was properly exercising its authority instead of being pressured by enraged commercials, it would have taken the steam out of the gamefish movement."

GCCA's Hilzim agreed that the recreational ban definitely hurt the commercials and at the same time helped his group by boosting membership by a few hundred and raising the interest level among the other members. The closure, said Hilzim, forced GCCA to become much more militant—and go for gamefish.

Ben Bagert put it simply, "The retaliatory closure made gamefish politically possible."

Once word got out that the push for gamefish status was on, the industry mobilized. Or tried to. As Henry Truelove said, "It's hard to spend money fighting when you can't pay your electric bill."

The January closure on redfish—their wintertime staple—had abruptly interrupted fishermen's incomes. Several months later, as the 1988 legislative session approached, many fishermen were simply too preoccupied with economic survival to support those who would fight for them.

Seafood dealers, too, offered reduced support. Like the fishermen, some were economically strapped as a result of the closure and were too engrossed with their immediate financial woes to fight to save their own industry. Others were apathetic since they had, after the closure, either turned to other sources for their redfish, such as Mexico, or had shifted emphasis to underutilized species like black drum and amberjack.

"The commercial fish dealer has lost interest," said Jane Black, who lobbied for the Organization of Louisiana Fishermen during the 1988 legislative session. "He no longer supports the commercial fisherman publicly and not too much financially. Token support, that's all."

So, except for a few involved dealers, the fishermen were on their own. But money's the name of the game in any Capitol struggle. This financial reality was driven home at a meeting where prospective lobbyists were being screened. One veteran lobbyist, who billed himself as a "hired gun," stated flatly, "I ain't cheap."

As one dealer attempted to pin him down as to exactly how much he would charge for a session's work, the crusty lobbyist responded that members of one of the recreational groups "took the entire Natural Resources Committee to dinner last night. They take them to lunch and they do it often. That costs."

It quickly became clear that the people in the coastal finfish industry, hamstrung as they were, were in no position to match this kind of action. But they'd damned sure try.

The same committed fishermen and dealers, the same familiar faces that each year fight the latest round of anti-commercial legislation, began to come together to discuss strategy. After a hard day's work—some still in their fishing clothes—the leaders of the inshore fishermen's groups from across coastal Louisiana would converge on some small hotel meeting room.

These meetings, attended by a few white-shirted city dealers but mostly by the work-hardened fishermen and dockside buyers, dressed in T-shirts and jeans, bore more resemblance to some junta of guerrilla captains than your typical industry meeting. By nature fiercely competitive, headstrong and clannish, the men made an heroic attempt to unify.

As Henry Truelove made clear at the commencement of an early meeting, "We have to set our differences aside." As the battle progressed, however, a rift over different fishing techniques appeared in their ranks and slowly widened, weakening their united front.

Typically, the fishermen's leaders travel to Baton Rouge to testify at hearings and to lobby the legislators themselves. They receive no payment other than the satisfaction of knowing that they're doing the most they can do to protect their livelihoods. While the recreational industry employs salaried executive directors and professional lobbyists to work the legislators throughout the session, the fishermen abandon their boats only at the last minute. Then, from Cameron to Venice, they pile into their pickups before dawn and, with their lunch money in their pockets, head north to Baton Rouge.

Committee members know the leaders by their first names; the hearings are informal and often comical as fishermen spin their down-the-bayou testimonies. But there's drama too, as the fishermen, overcome with the emotion and frustration at being backed into a corner and facing the loss of income or livelihood, burst into impassioned tirades against threatening legislation.

Initially the fishermen united as a bloc of organizations that included the Concerned Finfishermen of Louisiana, Concerned Shrimpers of America, Lake Pontchartrain Fishermen's Association, Louisiana Fishermen for Fair Laws, Louisiana Seafood Processors, Organization of Louisiana Fishermen, and Terrebonne Fishermen's Association. Because of the enormity of the impending gamefish legislation, they decided that this year they should supplement their own efforts with that of a professional lobbyist. The group pooled their resources and employed Mike Evans, a rookie, to represent them in the Capitol.

Evans had helped manage Manny Fernandez's election campaign in his unsuccessful bid for attorney general. Fernandez was now executive counsel and chief advisor on fisheries issues to recently elected Gov. Buddy Roemer. Evans' ties with Fernandez, it was hoped, would compensate for his total lack of experience both in lobbying and with the commercial fishing industry.

The group leaders concurred on a strategy of non-compromise. The bill was so ridiculous in its original form—it simply made reds and specks gamefish forever—that surely Governor Roemer would veto it.

According to Fernandez, the governor stated in several meetings that he would "look at vetoing the bill." He had even gone so far as to say on television that he would veto anything that was "unfair." The game plan—defensive, as always—was to not give an inch, go for broke and, hopefully, Buddy Roemer would save 'em.

The proponents of the gamefish bill, on the other hand, were prepared to go for the jugular. GCCA was in fighting form. Not only was the organization now perceived as a genuine conservation group but its war chest was growing daily as anglers, sensing an impending victory, wanted to be in on the kill. The Texas-based group also had two formidable allies—the Louisiana Wildlife Federation and Republican Sen. Bagert of New Orleans.

The 9,000 LWF members, added to the 7,000 that the Louisiana GCCA claimed, created a constituency of 16,000 recreationals. Disregarding the considerable cross-membership that existed between the two organizations, this represented less than eight percent of the 200,000 licensed saltwater anglers in the state. Still, they outnumbered the 2,000 commercial finfishermen considerably. And, with good jobs, they didn't have the fishermen's cash-flow problems.

Bagert was not only an eloquent trial lawyer but a member of the influential Senate Natural Resources Committee. He was the GCCA's gladiator who would fight like a pit bull to get the gamefish bill passed, albeit in a weakened yet still devastating form.

On June 2, Sen. Bagert introduced the gamefish bill before an overflowing crowd of sport and commercial fishermen. The commercials' worst-case scenario had begun. After Bagert's earnest introduction, members of both constituencies as well as LDWF biologists were called to testify before the Senate Natural Resources Committee.

Garden District attorney Maumus Claverie, who was vice chairman of the national Coastal Conservation Association and chairman of the Louisiana GCCA, testified in favor of the gamefish bill.

Claverie supported a cut in the recreational bag limit from 50 to five redfish but felt that the LDWF recommendation of a 900,000-pound commercial quota was all wrong. He then brought up the apples versus oranges argument used with so much success in Texas, comparing the "billion dollar" recreational fishery to just the dockside value of the commercial redfish and speckled trout fisheries which "are less than two percent of the entire commercial industry. Somebody said they're actually less than two tenths of one percent," added Claverie, for good measure.

The redfish and speckled trout combined harvest in 1987 totaled $6.8 million which was, indeed, two percent of the total $337 million worth of seafood harvested in Louisiana that year. The total landings included over 100 species of freshwater and saltwater finfish plus the greatest shrimp, blue crab, oyster and crayfish harvests of any other state in America. More to the point, of the total value of the seven major species that sustain the inshore finfish industry, redfish and trout contributed a solid 60 percent.

After Claverie, George Anne Bernard, president of the Louisiana Wildlife Federation and owner of a saltwater recreational marina near New Iberia, testified in favor of the bill. Bernard's comments revealed her group's prior reluctance to go for gamefish: "For the first time in our 49-year history we have voted to support gamefish status for redfish and speckled trout," she began. "We deeply regret the conflicts that have been caused over this issue by the different user groups but we feel that inconsistencies and irresponsible mismanagement of the resource has forced us to feel strongly about gamefish status as a viable and reasonable solution to the problem. It's the only way to manage these two species at this point."

After Bernard, representatives from the Louisiana Marine Trades Association and the Louisiana Association of Charterboat Captains spoke for the bill and then it was the commercials' turn. The fishermen testified against the bill, mostly pleading hardship and loss of employment should it pass.

Then it was the biologists' turn. LDWF biologists stated initially that the commercials probably could be allotted a quota of about 900,000 pounds of redfish for the 1988-89 season.

"You feel that if we reduce recreationals from 50 to five fish and give the commercials 900,000 pounds, that we could help the fish and preserve the industry?" asked Sen. Leonard Chabert, who represented the coastal parishes of Terrebonne and Lafourche.

"That's correct," answered Joey Shepard, LDWF fishery biologist.

But the 900,000-pound figure became more nebulous as questioning proceeded. LSU biologist Richard Condrey and recently appointed LDWF Secretary Virginia Van Sickle both emphasized that the 900,000-pound commercial quota was a very preliminary figure and that some amount would have to be pared off to compensate for the commercials' overharvest the previous year. As Sen. Chabert bore down, trying to arrive at some concrete figure based on good biology, on which a debate could proceed, the two offered only that the 900,000 would have to be reduced and that they didn't yet have enough data to recommend a firm quota.

Although the gamefish debate would go on for two months, this was the last time any quota other than a "zero quota" would be referred to officially. From there on out, it would be strictly politics and deals as the fishermen tried to cut their losses.

Before the 1981 gamefish fight in Texas, GCCA captured the attention of legislators by contributing generously to their campaigns through SPORT-PAC, the group's political action committee. In Louisiana, however, no contributions needed to be made. According to Mark Hilzim, "We have never made a single campaign contribution to anybody. We did everything with a grass-roots effort."

Jane Black, who represented the Organization of Louisiana Fishermen, a group of about 250 commercial fishermen including shrimpers, crabbers, oystermen and finfishermen, explained, "It's so easy to sell pro-conservation. We've got such a hard thing to sell. GCCA didn't have to spend much time trying to paint the fishermen as bad people—maybe one or two sentences the whole session—because it had already been done."

Hilzim and GCCA's two full-time lobbyists and Republicans Bagert in the Senate and Robert Garrity in the House spared no effort convincing legislators to go for gamefish.

The fishermen killed the redfish bill more than once but each time the magician Bagert revived it. Before a vote, he and friends turned to the computer. It was programmed to spill out preaddressed cards to thousands of sportsmen who would, in turn, relay them to the offices of their respective legislators. The resulting stack of mail from concerned citizens was sure to impress vote-conscious politicians.

"It was computer warfare," said Bagert. Of course, the fishermen had no computers.

Garrity, from the New Orleans suburb River Ridge, addressed a local chapter meeting of the GCCA after the fight was over. "We needed 53 votes in the House and 20 votes in the Senate to take it," he told the audience. "We had guys in North Louisiana who didn't care about redfish—they cared about cotton farmers. So we traded votes—they voted gamefish, we voted cottonseed."

Garrity also revealed how at least one attempt not to hurt the commercial fishermen had been foiled.

Pete Gerica, president of Lake Pontchartrain Fishermen's Association, related before this meeting, how he had convinced several of the black legislators to simply not show up for critical votes on gamefish. With many of their constituents unable to afford the equipment needed to catch their own seafood, several black legislators wished to support the netters, but with the negative publicity and pressure within the Legislature, it was difficult. A no-show was, at least, better than a vote *for* gamefish.

But, as Garrity played to the sportsman audience, he boasted that Gerica's efforts may have been for naught: "When some members of the black caucus got up to go to a meeting, one of our guys from North Louisiana pulled six of their machines for gamefish."

As the redfish bill progressed on its odyssey, it didn't remain in its original form. In fact, it went through so many transmutations that getting a hold on this piece of legislation was like trying to grab a wild redfish barehanded.

According to Jane Black, what Gov. Roemer was really saying when he commented on television that he would veto anything that was unfair was, "this bill better get cleaned up some."

"Cleaned up" meant compromise.

The attempt at gaining gamefish status for trout, which everyone agreed were quite abundant, was withdrawn. And, instead of trying to get gamefish status for redfish indefinitely, Sen. Bagert decided that a "sunset gamefish" designation would have a better chance of passing. Sunset gamefish meant that redfish would be decommercialized for only three years, when gamefish status would "sunset."

"I figured that Roemer'd veto it, that's why I only made it for three years," said Bagert.

Jane Black, executive director of the Organization of Louisiana Fishermen

Besides these two changes, an amendment was added, stipulating that, when the trout quota was filled, no net with a stretched-mesh size of less than 5 1/2 inches would be allowed in the water. This large mesh size was intended to protect trout and most redfish from capture during the closed season. But, if the trout quota was filled, as expected, in late winter or early spring, fishermen would be limited to using only this large-meshed net throughout the spring and summer, until September 1, when the next trout season would open. To catch what?

Many of the constituents of the fishermen's bloc were primarily shrimpers. They spent the summer months trawling from their shrimp boats; in the wintertime they tended set nets for redfish to help make ends meet. (Set nets are nets—usually gill nets—that are anchored out and checked periodically.) So, when the trout were closed, they had their shrimp. If the recreationals took the reds, they could still lay out their nets during the winter for sheepshead, flounder, black drum or alligator gar, all of which required nets with mesh sizes upward of 5 1/2 inches. So, no sweat. They'd still hold the line.

There were also some finfishermen, working primarily in the big lakes like Vermillion Bay and Lake Pontchartrain, who ran set nets year round. These large bodies of water are often rough or murky, which makes it difficult to spot fish. If they lost the reds, it would be tough but these boys too would try to make it with the larger, lower-valued species. They'd also hold the line.

But, there was a scattering of netters who were getting nervous. They were the full-time finfishermen who came from the west, in Cameron Parish; from down the Mississippi in Plaquemines Parish; from Grand Isle; and there were two clusters centered in St. Bernard and Lafourche Parishes. They were "strike" fishermen and they needed a smaller meshed net to harvest mullet, pompano and, perhaps, Spanish mackerel or bluefish during the spring and summer months.

Even if they took the reds, these fishermen wanted to make sure they could still earn a living. Some had already begun to distance themselves from the set netters.

"That was Gov. Roemer's first year," explained Jane Black, of the Organization of Louisiana Fishermen, based in Lafourche Parish. "And he had requested educational packages on Louisiana's finfish industry; how many boats were in it, who were the first finfish people that ever sold fish, the family names, and all that. LSU helped us put the package together and, while we were doing it, we included a recommendation that the strike net be identified separate from the set net because, in the politicians' eyes, strike netters were nonexistent. We had it drawn up as a bill but our board had agreed not to bring it up that year. We had a worse enough battle trying to save what we had, without confusing the issue.

"But it wasn't too long after we sent the package to the governor that our definition appeared right in the middle of the gamefish bill."

A strike net, defined within the Redfish Bill, "means any gill net, trammel net or seine net not anchored or secured to the waterbottom or shore and which is used off a vessel and actively worked while being used."

Along with this definition, the final draft of the Redfish Bill provided that fishermen could still use nets down to 3 1/2 inches if they used a strike net. Set nets, however, could be no smaller than 5 1/2 inches. The reasoning was that strike netting, where schools of fish are sighted and encircled, was a more directed fishery than set netting, where nets are staked or anchored in such a manner as to intercept passing fish. And, since the net is actively worked, the fisherman would be on hand to quickly release any redfish or trout he may incidentally catch.

The strike netters made a small victory, but it made for some bad blood among the fishermen.

"We had the strike net definition all the time, through all the redfish debates with the other organizations," said Black, "but we never brought it up because the OLF's board members had agreed not to. So when it all of a sudden appeared in the gamefish bill, the other fishermen thought we tricked 'em."

"There are only four or five of us who strike in the lake and we need an airplane to do it," explained a Lake Pontchartrain fisherman. "But Jane strictly represents strike fishermen. We were going to get the bill vetoed but she made an agreement to keep strike nets. She gave 'em a tool to bend."

The rift that appeared among the fishermen using different types of gear is a classic example of the sort of gear conflict that commonly sets fisherman against fisherman. Although it did weaken their united front at an inopportune time, it's questionable whether any tactic could have beaten the stiff odds the netters were up against.

The revised gamefish bill passed both Senate and House. Late in the summer, Gov. Roemer signed it into law. Reds were now off-limits to commercials for the next three years.

The concession to the strike fishermen may have been perceived by the governor as sufficient compromise to get him "off the hook" and not have to veto the bill, although Fernandez said that Roemer considered vetoing it even in its changed form. Others in the Capitol claimed that Roemer, in his first legislative session as governor, had too much at stake to veto the bill.

Roemer had just inherited a state with its budget linked directly to the price of oil. With the depressed price of the commodity, the state was in dire economic straits. Some parishes threatened bankruptcy; unemployment was the highest in the nation. The governor's foremost challenge during this session was to enlist support for a total fiscal reform. One lobbyist indelicately suggested that some legislative backing for Roemer's urgent economic programs might have been withheld if he hadn't gone along with the three-year closure: "If he'd have vetoed that bill, they'd have had his ass."

According to Fernandez, "The governor would have preferred to implement more traditional management techniques such as quotas, seasons and mesh sizes based upon biological data rather than votes, even if it would have led to a zero quota."

A zero quota, instead of gamefish status might have been followed by increasing quotas in subsequent years, which would have enabled the better redfish netters to pay some bills. Instead, the fishermen were left with nothing but the hope that the fishery might be reopened, three years later.

According to the law, the commercial redfish harvest was to resume on September 1, 1991, under a quota set by Louisiana's Wildlife and Fisheries Commission at a level to ensure a 30 percent escapement of juvenile red drum to offshore waters. "Under the existing regulations," explained John Roussel of LDWF's finfish section, "the annual recreational harvest should average 600,000 to 800,000 redfish. If we do our stock assessment and find that there are, say, 1.5 million fish available for harvest, above those required for the 30 percent escapement, then, under existing law, the commission is authorized to set a commercial quota up to a level equal to the surplus."

At the close of the session, GCCA's Mark Hilzim said that his group did not yet have a position on a reopening of the fishery, but that he felt a three-year respite would not be long enough to improve the brood stock. "I have no doubt that in three years the marsh will be crawling with reds, but that doesn't mean we'll have any more offshore. In six years, yes; in three, I'm not so sure."

The Louisiana Wildlife Federation's Randy Lanctot said, "We are committed to reopening the commercial fishery if there are enough fish to sustain it. We would also support an increase in the creel limit. If we should have the luxury of too many fish, we would support a one-half-million to one-million-pound quota and a ten-fish-per-day creel limit."

Fisherman Lonnie Black, who strongly resents being forced to defend his profession has, nevertheless, spent most of his life doing so in both Florida and Louisiana. Regarding the odds of reopening the fishery in 1991, Black warily remarked, "I've seen 'em take...and I've never seen 'em give anything back."

HOUSTON SERIGNY

Leeville is a small fishing village, a cluster of fish and shrimp sheds and wood-frame houses raised on pilings high above the salt marsh of coastal Louisiana. Once a thriving community of 2,000, its location proved disastrous in 1915 when a hurricane slammed ashore from the Gulf of Mexico, driving a dreaded *raz de marée*—a storm surge that leveled the town. When the water receded it left bits of seaweed in the branches of the live oaks, 12 feet above the ground. The Great Leeville Storm spurred the exodus of most residents who relocated to Golden Meadow, 10 miles farther up Bayou Lafourche.

Only a few hardy clans chose to remain on this slight oak ridge in the prairie—the Terrebonnes, Melançons, Cheramies, Griffins and the Serignys.

Fisherman Houston Serigny is the third generation of his family to live in this outpost seafood port. His grandfather, says Houston, immigrated directly from France rather than by the arduous trek that brought most of the Acadian exiles from Nova Scotia to South Louisiana. Like his grandfather's, Houston's first language is French and, except for electricity, gasoline engines and a few other conveniences, his life is changed but little from a century ago when his father's father supported his family on the bounty of the surrounding wetlands.

Felled recently by a serious heart attack, Houston still runs his crab traps, fishes a bit with the rod and reel and traps a few otter in the wintertime. Although many local trappers have trapped a lifetime and never caught an otter, Houston consistently took over a hundred of the wary animals each season. But he was more deadly yet on redfish.

Houston fished the reds with a trammel net and his "putt-putt." With the air-cooled engine and a two-bladed weedless propeller, he was able to get well up into the marsh, amid the shallow and grassy waters where these shy fish dwell.

His only son, Houston Jr., in his mid-20s, apprenticed at his father's side. Lean and industrious, he is now the family's chief provider. A skilled trawler, fur trapper and redfisherman, young Houston is trying to maintain his family's tradition—and the Cajun Way—by clinging to his independence and working the marsh.

On an autumn morning—three months after the Redfish Bill became law—father, son and I sat around the table in the Serignys' sunny kitchen. As he filled our cups with freshly brewed dark-roasted coffee, from a steaming white enamel pot, Houston began his story:

My daddy was born in Leeville. My grandfather was French, from overseas, but he came here a long, long time ago. In them days, mostly, the people would live across the Bayou. They used to plant corn, rice, sugar cane, you name it—what they got up the Bayou in that fresh water, they used to have it down here.

Our family made their living with redfish, shrimp and trapping. That's all we could do here. But we made the most with redfish.

I'd say it was about 45 years ago, we were gettin' eight, nine cents a pound for redfish. We'd sell to Eddie Martin, here in Leeville.

Houston Serigny

Houston "Goo" Serigny, Jr.

Eddie'd take 'em 'cause he had the trucks, you know. He'd buy fish for three or four days and he'd go up to French Market in New Orleans.

In those days we used to oar our boat. From down here we'd leave at twelve o'clock at night and go in the Fourchon Pond. We'd leave at twelve o'clock and oar all night and we'd get down there around six, seven o'clock in the morning, you know, daybreak.

And we had a little piece of *tramail*—maybe 150 feet—short so we wouldn't catch too much fish. What we'd do, we'd fill up half o' the boat with oysters and then when we'd come back in we'd make a couple o' sets, catch 200, 300 pounds.

We'd spot the fish but we were too small to oar the skiff and get the fish so my daddy would say, "Well, let me get at it." He was young and full of energy, you know. So he'd take it and he'd circle the fish.

And then we was two, three of us in that little boat and, on the way comin' back, my daddy'd open the oysters, that we could sell them for a dollar or a dollar-and-a-half a gallon. And the only thing we had to eat, my momma used to make bread—that homemade bread—and we'd eat raw oysters and bread for our dinner.

I think our first motor was a three-cylinder Fairbank. It was with a crank. To keep it cool, it had a big old head and you had to fill it up with water. You'd just fill it with a big bucket, the head of it, you know, it was open. You'd run it for a couple of hours and when that motor came hot, that water would boil. And when we'd fish crab we'd put us some crabs in there and we'd eat boiled crab!

In our days, we didn't know what was a gill net. We didn't know what was a set net. We didn't know what was a seine. Well, we had seines for shrimp but they got seines for fish now. We didn't know until those people there came and brought all o' that here.

My daddy used a *tramail*. He used to make his own nets, out o' cotton. And every time we'd use it we had to dry it in the sun so it wouldn't rot. When the nylon net came out...we had bought an old nylon net from somebody, and we used it for maybe five years. And then we made a little money—I guess we saved maybe $400 or $500 in the year. So my daddy went up there to LaNasa's—that used to be a hardware by the French Market—and bought some new twine. So we threw the old one.

It stayed there four or five years and then I decided I wanted to fish for myself. So I went back down there and took the net out o' the mud and the grass. My daddy patched it up and I worked that net maybe four, five years. And I made money with it.

Raoul Martin—he's dead now—well, he came here one day and my daddy had bought a brand-new cotton net, maybe 300 feet long. I'm the first one that used it. He came here and he said, "Houston," he said, "I got my brother-in-law and my sister and we can take my little boat"—he had a little skiff with a six-cylinder Chrysler in it— "we're goin' to go catch some fish, we're goin' to go catch some fish in the lake down there." And he said, "I'll give you 10 dollars. You come with us and we'll use your net." And boy, 10 dollars was plenty money.

So we went down there around Fils de Bruce Island and they had a big bend in the bayou with a big cove and man, I could see that muddy water and I could see the fish. Raoul, he said, "Houston! Let's circle them, let's circle them!" I said, "Naw, that ain't redfish." He said, "Let's circle them anyway." So we circled them.

It was garfish that weighed from 100, 150 pounds, and tore my daddy's net up, I mean no more good at all! And then I was in trouble.

It was holes from one end to the other.

Before, we couldn't even buy no net. When we started, we started hand fishin'. With cane poles, with that bamboo. We used to go out in the lake right here and fish redfish with bamboo. And we'd string 'em up on a string we'd take from those *lataniers* [palmettos]. You'd take the stem and peel two of those things off—they might have 30 or 40 strands—and tie 'em together at the bottom. They'd be about three feet long.

And we'd open up the gills and we'd string 'em up on both sides. You could put about 10 redfish on each side. And then you'd tie the other end. And, if we'd be, say, three people fishing in the little boat, OK, me, let's say I'd make one knot at the end, and, now, if you're with us, you'd make two knots, and the other one, well, he'd make three knots at the end. That way, whenever we'd come sell, everybody knew whose fish were for who, 'cause all the fish were iced up together—we couldn't afford enough ice to ice 'em up separate.

I hate to go with the line today—it makes me sick. I mean that marsh is full o' redfish. I just go if somebody wants me to catch 'em some to eat. It just takes me about 10 minutes to catch the five.

But I can bring you where you can load up your boat three times a day. I just wish they'd let me at 'em for two days!

Now the sports, they still got the authority to fish in the water. And catch five redfish. We can too, but if we catch five redfish, that's for us to eat.

But what we call "sport" in Louisiana, there's no such thing as sport. Because the sports sold more fish than the commercial fishermen. I've seen that at every shed on the Bayou and if they didn't sell it here, they sold it in New Orleans or Baton Rouge.

When we was doin' it—sellin' the fish—it was to feed our families. But they got good jobs, they make a lot of money and that's why they call 'em "sports." They got $25,000, $30,000 boats.

This is the first winter ever we won't be able to fish the reds. But we have to watch them come in with ice chests full o' fish. If they wanted to close the fish, close it for everybody. *They're not more than us, them.*

I'll tell you, it hurts me. It hurts my boy. It hurts everybody from Lafourche Parish. I mean all the poor people that used to make a livin', they can't no mo'. And it's gonna get worse than that, the way it's goin'. I don't see no future where the people can make a livin'.

LOUISIANA REDFISH BLUES

There's no more Louisiana pride down here. The fishermen are now at the lowest point, morale-wise, stressed out and broke.
                    —Henry Truelove, president,
                      Louisiana Fishermen for Fair Laws

Golden Meadow fisherman Russell Black was making it. First he financed a $5,000 lot and paid that off. Then he saved for four or five years and in 1986 mortgaged his land for a down payment on a brand-new mobile home for himself, his wife and two kids. In two years, he paid the bank another $7,500.

In the summer of 1989, they repossessed everything.

"When they closed the redfish, I got too far behind," said Black. "I burnt a thousand dollars worth of gas trying to catch something else—for two months. I didn't make a dime.

"The bank even came back later. They told me I always paid my bills on time and offered me my land back. But you can't fish, and there's no jobs. I told 'em I just couldn't do it."

Black was not alone among the finfishermen. By the summer of 1989, those who hadn't lost their homes were rare indeed. It had been less than a year since the Legislature imposed a three-year ban on the commercial harvest of redfish.

"There's a lot of car notes in three years," remarked Henry Truelove. "It's no longer economically feasible to fish. If you're making $100 or $200 a day—and half of that's redfish—your expenses are 50 or 60 bucks and they cut your gross in half? You can't put a $15,000 rig in the water for that. One breakdown and you're out."

After their first entire winter without redfish, the netters were reeling. "Fishermen all over the state are really havin' a helluva time," said Vernon Cubbage of Deep Delta Fisheries and Marine Supplies in Boothville, near the mouth of the Mississippi River. "Their families are on food stamps, welfare, they're losin' property and gettin' thrown out of their houses."

Not only did the loss of redfish deal an immediate and crashing blow to the state's nearly 2,000 inshore netters, but it reverberated throughout a myriad of related businesses—in the coastal communities and beyond—that depend upon the fishermen: dockside buyers, wholesalers, processors and retailers, marinas, grocery stores, ice plants, lumber yards, hardware and auto-parts stores, net shops, banks....

"All businesses in the coastal parishes are hurtin' because of this," said Larry Loga, owner of P&L Seafood, a dockside operation in Venice. "Nobody has any money to spend. My income dropped by a third but what we lost in fish business was minor compared to what was being spent in these other businesses."

Older fishermen recall traveling to LaNasa's Hardware on Decatur Street in New Orleans to buy webbing to make their redfish nets. LaNasa's is gone now, replaced by Santa's Quarters, a shop that sells Christmas ornaments to French Quarter tourists. But there are about 40 net shops in the state that supply fishermen with the tools of their

LaNasa's French Quarter net shop, 1025 Decatur Street

trade.

Benny Champlin of the Fish Net Company, in Jonesville, up in North Louisiana, lost "a couple hundred thousand dollars" due to the closure, "20 percent of my gross revenues," he said. About 70 percent of Champlin's sales volume is mail order. His out-of-state business, half of his total, enabled him to keep most of his employees.

Vernon Cubbage of Boothville started his fishing supply business in 1961, after retiring from the Navy. "My gross sales for 1988 were down over a quarter million dollars from 1987," said Cubbage, "from about $700,000 to $400,000. That's not just webbing, that's everything including rope, leads, corks and hanging twine.[1] Not only did I lose those sales," he added, "but I had already bought a container load of webbing which I now have to sit on. That's 40,000 pounds that I paid $5 a pound for, plus a 25 percent duty. I've sold a little but I'm still sitting on most of it. Normally I'd have sold all that plus another 50,000 pounds."

Warren Delacroix of Fisherman's Net and Supply Company, in New Orleans, also had a problem with inventory. "I stocked about $40,000 of webbing, primarily for redfish. Some of it I'm slowly selling—the 5 1/2- to 6 1/2-inch mesh—which they're using some for drum and sheepshead. But there's $10,000 worth of 4 3/8-inch that they don't use for anything but redfish—the smaller, about 3 1/2-pound fish.

"Besides webbing, we may have lost $20,000 to $30,000 on related items like corks, rope, leads, life preservers, knives, gloves, baskets, anchors, rainsuits—you know—everything that fishermen need.

"The people who make leads for us? They used to sell us a thousand pounds a week. Now we're lucky to sell a couple hundred pounds."

A New Orleans lead manufacturer, who supplied many Louisiana net shops with molded leads, saw his thriving cottage industry nosedive after the ban. The proprietor wished to remain unnamed because he also serves recreational-fishing businesses. "I supplied 30,000 to 40,000 pounds of molded leads to net shops monthly," he said, "at 80 cents a pound. Before the ban I employed three full-time employees and a sales representative; now I've got one part-time worker. And myself? I have a lot more time to go fishing."

Fish buyers and processors across the state were naturally hit hard by the closures. New Orleans processor Harlon Pearce lost more than $1 million and 20 employees. Terry LeBlanc in Chauvin, down on Bayou Petit Caillou, went bust, laying off 15 workers. Henry Truelove, who buys freshly caught fish in Charenton, said, "I deal in both freshwater and saltwater fish, which was lucky for me because my business fell one half after the closure, from $500,000 down to $250,000." Truelove had employed six to eight full-time workers but

Henry Truelove, president of Louisiana Fishermen for Fair Laws

he said, "After 20 years in business, I'm back to where I started—just my wife and I. And the way it looks," he joked, "one of us is gonna have to get a job."

Dockside buyers either shipped their reds out of state or trucked them to wholesalers in larger cities who exported the fish or distributed them to local retail markets and restaurants. The redfish closure rippled along this market chain, from fisherman to consumer.

The National Marine Fisheries Service reported that Louisiana fishermen landed 4.57 million pounds of redfish in 1987 with a dockside value of $5.16 million. In 1988, landings fell to 245,365 pounds, paying $344,824 to the fishermen.

Economists estimate that each dollar of dockside value of seafood translates into about $3.50 of retail sales value. Applying this multiplier to the redfish industry suggests a decrease in value from $18.1 million in 1987 to $1.2 million in 1988, a loss to the state's economy of nearly $17 million.

Meanwhile, fish are imported from Latin America to replace the void in local production. Harlon Pearce claimed that by 1989, dealers were importing 5,000 to 10,000 pounds of *corvina* or "Central American redfish" into New Orleans each week. Most of these fish, said Pearce, were caught on the west coast of Costa Rica and Panama and imported as fillets for which dealers paid about $4 a pound.

The inshoreman was decidedly down, but not out. Not yet. A natural stoic, he tried to hide his sea of troubles. But as he talked to you, he avoided your eyes, gazing toward the horizon or down at the ground instead of drilling you with his usual self-assured stare. He even talked about getting out of the business. "Ain't no future in this no more," he sighed, shaking his head.

But, fishing's all he knows how to do and it's all he *wants* to do. So there's really only one option—scale back and start over.

He would not get a lot of outside help. Coastal bankers, even with their understanding of the capricious fishing industry, have generally learned to shun the finfishermen who, unlike the larger operators, can rarely lay aside enough savings to keep up with their notes through the inevitable lean times. Instead, the netters rely on their fishhouse or on finance companies for equipment loans. But the fishhouses had their own problems and the finance companies were leery.

"Fishermen don't borrow anymore because they can't fish anymore and don't have any income," said Tina Crosby of Tideland Finance Company in Galliano.

With the house repossessed—and $10,000 of hard-won equity out the window—the fisherman rented another house or moved his family in with friends or relatives. And that shiny Ford pickup, with only one more year of payments to go? Well, it was sure nice but a

'78 model would do just fine. Besides, after months of hounding by insistent bill collectors always asking that impossible question— "When?"—it was sort of a relief to be out from under all that pressure.

"And hell, Beb, we don't need no phone neither." Most fishermen already had VHF radios onboard their skiffs, to compare notes with other fishermen and to call for help when they break down far from home. But, after the closure, whip antennas began to spring up from rooftops like cane. Instead of the usual brief ship-to-shore messages like, "Go get us some steaks, momma, 'cause I'm comin' in with a load," the airways filled with feminine voices as housewives gabbed with mothers-in-law, sisters and friends until, finally, an impatient fishermen would cut in, "Damnit, this ain't no party line, we're tryin' to work out here!"

To the victors go the spoils. While the fishermen walked around like dead men, Sen. Bagert and Rep. Garrity went to bat again for GCCA in the 1989 legislative session, authoring identical versions of a bill to create the Louisiana Marine Recreational Fishing Development Board. Now that the recreational industry finally had control over the redfish, it was wasting no time gearing up to exploit them.

Excerpts from the proposed law read:

> The marine recreational fishing industry in Louisiana contributes significantly to the economy of the state and could have an even greater economic impact in terms of tourism if improvements were made in recreational fishing facilities and capabilities. However, there has never been a cohesive, comprehensive strategy to promote, market, and develop marine recreational fisheries....The purpose of this

Subpart is to provide the means to expand public awareness of marine recreational fishing opportunities in Louisiana, to establish new and improve existing marketing channels and concepts, to identify and remove impediments to the development of marine recreational fishing in Louisiana, and to assist the industry in improving the quality of its services and products....The board, working with the Department of Wildlife and Fisheries, shall plan and conduct a campaign for advertising, publicizing, and promoting marine recreational fishing in Louisiana, and may contract for any advertising, publicity, and sales promotion services. The board may take any other action which it deems necessary to promote and to improve the well-being of marine recreational fishing in Louisiana.

The bill also requested that the Legislature grant the board the authority to either lend the money directly or guarantee the loans for up to $3 million for "the purchase, construction, or necessary improvement of any equipment, machinery, or structure used in the operation of a guide service, marina, launch, or other marine recreational-fishing-oriented business in Louisiana."

This eager request for funding caused the bill to fumble. With the state in severe economic depression, the timing wasn't right for SB 570/HB 1401. But, "getting the bill wet" would facilitate its passage in the future.

Before the GCCA brought around its bill to promote recreational fishing for the second time, it paved its way by staging a media event. A private one.

Not long after Gov. Buddy Roemer had been elected, he appointed fisheries economist Jerry Clark to the department's top fisheries post, assistant secretary of fisheries. Prior to his appointment, Clark was coastal fisheries chief at the Texas Parks and Wildlife Department.

Just prior to the 1990 Legislative Session, according to the Associated Press, Clark spoke to "a gathering of legislators and sport fishermen of the Gulf Coast Conservation Association at a camp deep in the marshes off the Barataria Waterway." He told them that recreational fishing may have an economic impact on Louisiana more than 50 times greater than the commercial fishing industry.

During the 1990 session, a revised bill, minus the funding provision, sailed through the Senate and House and was signed into law by Gov. Roemer. The 15-member Louisiana Recreational Fishing Development Board includes, among others, the Louisiana GCCA, Louisiana Travel Promotion Association, Louisiana Hotel-Motel Association, Louisiana Association of Charterboat Captains, Louisiana Marine Trades Association, the lieutenant governor or his designee, a marketing specialist, someone engaged in the retail business of selling fishing tackle, and a representative from both the transportation and banking industries.[2]

GCCA got its recreational fishing promotion board, but the Texas-based group was less successful in its quiet attempt to have red drum declared a gamefish *permanently*, a year before the fishery was to reopen.

Garrity and Chris John of Crowley drafted identical bills for the House; Baton Rouge Sen. Larry Bankston introduced GCCA's bill on the Senate side. (Bagert was distracted: He was locked in an interesting three-way U.S. senatorial race against Rep. David Duke and incumbent J. Bennett Johnston.)

Attendance at the Senate Natural Resources Committee Hearing by recreational fishermen was extremely light. Their tempers had cooled since the heated battles of two years before; some had even begun to sympathize with the inshore netters while others had come to realize that any new restriction imposed on the commercials was always accompanied by a cut in their own catch—and they were already down to only five fish. GCCA would go for permanent gamefish status, but the state's recreational fishermen would sit this one out.

The commercials, on the other hand, showed up in force to protest GCCA's sly tactic.

After Bankston introduced the bill, and its proponents testified in its favor, LDWF Secretary Van Sickle declared that no change in the three-year ban was warranted at that time. "We are working on a redfish management plan which should be completed by early next spring."

The fishermen testified against the bill, with the general theme that, "Enough is enough." Then, help came from an unexpected quarter.

Powerful Sen. Don Kelly of Natchitoches, in North Louisiana, regularly threatens to make both redfish and trout gamefish simply out of impatience over the time-consuming squabbling that has taken place over these two species each year since the early 1970s. In 1990, Kelly gave the fishermen butterflies again with the same threat, but he ended up rebuking GCCA's Hilzim: "I can understand bein' on a roll, but y'all better slow down a little."

The fishermen cast eyes at each other, grinning. GCCA's ploy was almost unanimously voted down. With nothing to gain but the possibility of appearing too greedy, the Texas group pulled its redfish bills from the House and didn't even bring up its trout initiatives, which would have slashed the commercial quota from 1.25 million to 500,000 pounds.

LOUISIANA REDFISH FIGHT II

T he man with the gold gets the fish? Well, let me ask you up here, who represent all the people o' Lou'siana, is that the way it operates? Well it shouldn't....And if that's the way it operates, we need a change. And the people's gonna have to make a change, 'cause we got to survive!

—Monroe Gray, Cameron Parish fisherman,
Senate Natural Resources Committee
Hearing

It's time we realize these resources have substantially greater socioeconomic impacts outside their relatively insignificant commercial use, and that allowing enough commercial take to be meaningful to that sector adversely impacts the recreational sector.

—Mark Hilzim, executive director,
Gulf Coast Conservation Association

When I worked at the paper, the tackle companies, the sporting goods dealers, they loaded us up. Rods, reels, all the latest. I guess they wanted us to come around to their way of thinking and, with all the stuff they gave us, it was kind of hard not to.

—former sportswriter
New Orleans Times-Picayune

After a hiatus of more than three and a half years, commercial fishing for redfish was scheduled to resume on September 1, 1991, if warranted by biological data. But no fisherman was surprised when GCCA announced that it would try to prevent the reopening of the fishery by convincing the 1991 Legislature to declare the species a gamefish permanently. Nor was anyone in the industry surprised when the group went after the trout, as well.

Though GCCA gave it their all, the fishermen, with the help of some new allies, rose to the occasion, putting up their best defense ever.

Still, after more than three years of anticipation, the outcome of the 1991 gamefish fight proved anticlimactic: Fishermen and consumers hung onto their trout, and the redfish, they would have to do without. The campaigns that both the recreational and commercial industries waged before and during the legislative session, however, were anything but dull.

Though GCCA was not to introduce its gamefish bill to the Legislature until May, the group kicked off its campaign early the previous autumn when chapter presidents convened for their briefing at Zemurray Gardens, the posh St. Tammany Parish estate built in the late 1920s by Samuel Zemurray, founder of the United Fruit Company.

With instructions in hand, the 14 chapter presidents returned to their districts to spread GCCA's message to members and the general public. Their first efforts didn't appear too promising.

At a November, 1990, meeting, executive director Mark Hilzim, along with outgoing chapter president Don Duplantier, unveiled GCCA's gamefish scheme to the Delta Chapter, which encompasses the strategically important New Orleans area.

"Besides our ads, we sent out 1,500 letters telling people about this meeting," said veterinarian Duplantier, visibly disappointed at the pitiful gathering of about 35 amateurish anglers. The professional Hilzim, however, cooly remarked, "This issue's not hot yet. We have to heat it up...a new video, radio and TV spots, billboards, it's all comin' up."

Less confidently, Duplantier exhorted the group, "We need to build the momentum for gamefish. Build, build, build!"

And they did. Six months later, as the debate in the Legislature ensued, the gamefish bill was recognized as the most lobbied of the session, surpassing even the pro-life issue.

Louisiana GCCA claimed a membership of 7,500; these people needed little convincing to go for gamefish. But 7,500 represents only about two percent of the conservatively estimated 350,000 Louisiana marine anglers.

To raise support among non-committed anglers, GCCA hired marketing consultants to help with its campaign. A crucial aspect of this campaign was the development of concise sound bites, easy to grasp and to repeat.

Spelled out in newsletters mailed directly to members, these selling points were virtually identical to those employed so successfully in Austin, 10 years before. Then, to compensate for the lack of a sound biological justification for gamefish, recreationals minimized the value of the commercial industry while glorifying their own.

In 1991, GCCA's three major arguments in favor of gamefish were:

• "The recreational fishing industry in Louisiana is worth at least one billion dollars."

• "Historically, redfish and speckled trout have accounted for less than two percent by volume and one percent by value of the commercial fishing industry's total annual harvest."

• "We need to protect these two species the same as we now protect other species such as ducks and deer."

The effectiveness of these sound bites was demonstrated at the 52nd annual convention of the Louisiana Wildlife Federation. Held in Covington in early March, the convention predated the release of the first-ever LDWF redfish and trout management plans, which had been in the works for a year and were to include stock assessments of the two species. Even so, before this meeting was over, the delegates needed to adopt a position on gamefish that LWF would support in the upcoming legislative session.

The lack of biological data hadn't influenced GCCA's course whatsoever: "We feel that gamefish is the way to go and we'll push that no matter what the reports say," declared Hilzim. The interests of LWF, however, are substantially more broad than that of single-issue GCCA.

As an affiliate of the prestigious National Wildlife Federation, LWF is actively involved in a variety of outdoor issues ranging from pollution and coastal erosion to habitat acquisition, hunting and fur trapping. Some delegates on the saltwater fishing and boating committee felt uneasy about making a hard decision on the gamefish question without the benefit of any scientific data, particularly in light of the federation's 1988 promise to fishermen to not oppose a reopening if the biology warranted it.

GCCA had prepared for this eventuality. One by one, delegates popped up, each attempting to sway the others toward gamefish.

Eerily, their arguments were laced with the same mantras: "billion dollar industry, billion dollar industry, less than one percent, less than one percent, ducks and deer, ducks and deer."

Commercial fisherman Pete Gerica described a GCCA video that was shown around to sportsmen's groups prior to the convention. The video opened with a shot of a conveyor belt carrying dead bull redfish off a purse seiner. "Do you want this to happen again?" asked the narrator. After this rekindling of passions ignited by the redfish fights back in the mid- and late 1980s, the sportsmen were hit several times with the "billion dollar industry" line. The movie concluded with an angler and his son wistfully riding off into the sunset.

Several of the sportsmen's groups were seduced by GCCA's effective campaign and joined its coalition. But after heated debates that went on into the night and the following morning, the Louisiana Wildlife Federation resolved to honor its word: "Basically our position is that if the state determines the resources are at the point where there are enough fish to support both groups, and the commercials can be allowed a portion without causing a negative impact on the recreationals, then we have no problems with the commercials having a season," stated executive director Randy Lanctot.

This was a blow to GCCA; the Texas-based group coveted the endorsement of the respected LWF. In a March 31 article, *Times-Picayune* outdoor columnist Bob Marshall weighed the strength of GCCA's position relative to that of the fishermen. Though Marshall jumped the gun by inaccurately reporting that GCCA already had the federation onboard, he nicely described the advantages to the group had it been successful:

For the first time, the Gulf Coast Conservation Association

has succeeded in lining up support from a broad coalition of other sportsmen's conservation groups. That list has been joined for the first time by the Louisiana Wildlife Federation, which remains the most influential of sportsmen's lobby groups in Baton Rouge. The alliance will help the GCCA shed its undeserved image as "a bunch of rich doctors and lawyers who want all the fish for themselves."[1]

Spearheaded by Houston-based GCCA, the recreational industry's coalition included the Louisiana Marine Trades Association; *Louisiana Sportsman*, a regional outdoor publication; some 15 sportsmen's groups and a handful of the state's many outdoor columnists. According to GCCA, more than $30,000 was donated by a number of sponsors that included the First American Bank of Monroe; Texaco; Freeport-McMoRan, a New Orleans-based petroleum and mineral extraction company; at least one coastal real estate developer, and two members of the Louisiana Wildlife and Fisheries Commission. In addition to these donations, local banquets generated over $130,000, while the 1991 Louisiana GCCA Boat, Motor and Trailer Raffle raised an additional $39,000.

If the fishermen had been on their own, as they were in 1988, they wouldn't have stood a chance against this powerful and aggressive coalition. But with some new allies—the Louisiana Seafood Promotion and Marketing Board (LSPMB), the Louisiana Restaurant Association and some members of the media—they managed to hold their ground.

The finfishermen had never before attempted a public relations campaign. To the man on the bayou, keeping his mouth shut is basic. To anyone naive enough to ask him, as he unloads his catch, "Where'd you get those?" the taciturn fisherman typically answers, "Oh, I got them in the water, the fish are most gen'rally in the water."

Further, information that fishermen volunteered to the media in the past had often been reported in a biased fashion that only hardened public attitudes against them, until the unofficial motto throughout the industry had become, simply, "Don't say nuttin'."

But, confronted with the annihilation of their industry by the permanent loss of their keystone fisheries, some of the leaders decided they had nothing to lose by telling their side of the story.

To do so and, at the same time, to counter GCCA's slick propaganda campaign, the Organization of Louisiana Fishermen and LSPMB prepared a 21-page information packet which they mailed to over 150 Louisiana newspapers and magazines, and to about 25 television stations. After reading the cover letter and the four short articles, including tables that compared recreational and commercial harvest levels, anyone could understand that "gamefish" was a matter not of "conservation" but of allocation.

For the first time, members of the media had the other side of the story in their hands.

As the media kits went out, LSPMB hired a clipping service to collect articles containing key words such as "gamefish," "redfish," "trout." Relatively inexpensive, the service proved invaluable in monitoring statewide coverage of the gamefish fight.

As the battle escalated and the clips began to come in, the positions of the media crystallized.

A few publications, primarily in New Orleans and New Iberia, continued to promote GCCA's aim. A column in *The Sunday Iberian*, for instance, was headlined, "It's time for legislators to make specks, reds gamefish."

But, as if a levee had burst, newspapers from Shreveport to Franklin, Lafayette to Covington, began to, at least, cover the gamefish issue in a balanced fashion. Several writers went further, clearly supporting the fishermen and the principle that the fish should continue to be shared among all user groups.

One of the first was Topot Morrow, whose columns appear in the south central Louisiana *Crowley Post Signal* and *The Gueydan Journal.* Under the caption, "Trout, Redfish Debate," Morrow wrote:

> There is no doubt, G.C.C.A., whose membership consists of sports fishermen, wants the whole fishery for themselves. Many of their members do not feel this way. There is a group within who believe there is room for both. The truth being, there is room for both.

In an April 17 article in the business section of *The Times of Acadiana*, titled "Who Gets the Fish," Marcell Tessier balanced some of the plausible-sounding claims made by GCCA:

> GCCA says that redfish and trout constitute a small part of the commercial industry. GCCA figures prior to the redfish ban show that both fish accounted for less than half of one percent of Louisiana's commercial landings and less than two percent of its value. What GCCA does not mention is that the vast percentage of the commercial take is composed of menhaden, a non-edible species that is harvested by corporate fishing fleets for fertilizer, pet food and other use....It's interesting to note that GCCA appears to be increasingly interested in the economics of the issue, but only as it applies to recreational fishing. The organization figures that sportfishing enthusiasts pump $1 billion annually into the state's economy, a fact prominently emphasized in the group's

most recent press release. Yet three years ago, commercial fishermen's pleas for their livelihood fell on deaf ears. According to the organization's own literature [at that time], "conservation of the resource must take priority over economic considerations."

In the past, reporters had neglected to interview either fisherman or biologist. Tessier talked to all parties, however, and allowed fisherman Daniel Edgar to have his say: "The people who want to save the whales don't go kill the whales. GCCA call themselves conservationists and act like hogs." Tessier also reported that there was no evidence from LDWF to indicate that the commercial industry was solely responsible for depleting the resource:

> To the contrary, a department study...indicated that 73 percent of the saltwater finfish [redfish] harvest in the state came from the recreational sector, with only 27 percent collected by commercial means....Sports fishermen loudly discount this information, maintaining that commercial fishermen notoriously under-report their catch. But John Roussel [LDWF marine finfish division chief]...stands by the numbers. "If you look at it in detail, it makes a lot of sense. The sheer numbers of recreational fishermen make their cumulative catch quite large."

GCCA's public education campaign was in full swing by March. Spots were appearing on radio and TV, billboards were prominently posted along the state's highways and pro-gamefish letters to the editor, written by members and staff, had begun to appear in newspapers.

Nothing from the commercial industry, however, which had to save its ammunition and make its shots count. Then, in late April, the industry launched a smart bomb.

The Louisiana Seafood Promotion and Marketing Board had contracted with noted pollster and Loyola University professor Dr. Ed Renwick for a study to determine consumers' attitudes toward seafood. He conducted the poll over the telephone by asking voters 24 questions. Three weeks before GCCA was to introduce its gamefish bill to the Legislature, at a press conference sponsored by the Louisiana Restaurant Association, Renwick and LSPMB released the results of "Opinions and Attitudes of Louisiana Voters Regarding Seafood."

The survey yielded much important information. For instance, 93 percent of voters polled ranked the seafood industry as the most important industry in the state, 84 percent tourism, and 79 percent the petrochemical industry. But the most useful information for the gamefish fight came from voters' responses to the following question:

Some people want to allow only sport fishermen to catch redfish and speckled trout. This would mean that these fish could not be purchased by consumers in restaurants or retail stores. Other people would allow commercial fishermen to catch a certain quota of these fish, which would then be available to all consumers. Which one do you favor— allowing only sport fishermen to catch and eat redfish and speckled trout or allowing both sport and commercial fishermen to catch them so all consumers could purchase them?

Eighty-one percent came out against any legislation that would limit access to reds and trout strictly to recreational fishermen. Of the 750 households surveyed, 42 percent had at least one sport fisherman in the family. Even in these 315 households, again, 81 percent of the respondents were in favor of some commercial fishing to provide all consumers access to redfish and trout.

While the carefully worded question immediately educated 750 Louisiana voters as to how "gamefish" would affect them, more than a million others were tipped off when nearly 50 newspapers around the state reported the results of the survey under eye-catching headlines such as the Franklin-based *Banner-Tribune*'s "Consumers want specs, reds available," or the Lafourche Parish *Daily Comet*'s, "Voters want chance to buy reds, specks."

Most of these articles concluded with a quote by LSPMB executive director Karl Turner, who explained, "This issue is allocation, not conservation. The issue is having access by consumers."

Renwick's study and LSPMB received swift retribution in the *Times-Picayune*. On April 28, Bob Marshall denounced the question pertaining to gamefish as "inaccurate to the point of being a lie." He then explained to his sporting readership:

> GCCA's legislation has never meant these fish could not be purchased by consumers in restaurants and retail stores. It allows for the sale of fish legally caught outside of Louisiana to be imported into the state.

Two days later, the New Orleans journal, in an editorial headlined, "Befouling fisheries again," reiterated its outdoor columnist's accusations to those of its readers who may have missed the sports pages.

In "Befouling...," the editors clarified the paper's stance on the gamefish issue: "To understand the overall economic importance of the state's fisheries, it is essential to know that recreational fishing, the force that drives the sales of boats, boat motors, fishing gear, etc., occupies the top place."

They then assailed LSPMB, an affiliate of the Louisiana Department of Wildlife and Fisheries:

> The board has taken a position in the current legislative session in direct opposition to the efforts of recreational fishermen to have speckled trout and redfish designated as gamefish....A state agency should not...conduct a poll in behalf of the commercial industry's own interests and directly contrary to the interests of recreational fishermen.

In actuality, the interests of the local commercial fishermen and the local recreational fishermen are precisely identical—both groups desire an abundant supply of fish. The major deterrent to their working together toward this goal are those whose interests lie best in pitting the two groups of Louisianians against each other—the recreational fishing industry. Until 1991, only one other of the parties in this old conflict had been less regarded—the consumer.

No one in the press did a better job of bringing the consumer into the gamefish equation than did Tommy Simmons, food editor at the Baton Rouge *Morning Advocate*.

Seafood has long been Simmons' specialty; of the several national press awards she has received for her writing, three involved seafood— one on redfish, another on speckled trout. Simmons also knows the fishermen firsthand. In 1989, Gov. Roemer appointed her as media representative to the Limited Entry Task Force, where she played an active role in helping the fishermen design a plan to limit their numbers.

Though she herself is a lifelong sport fisherman, "I don't represent either recreational or commercial fishermen," she said. "I have to represent the consumer because that's who I write for. So my approach was, 'If gamefish goes into effect, how's it going to affect consumers?'"

After several months of research, Simmons presented the answer to this question, in a six-article package in the *Morning Advocate*'s food section.

In the first, "To be or not to be, on the menu," an elegant Garden District matron and her granddaughter were being seated at one of New Orleans' classic restaurants. "She and her husband had taken their daughter to Galatoire's for her 16th birthday and she was carrying on the tradition with her granddaughter," wrote Simmons. In keeping with tradition, they ordered trout *meuniere*.

The debutante-to-be had better have enjoyed it, insinuated Simmons:

> What is ironic is that the young lady's lunch last week may end up being a memorable meal, just that, nothing more. Her first taste of a classic Creole entrée, a perfectly sautéed and lightly sauced speckled trout, fresh from the Gulf, could possibly be her last if legislation being considered in this session of the Legislature is passed.

After this stirring lead, Simmons' readers encountered, "Louisiana landings reflect 'Specks' historical value"; "'Specks' are 'fish of choice'"; "Are specks safe?"; "Dollars favor recreational interests." Each of these articles was informative and balanced. So what set the phones ringing off the hook less than an hour after the paper hit the stands?

In her concluding piece, "Are consumers left out?" she wrote:

> Most of the special interest groups have portrayed the speckled trout issue as a conflict between user groups, commercial and recreational. Left out of the equation are the consumers, those Louisianians who don't own boats, don't fish either recreationally or commercially, and who on occasion, like to dine on speckled trout....A neglected point of consideration is that Louisiana restaurant patrons and seafood market customers, like the commercial fishermen, have an established historical record of access to Louisiana's speckled trout resource. Those fish and that resource need to be managed for the consumer, whose right to a sautéed speckled trout is as much a part of his cultural heritage, as is the recreational fisherman's right to catch 25 fish and the commercial fisherman's right to a way of making a living.

By bringing into the debate the consumers, who far outnumber the angling constituency, Simmons awakened the worst fear of the gamefish advocates.

Five days later, with the phones still ringing in response to Simmons' series, the family-owned *Morning Advocate* followed up with an editorial, "Manage specks for everyone."

> Sport fishermen have no basis for claiming exclusive rights to the speckled trout—no basis, that is, except selfishness. That kind of selfishness makes sportsmen look bad to the general public....The fishery resources of our state must

continue to belong to all, not to a select few.

"After the editorial, the phone calls started getting nastier," recounted Simmons. "There was a lot of calling and hanging up at work and at my home. My boss got a lot of calls, too, from people complaining about me but, in the newspaper business, that's the best thing that can happen to a writer!

"I got a lot of threats but the two most frightening were when someone called and asked me some things about my husband's work. They were threatening to hurt *his* business, which really made me livid. Then, when I wasn't at home, two guys showed up at the house 'to fix the septic tank.' But we don't have one! When my son told them that he'd have to call me, they got out of there.

"It was the publisher's son who wrote the editorial but, right after it came out, Mark Hilzim called me up and said how disappointed he was in me, 'How can you say we're selfish?' he asked. They thought I wrote it."

Baton Rouge is the state's capital and second largest city, with 400,000 residents. That city's *Morning Advocate*, with a circulation of about 100,000, was the largest of the many Louisiana newspapers to adopt an editorial stance against GCCA's gamefish bill. In the New Orleans area, however, where more than a quarter of the state's 4 million residents reside, editors skirted the issue or came out *for* gamefish.

Published by New Orleanian Ashton Phelps, Jr., the *Times-Picayune* is owned by New York-based Newhouse Newspapers. The T-P is the city's major newspaper, with a daily circulation of nearly 300,000. The weekly tabloid *Gambit* was launched several years ago as an alternative, but in an editorial captioned, "Protect Reds and Trout," it urged the Legislature to "protect" the two species by keeping redfish a gamefish and to, "at least, reduce the quota on speckled trout."

CityBusiness, a weekly business tabloid, also shunned analysis of the gamefish issue; instead its publisher wrote:

> One of the most hotly debated issues among those of us who love the outdoors is whether redfish and speckled trout should be given gamefish status and barred to commercial fishermen....I don't think the Louisiana commercial fishing industry—which takes over 2 billion pounds of fish a year, of which redfish and specks are a minute part—will be damaged by a gamefish bill.

It didn't take long to see that New Orleanians would receive little information that did not further GCCA's cause. Stonewalled by the Crescent City media, fishermen realized that if they wanted to alert the people that access to their fish was threatened, they'd have to tell them themselves, even though it was already late in the game.

Several of the fishing groups pooled their resources and, for less than $1,000, hired a printer to make up some good old-fashioned fliers and deliver them door-to-door to 10,000 households within Jefferson, a New Orleans suburb. Why Jefferson? It was the turf of long-time GCCA advocate and House sponsor of its gamefish bill, Rep. Robert Garrity.

"We got good positive feedback immediately," recounted Harlon Pearce, coordinator of the commercial industry's campaign. "We even heard from some people who live in that area and work for a major PR agency who told us what a good job we did and how they appreciated hearing some truth on this issue. 'If you're responsible for this, this is great,' they told us. Of course, Garrity didn't think it

NOTICE TO VOTERS OF DISTRICT 78

If you want to buy fresh natural-caught Louisiana speckled trout or redfish in a store or restaurant again let Mr. Garrity know by calling him at **738-1111** or writing him at 981 Hickory Ave., Harahan, LA 70123

Your representative in the Louisiana Legislature, Robert T Garrity, Jr., has introduced the following legislation into this year's legislature:

HB 440 Declares redfish gamefish permanently

HB 441 Reduces commercial harvest of speckled trout by 60% without biological justification

HB 749 Declares speckled trout and redfish gamefish permanently

HB 750 Declares redfish gamefish and provides for mangement for sportsmen only

If passed these bills would:

*Prevent the consumer from buying fresh natural-caught Louisiana speckled trout and redfish forever.

*Prevent a restaurant from serving fresh natural-caught Louisiana speckled trout and redfish forever.

*Give **all** rights to speckled trout and redfish to sportsmen wealthy enough to own a boat or healthy eough to fish.

*Ignore scientific information that says that speckled trout are not overfished.

was so great. He got pretty hot."

The representative fired back with a flier of his own. Under the head, GAMEFISH—BECAUSE IT WORKS, his response listed GCCA's arguments for gamefish, with the sincere assurances, "You will still be able to eat imported or pond-raised redfish after HB 749 passes...Don't be misled!! HB 749 is good for Louisiana and good for Jefferson."[2]

"We should have come back a third time after GCCA did theirs," said Pearce, but at that time, we were in the middle of the legislative session, and we were fighting a losing battle as far as redfish was concerned."

With the session well under way, fishermen had to concentrate their efforts on working the legislators. They couldn't afford to put much more of their limited resources into trying to educate the public. But, thanks to their allies, they learned what the New Orleans Saints already knew—that a strong defense can be almost as effective as a good offense.

GCCA had their billboards up around the state by late winter. The group's suggestive 1991 campaign slogan—"GAMEFISH, Because it's working"—was prominent; a drawing of a redfish and a trout, plus a toll-free number completed the simple and straightforward message.

The Louisiana Restaurant Association came up with a way to level the playing field.

With 2,500 dues-paying members representing 4,000 operations, LRA is the largest trade organization in the state. The powerful group had stayed out of the vicious 1988 redfish fight, but in 1991, executive vice president Jim Funk said, "We're strongly opposed to gamefish. There's no doubt about its hurting restaurants. The number one

The meaning of GCCA's roadside billboards may have escaped the general public but recreational fishermen got the message.

reason people come to Louisiana is to eat in our restaurants and we don't feel we should be serving them seafood from Alaska or New England. Our position is that the resource belongs to all the people, not just one select group."

Restaurateurs are hardly unaware of the high costs of outdoor advertising—nearly 75 percent of billboards promote restaurants. "It just hit us all of a sudden...Who's paying for all these billboards?" said Funk, who called the major outdoor advertising companies and learned that they were donating the signs. "They just didn't realize how politically hot an issue it is," said Funk, who explained it to them and who also politely suggested that if they were going to continue to give GCCA free exposure, then they should extend the same courtesy to LRA members as well—all 2,500 of them.

Two days later, the GCCA billboards began to come down.

Television coverage of the most lobbied bill in the 1991 Legislature was scant. The little there was, reflected the medium's preoccupation with being first, rather than best.

Outside the chamber where the Senate Natural Resources Committee was about to hear GCCA introduce its gamefish bill, a representative from the commercial industry approached a reporter from New Orleans WVUE:

"Here's my name and number. If you'd like some more facts on this, please feel free to call me."

"Facts? I don't have time for facts. We've got to go with this story tonight at five."

When the story played that evening, Channel 8 dusted off its footage from the mid-1980s and portrayed the redfishermen by showing aerial shots of a purse seiner taking in a school of bull redfish.

GCCA, meanwhile, was having a lot better luck with the visual medium. New Orleans Channel 4 had started running two spots for the group in the first week of March. Both portrayed scenes of recreational fishing in the marsh.

A 30-second spot touted the "billion dollar" saltwater recreational fishing industry, which might "go away," suggested the narrator, unless viewers "send what you can now" to GCCA.

The 10-second spot was more to the point:

> In Louisiana, it's time we stop to hear the music. Let's save our billion-dollar-a-year saltwater fishing industry by protecting both redfish and speckled trout. Let's go gamefish. It works!

Both spots ran for several months, until LSPMB Executive

Director Karl Turner telephoned WWL-TV Community Affairs Director Mary Beal. During their conversation, Turner asked Beal how much GCCA was paying for their spots.

"We're running them as public service announcements," she answered, "free of charge."

When Turner suggested that promoting the monopolization of the state's natural resources may not qualify as a public service, Beal advised him to draft a letter to the station's general manager.

Turner immediately did so. After explaining the political nature of the gamefish issue, he requested that WWL stop running the spot promoting gamefish.

The station immediately yanked both off the air.

"We wondered about it," recalled Beal, after the campaign. "But since there was no political candidate, we ran it. We run PSAs as a community service, for non-profit groups who need to get their message to the people. We just didn't know what was involved with this issue."

GCCA did not report any campaign contributions to Louisiana legislators prior to 1991. SPORT-PAC did lightly disburse $4,650 to a dozen members of the 1991 Legislature, however. These funds, nearly half of which were sent over from Austin, were directed primarily to members of the influential Senate and House Natural Resources Committees.

During the dynamic legislative session, the date for introduction of a bill is typically firmed up only a few days beforehand. But not for the gamefish bill. GCCA sent out letters to its membership more than a month ahead of time: "We're gonna do it on May 16. Be there."

Then, on May 2, the Wildlife and Fisheries Commission, chaired by one of the founding fathers of the Louisiana GCCA, set the opening date for the inshore shrimp season...Thursday, May 16.

Shrimpers faced an agonizing choice: attend the committee hearing and show their opposition to the gamefish bill or, after a long winter with little or no income, go shrimping on the most profitable day of the season.

When the sixteenth arrived, there was a fair showing of fishermen. Likewise for GCCA members, who were easily identified by their redfish nametags and "GAMEFISH IS WORKING" T-shirts.

As SB 534 was first introduced to the Senate Natural Resources Committee, it called for a permanent ban on commercial fishing—gamefish status—for both redfish and speckled trout. It also sought to give to the Wildlife and Fisheries Commission the authority to set size and bag limits for recreational fishermen, who would continue to harvest both fish.

WFC had this authority for virtually every other species of fish and game in the state, but the Legislature had never entrusted management of these two hotly contested species to the body.

Unlike in Texas, Louisiana law requires that three of the seven members of the commission be from the coastal parishes and representatives of the commercial fishing or fur industries. "The other four shall be electors from the state at large, other than representatives of the commercial fishing and fur industries."

The seven members of the commission in 1991 had been appointed by Gov. Edwin Edwards during his 1984-1988 term, and by Gov. Roemer, who was still in office. Presiding as chairman was Baton Rouge sportsman James Jenkins, Jr., president of Jenkins Construction Corporation, GCCA contributor and former CCA trustee. Other commission members included Baton Rouge sportsman and GCCA contributor Warren Pol, a mechanical contractor and chairman of the board of Airtrol, Inc.; Loranger businessman and sportsman Jeff Schneider, a former CCA trustee; Norman McCall, owner of an oilfield supply boat business in Cameron; Ruston sportsman Bert Jones, former professional football player and head of Mid-States Wood Preservers, a lumber-treating firm. Cocodrie shrimp processor Houston Foret and New Orleans oysterman "Captain Pete" Vujnovich represented the commercial fishing industry. There were no representatives from the commercial finfishing industry.

GCCA led off in testifying for the bill. Having already studied the LDWF stock assessments, GCCA spokesmen agreed with the results of the redfish plan and disagreed with the spotted seatrout plan, to be presented later in the hearing. Among the arguments for gamefish status for the two species, executive director Hilzim further justified it by telling the senators, "We're very concerned about the tourism industry and we think that fishing's another good draw."

But Henry Truelove, of Fishermen for Fair Laws, said, "We got in this problem together, we want to get out of this problem together. But so far, for the last three years, our people have carried the brunt of that problem. We have been the ultimate conservationists in the fact that we have caught *no* fish. We can't do any better than that."

Nick Perez, representing the Louisiana Retailers Association, told the committee that GCCA was asking the Legislature to choose between the commercial interests and "a privileged few who can afford to go fishing...They're asking you to put someone else out of business. That's not fair...The issue is saving the species of redfish and trout, not the species of recreational fisherman."

Morning Advocate food editor Tommy Simmons also testified. Unnerved by recent threats, she was reluctant to leave the side of her husky son. Simmons had been further shaken as she walked down the crowded hallway toward the committee room, when a shoving match broke out between a commercial fisherman and a sport-fishing guide. Seated before the panel of senators, Simmons explained that her publisher requested she testify because of the harassing phone calls she had received from sport fishermen over her recent series of articles.

"I wasn't prepared for the reaction," she said, her voice breaking with emotion. "I was warned, yelled at and harassed at the office and at home during the evenings...This has nothing to do with fish, this has to do with power."

While the bullying of the fishermen occasionally offends some legislators' sense of fair play, when confronted with the treatment that this sincere and attractive lady had received, almost everyone in the chamber was moved.

"At least 50 people called me afterward, and apologized to me," recounted Simmons. "They were in the GCCA and they thought that other members had called me. They were embarrassed."

Following Simmons was Tee-John Mialjevich, president of Concerned Shrimpers of America. After suggesting that the most equitable solution would be to divide the available fish 50-50 between the two industries, Tee-John couldn't resist getting in a dig. "Mrs. Simmons has me upset, too. I didn't think the other side was that kind of people. I thought they were rich people, they were well-educated and well-mannered. And now I've lost my respect for them. I see that the poor people, with a lower education, are better mannered than they are."

After the opponents, LDWF biologists were called up to disclose the results of their long-awaited redfish and speckled trout stock assessments. Assistant Secretary of Fisheries Jerry Clark told the committee, "The status of red drum...is that we are making a recommendation that no increase or decrease in the current harvest rate of that species take place."

"Well, by sayin' that, do you mean to maintain the moratorium, as far as commercial fishin'?" asked Sen. Don Kelly.

"No. We're not recommending that. What we're saying is that we have a fixed amount of fish that we think should be harvested and that's what we recommend should be harvested. It's not *our* role to determine how that should be distributed. That's *your* job."

"Well, how you gonna distribute it?"

"It's currently distributed all to recreational fishermen," said Clark. "If you wish to change that, it's our recommendation that whatever is removed from that, to add to a commercial quota, be reduced from the recreational harvest."

With that statement died the fishermen's hope of reopening redfish in 1991. Clark's testimony, with regard to trout, sounded better for them:

"The bottom line in the plan on the status of the spotted seatrout is that the department has looked at the history of the harvest and the history of the stock over the last 10 years and it's our conclusion that the harvest rates that have taken place over that 10 years have not depleted that stock and that the current harvest rates in total are safe....With regard to the freeze of 1989, it is our prediction that the spotted seatrout will rebound from that freeze as they did after the 1983 freeze. We expect this year to be an average fishing year, and we expect next year to be even better."[3]

When the testimony was completed, Sen. Leonard Chabert of Chauvin offered an amendment to delete gamefish status for speckled trout. The provision to give the Wildlife and Fisheries Commission the authority to manage both the recreational and commercial trout fisheries, however, remained, as did that to keep redfish gamefish.

The senators voted 7-0 to pass the bill out of committee.

It then moved to the Senate floor where Sen. John Hainkel of New Orleans signed on as co-author with original author, Baton Rouge Sen. Larry Bankston. The Senate heard the bill on May 21. It also heard a lengthy denunciation of the bill by Senate President Sammy Nunez of Chalmette.

"I'm sad to see this day come," said Nunez. "The LDWF study showed that the redfish population was in no danger and the department biologists didn't recommend gamefish status to protect reds...but I can count," he said, referring to what he predicted would be an overwhelming victory for GCCA. "The numbers game will prevail...It's a powerful group...Pure greed. Pure greed."

The Senators approved the bill by a 32-5 vote.

On June 12, the gamefish bill was presented before the Natural Resources Committee on the House side. Rep. Garrity handled the bill for GCCA. After a short discussion, the committee passed it by a vote of 14-2.

Also passed was a companion bill, HB 1592, by Rep. Randy Roach of Lake Charles. With wording based on the Magnuson Act, the 1976 federal law that set standards and policy for management of offshore fisheries, the bill provided that regulations "be fair and equitable to all fishermen and executed in such a manner as not to exclude any 'historical user group.'"

Even more important to fishermen, HB 1592 also made biological data a necessary condition for continuing gamefish status for redfish:

> The commission, through its secretary, shall make an annual report to the Legislature no later than March 1 of each year, which contains the following information on red drum:
> (a) a biological condition and profile of the species and

stock assessment, a total allowable catch with probable allocation scenarios, based on the most current information available, and

(b) a recommendation to the Legislature as to whether or not gamefish status for such species should be continued and a detailed explanation for such recommendation.

On June 25, both bills moved to the floor of the House where Rep. Frank Patti of Belle Chasse amended the gamefish bill to include the same conditions regarding redfish that were put in Roach's standards and policy bill.

"We wanted it in both bills," said OLF's Jane Black, of the Patti Amendment, "just in case it disappeared from one along the way."

The House voted 94-4 in favor of the amended gamefish bill. The representatives also passed Roach's companion bill 100-0.

Two days later, the gamefish bill went back to the Senate floor. The senators, who had already debated and voted on the issue once before, concurred unanimously on the amended bill and sent it on to the governor.

On July 2, SB 534 became Act 157 upon the signature of Gov. Roemer.

In its final form it provided:

- Indefinite gamefish status for redfish
- Commission management of the recreational redfish fishery
- Commission management of both commercial and recreational speckled trout fisheries
- The Patti Amendment

After the session, Harlon Pearce commented on how he felt it went for the fishermen:

"The session was not a winning session for us, that's for sure. The only thing we can say is, we didn't lose trout. GCCA really wanted the trout, no doubt about it. We were amazed, actually, that we stopped the trout gamefish in the Senate committee. But the power of the testimony is what stopped it. That and that alone. Tommy Simmons' testimony was probably the most powerful I've seen.

"As for the redfish, well, the study said that there should be no more, no less catch. Actually it shouldn't have hurt us because we could have said, 'Hey, no additional catch, but there are still fish to be caught and we should get our share of them.' But nobody'd listen to it.

"When I got up there, it was clear to see that it was an election year; it was clear to see that there was nothing I could do to save the reds for this year. When legislators tell you, 'Hey, I can't do it, no matter what,' you know you're in trouble.

"The deal that we cut with Rep. Roach was that if he gave us HB 1592, intact, the way we wanted it, and if he put the Patti Amendment on the gamefish bill, we wouldn't fight it anymore this year. We opted for those two, knowing that we could not stop gamefish for redfish.

"We came out of it OK with the Patti Amendment. It structured us for down the road, it gives us an opening. If the biology says we should have any fish at all, you *will* see my face up there again next year.

Fishermen expressed confidence that redfish populations would soon permit a reopening of the fishery. They blamed the 1989 freeze—and the accompanying frigid Northwest winds that drained the marsh by literally pushing out the water—for killing many redfish, and forcing even more to take to the deeper waters of the Gulf, beyond biologists' sampling nets.

They had witnessed a similar phenomenon following the December 1983 freeze which, apparently, had killed most of the fish in inside waters. Redfishermen resigned themselves to wait until the brood stock spawned new crops, which would take a few years to reach marketable size. But then, in October 1985, came Hurricane Juan. This storm of only moderate intensity hung off the Louisiana coast for days, blowing Gulf waters into the marsh. When it did finally come ashore, it did so on the full moon, forcing tides even higher, and covering the marsh with six feet of water. When the waters receded, residents of some coastal fishing villages were astounded to find redfish stranded in the streets, and fishermen were pleasantly surprised to find their grounds completely repopulated with marketable fish.

In the absence of a similar storm, fishermen in 1991 again waited for fish to trickle back inside on wind-driven spring tides, and for the brood stock to replenish the marsh with enough fish to satisfy biologists.

In the meantime, as they faced another winter without access to their wintertime staple, their outlook was grim. Although there was a bumper crop of trout, most were still undersized. And, with most everyone forced to chase mullet, that short season held little promise.

GCCA, however, was not missing a beat. Autumn fundraisers were planned for chapters in Shreveport, Monroe, the North Shore, and River Parishes. And "Rock for Redfish III," a GCCA benefit, was scheduled at an uptown New Orleans nightclub for November, 1991.

But because the Legislature granted control of the trout fishery to a biased commission, GCCA would not need to spend as much money to get its way.

The commission wasted no time in running with its new responsibilities. Its Finfish Subcommittee, comprised of highway contractor Jimmy Jenkins and two other GCCA supporters, met to seek solutions to the speckled trout "problem." On September 5, 1991, the commission adopted the following proposed changes in the commercial (only) fishery:

• Cut the commercial quota from 1.25 million pounds per year to 1 million.

• Set a fixed commercial season that commences on September 15 (rather than Sept. 1) and ends April 1, whether the quota has been filled or not.

• No commercial trout fisherman to be allowed on the water from sunset on Friday until sunset on Sunday.

The proposed management measures required an accompanying economic impact statement. "Typically, we would prepare that," said a biologist within the marine fisheries division. "But in that particular case, they didn't want to involve us. We didn't see any biological reason for what they were proposing so they got someone higher up in the department—one of Gov. Roemer's appointees—to prepare it."

If the commission's proposed measures were adopted, said the impact statement, "Benefits are likely to accrue to recreational fishermen anticipating enhanced fishery experiences, and to the industry that supports recreational activities. For instance; bait, tackle, auto transportation, boat launches, lodging, food and beverages likely will be positively impacted (approximately $91 per fisherman trip). Due to the reduction in spotted seatrout quota by 250,000 pounds, there will be a reduction in income at dockside to commercial fishermen in the neighborhood of $250,000."

Keeping commercial trout fishermen off the water from April 1 until September 15, and weekends during the season that they could fish, was justified in that "The historical commercial fishery is a fall and winter fishery, and the historical recreational fishery is a spring and summer fishery, and mostly on weekends." And because, "There are continuing and potentially dangerous conflicts occurring on the water between commercial and recreational fishermen that can best be reduced by separating them in time and space."

This separation "in time and space" was applauded in a GCCA newsletter in that it would "provide a greater opportunity for families to go out and safely enjoy fishing for specks."

But, said Major Inspector Tommy Candies of the LDWF Enforcement Division, "We're not having any physical confrontations."

"There have been no physical confrontations that we're aware of," stated Keith LaCaze, public information officer, LDWF Enforcement Division. "Any 'escalating problems' will be seen by us only as increasing competition between two user groups over a limited resource."

Major Candies added, "The commissioners only set seasons and limits and things like that. They don't tell *us* what to do. We take our orders from the secretary."

Louisiana's Wildlife and Fisheries Commission is not authorized to hire the secretary of Wildlife and Fisheries, undersecretary, or assistant secretaries. (Assistant secretaries of both the fisheries and wildlife offices have control over the direction of research; internal organization; approval or cancellation of programs; and hiring, firing, and promotions of employees.) Currently, the governor, upon entering office, appoints these top posts.

As Cajun Governor Edwin Edwards was about to take office, in early 1992, this system was criticized for disrupting continuity within the department.

"You see good programs being put into place, and you know they could all be undone with the next election," said commission Chairman Jenkins, in a *Times-Picayune* interview. "That has a pretty destabilizing effect on the agency, in my opinion."

A better way, suggested Jenkins, might be for the commission to recommend the secretary, and for it to hire the assistants.

According to the Wildlife Management Institute, most Southern states have already gone to such hiring practices. And that's just what has fishermen scared. Because that's how they did it in Texas.

OCTAVE TOUPS

"Back o' Bayou L'Ours," "The Woods," "The Stumps," "The Ridge"...all these names refer to roughly the same region. Just east of Bayou Lafourche, this is choice country. Or was. More than 20 miles inland from the coastline, and elevated on the floodplains of Bayous Lafourche and L'Ours (pronounced Loorse, French for bear), the Woods were high enough to bar entrance to all but the highest tides. Protected from the Gulf's lethal brine, the lowest-lying land grew a special freshwater marsh; bayous that traversed this marsh flooded each year, piling sediments into high, bayouside ridges that grew island forests of oak and palmetto.

But in 1904, Bayou Lafourche—a branch of the Mississippi River—was dammed off at its mouth, upriver at Donaldsonville. Deprived of its supply of nourishing fresh water and sediment, the Woods ceased to build. Salt water began to creep in from Barataria Bay, to the east, and while the marsh tried to recover, the oil companies moved in to rip the area with canals, and to suck out the oil from beneath.

The freshwater marsh between the wooded ridges had been firm enough to support a running deer; the vegetation wove a thick mat that floated upon the soupy mud beneath. When the hunter or trapper

A land dying

walked upon it, the *flottant* shook like jello.

Cajuns hunted this area for deer and bear. But the last bear seen on Bayou L'Ours is legendary and now, says Octave Toups (pronounced Ock'-tov Toop), 73, "Where we used to hunt deer, we fish."

The floating marsh was the first to go. As the vegetation died and the land sank, potholes appeared, and grew, coalescing to form ponds and then bays. As the ridges sank, the salt water poisoned and drowned the great moss-laden oaks; their haunting gray skeletons now form a gloomy landscape.

This is a land dying. Unless checked by the hand of man, the future of the Ridge is open salt water. But, as it not-so-slowly vanishes, some species benefit, temporarily.

Owls stare from their nests in the hollowed trunks of the decaying oaks. The brackish ponds grow thick beds of widgeon grass and other submerged vegetation which attract concentrations of overwintering

Octave Toups

ducks. And just beneath the rafts of floating ducks, amid the sunken stumps, roots and long-fallen branches, swim even greater numbers of redfish.

Octave Toups grew up back here, in a remote camp, accessible only by boat. He's probably the best known *tramailleur* along Bayou Lafourche. A redfisherman myself, I was always curious about this old-fashioned Cajun in high-top sneakers, who so regularly pulled up at the fishhouse to unload baskets of handsome redfish from the bed of his pickup.

Then, one July morning, Pagaie and I ventured out of our usual territory and rode north, to the Ridge. We had just tried to make a set for about 20 nice reds, laying out the net by gently pushpoling the boat through a minefield of stumps. The fish had coolly outrun us, and as we picked up the barren webbing, we heard the approaching hum of a muffled and well-tuned...Ford Fairlane?

It was Octave. Planing smoothly through the same little bay, his fan-tailed skiff threw a roostertail of pure mud. Once in a while, the boat lurched sharply as it jumped a stump or log. Standing toward the rear, eager to throw the net, grandson Vhores Trosclair and another boy shouted excitedly as they pointed to the telltale wakes of the fish that we'd missed.

Octave keeps his fishing boat tucked away, like a secret weapon, in a shed along a little canal that leads to Bayou L'Ours. The culmination of years of innovation, his skiff, with freshwater-cooled inboard engine, tunnel drive and special weedless wheel, runs shallow.

While the ideal fishing machine for this difficult terrain, each of the mosaic of patches on its plywood bottom record a day when some jagged snag punched through, compelling the fishermen to gun the little boat for the bank, hoping to beach her before she sank.

But a little thing like that hardly slowed down Octave. He'd jump to the shore, find a piece of driftwood, nail it over the hole, bail her out and go back to fishing. "Tov" is hard to stop. The Stumps couldn't stop him. And a heart attack while deer hunting several years ago couldn't stop him. It took the House, the Senate and a governor to stop this Cajun.

"He still wants to fish," said grandson Vhores. "He could do it. He could fish trout and other stuff, but he doesn't want to do that; redfish is what's in his blood."

It was a gray and raw afternoon in November 1991, when I visited Octave. The wind was picking up from the Northwest and whitecaps rolled down the Bayou. To me, it seemed a pretty good day to sit around and shoot the bull. But Tov didn't have much time to spare. He'd been up early to hunt deer in the marsh with Vhores, and after coming in for dinner and a nap, he was getting ready to head back out for an evening hunt.

My daddy? No, my daddy was not a fisherman. Daddy was a farmer and a trawler. A trapper and a pirogue maker. He fished a little bit but not much. He was from Cut Off, but he went and lived on Bayou L'Ours in 1909. In a camp. I was born and raised back there.

He bought some land and we still got it. There's a little bit o' marsh but not much, it's mostly on the ridge. He was a farmer, you know. He could've bought some marshland but, in them days, it was free—it was for *everybody*. In them days, as long as the water covered the marsh, you couldn't stop anybody from goin'. That's the way it was.

But now they're closin' everything off. It started a good while back but it's pitiful now. Lac Enfermer, Lac Ronde, that's all closed up now. You can't go in there no more at all. At King's Ridge they got a fence, they got fences *all over*.

I started trammel nettin' when I was about 35; almost 40 years ago. And since then, I've caught a lot of fish. I've caught my share of fish.

And in all that time, I've seen it when they didn't have no fish and I've seen it when there was a lot of fish.

But everything that happen, it's blamed on the fisherman. You know, when there gonna come a red tide—clean out all the fish, you don't hear nothin' about that—they don't blame the red tide. A big ice come, like in '89, clean out everything from Texas to Alabama. It didn't clean out a little bit, it clean *everything*. I saw enough fish dead, it was unbelievable, the fish that was dead. But it's not the ice that kill 'em, it's me!

When I first started trammel nettin' there came a ice, and I mean a ice. I believe it dropped down to nine. That was about 40 years ago. Everything ice up, and it stay ice up for about 10 days. I tried to go in the Back but I couldn't. When the ice broke up, it melted in the night.

That mornin', I went in the Back. The oil company had made a canal back there and they had a little patch of dirt. And when I got there it was early in the morning. And man, I saw that white boat. Daggone, I thought I was gonna be by myself this morning and I see there's a guy there already.

It was white but it was a block of ice that hadn't melted yet. The water had splashed over that little island, and it had maybe three or four feet of ice that was solid.

And that day there was not one fish left in the Back that was not froze. I don't believe that not one fish save his life.

A little more than a month after, I went back of Bay Harrison; I caught 10 redfish in a strike. And it weighed 190 pounds. They averaged 19 pounds apiece. That was a little gang of bulls that had followed in after the ice. That's the only time I had caught big fish inside—you know, worthwhile. A lot of time I'd catch one, but that time I caught 10. I remember I brought it to old man Dovic, and he gave me 10 cents a pound for it.

Sometime I'd fish a whole week in Little Lake by myself. I wouldn't see nobody.

And you'd go there and you'd make you 10, 15, 20, 25, sometime 50 dollar. It was not much, but you was workin' at a dollar, $1.50 an hour, carpentry work. I was building boats for $1.50 an hour but I made better fishing, you know. So I just quit working outside, and I started just fishing.

But I worked for 17 years building boats. I was building some little boats over here at the house, and I was workin' with Neil Covacevich, when he come from Biloxi and build boats down here. I worked for a year with him—a dollar an hour. And I worked with Cleo Adams. I was working for Cleo Adams for $1.50 an hour, and then Roland Duet. When I started working by Roland, two dollar an hour.

When I used to build boats over there, I'd knock off, and I'd build me some little boats over here. After hours and before hours. I built a lot o' little boats. I all the time work hard, all my life. I never made money, but I made a living. I all the time work hard.

A lot of people say, "Man, you got to know what you're doin' to build a boat." I say, "No, you don't need to know nothing. All you have to have is a strong back and a weak mind."

My little boat? Oh man, it just come natural. I had never seen a boat built in my life, before I built the first one. I made it out o' lumber. I built my first little boat when I was livin' in Bayou L'Ours. My brother had a little saw mill and we sawed some lumber. That's when I made the first boat.

And after that, I believe, I'm almost sure, that I'm the first man around here that made a mud boat. I just bought some plywood and I say, "Well, I'm gonna make a little boat." And I had seen that weedless wheel work already, you know, in them water lilies and all. "I'm gonna try that," I said.

I put in a six-cylinder Ford and, at first, I put it with a water pump. I run it a long time with a water pump. I had the intake on the side where I could bend with my hand and get the grass out. Then I put a radiator.

My fishing boat is almost 20 feet long on deck, but it's wide—I made that special for trammel nettin'—it's 8 1/2 feet wide, on the top. On the bottom, almost 7 feet. And I got a tunnel on there. And

I mean it run—if a redfish can swim, I can go after it. Unless it's real hard bottom. Soft bottom in the marsh there, I can go anywhere.

The first boat I made with a tunnel, it was for a guy that had a little flat boat, a little jo-boat. He was hunting in Grand Bois, and he'd pass in that hard clay bottom there, and the wheel, when it would touch that clay, it would stop the engine.

So he came see me. He say, "Do you think you could build a tunnel?" I say, "I never built none, but I know I can."

So I build him a little boat. I put a three horsepower Wisconsin in there. After he had it, he came told me, he said, "Man, I want to bring you, I want to show you how that little boat pass in that shallow water with that tunnel."

When I first started trammel nettin', I didn't have no slicker suit. Man, I'd get in that water...cold! The first man gave me a suit was old man Dovic. He came there one day and he gave me one of them suit that come up to here. He say, "There's some guys that went and work on a pipeline by Bird Island, and when they stop the job, one of 'em gave me one of them suit." He say "I want you to try that."

Man, I never did trammel net without that since then. Boy, I got cold in my life trammel nettin'...get wet!

For the redfish, we were getting, from 8, 10 cents, 12 cents, very seldom you'd get more than 12 cents. In them days, when I first started, I was fishing for old man Dovic, in Golden Meadow. Then Estay—the one had New Orleans Shrimp Company—he came see me over here, and he told me, he say, "How much you getting from Dovic?"

"Well," I say, "I'm getting 12 cents for the redfish and I'm getting 15 cents for the trout. He say, "I'll tell you what, if you want to fish for me, I'm gonna give you 15 cents for the redfish and 17 cents for the trout." It doesn't look like much now, but it was a big difference then, you know. If it had been $1.12 to $1.15, it was not much difference. But 12 cents and 15 cents, that's a lot of difference right there.

So I fished for him, oh, a good while.

Lots of times, when you'd come around Christmas or Thanksgiving, you couldn't sell the redfish at all. You hardly couldn't sell *no* fish at all. And sometime—me and my brother was fishin' together—when we'd see a big school of redfish, and we knew we couldn't drop our net, we'd say, "Look, look at that big bunch o' ducks!" That was a big joke, you know. We didn't like to go back there and have to leave that, and not be able to catch it, *mais* you couldn't sell it at all.

And one time me and Tom Kiff, my nephew, the year that, maybe you saw that tall boat already—the Frosty Morning—the year that trawl boat was made, he trammel net with me. And we went there, to Bay L'Ours, we went there and we was fishing for trout—you couldn't sell anything else but trout—no drum, nothing but trout. Twelve cents a pound. And we went there and I dropped my net, and I hit a little bit, "toc, toc," on the boat. And I heard, "splash, splash." "Oh Lord," I told Tom, I say—it was at night—I say, "let's not make no more noise, let's pick up that net." And we pick up that net, makin' sure that we didn't make no more noise, so for them to not tangle up too much. And we save 520 pounds of redfish.

I brought 'em to old man Bell, in Larose over there, and he told me, "I don't want 'em." And I say, "Well, if you don't want 'em, I'm gonna dump 'em in the Intracoastal Canal." He say, "No, don't dump 'em." He say, "I'm gonna give you five cents a pound." I never will forget that...520 pounds of redfish...$26.00. Twenty-six dollars!

Did it hurt me when they closed the fish? Man, it hurt *everybody*. The only thing it didn't hurt is the sports. But they got mad just the same because they thought they was gonna catch the fish and sell it. But now they can't sell it no more. That's what happened. They thought they was gonna get all the fish for them, and then they was gonna catch it and sell it.

This is the first year I didn't get a fishing license. Because the last time I went gill net, it was after you couldn't catch the reds. They had closed it, and it was just before the freeze. I went there and if I would've had a net three miles long I could o' drop it in redfish. All the time, all the time, there was no place that I pass that I couldn't catch no redfish. I came here, I hang the net right there where it is and I told my wife, "I'm not going back."

They had a few drum—maybe I could have caught a few drum—but too many redfish to bother me. So many fish...all them ponds in the back, that was all full of fish. Everywhere you looked they had some fish. And I'm not tellin' you two or three fish. They had fish everywhere.

I came here, hang my net, and it's still there. You can see it's all mildewed there. I never did touch it since then.

SPOTTED SEATROUT

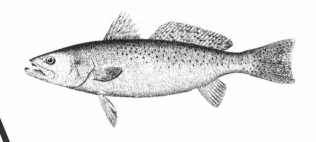

Louisiana coastal fisherman sat on the porch of his small home of cypress and pine. It was a sunny day, late in March 1988, but a 25-knot South wind coming in from the Gulf kept him off the water. Not that there was much to do out there anyway.

It's been a long damned winter, and it ain't over yet. They shut us down on the redfish in January. That was it—zip, no income. We weren't used to that; it kind o' put us in shock.

January's about our best month for reds, and February's pretty good too. March? Well, it's not great but when the weather'd get right, when the wind would die down—maybe two days a week—you could ride the beach and maybe luck into a good school o' reds up on a bar takin' the sun. It was a long shot, but at least it was there.

Now we're fishin' sheephead and black drum a little but the markets aren't there yet. You make one fair day and the fishhouse won't let you go back out for a week. You can't make it like that, not with the prices they're payin'.

March has never been a money month for us. It's a survival month. But this one's been about the toughest I've ever been through. I'm pretty much on a steady diet o' Maalox now. Last week, I got calls from Ford, the mortgage company and the finance company. I mean they wanted to take my truck, my house and my outboard all in the same day!

And I didn't have much to tell 'em either. It's probably just a matter o' time. I feel like I got two sisters pregnant, and I'm just waitin' for the one to tell the other.

But a fisherman's supposed to be able to take it, you know what I mean? It's hard to keep a fisherman down, but there's always somethin' or somebody tryin'. This year it's the sports—well, it's always the sports but this year they're worse.

Back in late '82, early '83 it was the worst el niño *in a hundred years. It didn't get cold, it flooded, and we had these winter storms that blew the water in from Barataria Bay and covered the marsh. The reds were there, yeah, but under four foot o' water they were harder to find than a pearl in a mud oyster. Then, the next winter, we had record* low *tides and a freeze that killed a bunch o' the fish and ran the rest of 'em out into the Gulf.*

Winters are always rough, it's just that some years they're rougher! I guess the only thing that's keepin' me goin' now's the trout. It won't be long and they'll be here. They always are.

The spawning run of spotted seatrout marks the official end of winter for South Louisiana netters. As the southerlies of March and early April drive the replenishing waters of the Gulf into the winter-worn marsh, fishermen know that there will soon be money to spend. But there's a lot to get ready first.

A new net will have to be hung—a 1,200-footer might take a good week of dawn-to-dusk days. The boat will need to be pulled and dried, scraped, sanded and painted. And the engine will need a good going over, a tuneup and a fresh prop. You don't want any downtime once the fish start.

The trout usually begin to show around the end of March or early April; by mid-May, they're coming in hard. The timing depends on water temperature, salinity and day length.

According to biologists, spawning normally begins when the water temperature gets up to at least 68° and salinities reach at least 20 parts per thousand. The fish lay their eggs just off the beaches, in and around tidal passes and in the estuaries. Although most of the trout showing up in these locations are coming in from the Gulf, some biologists and commercial fishermen suggest that their numbers are augmented by a large population of inshore fish. Having overwintered deep in the marsh, these trout migrate southward to the beaches and mix with the bright fish that spent the winter offshore.

"I know that in the spring, when trout start showin' up on the beaches, some of 'em are comin' in from offshore and some are comin' from inshore," said Claude McCall. A veteran commercial fisherman and sport-fishing guide, McCall pursued the species in both Florida and Louisiana. "It's harder to tell here, but in Florida those that came from inshore were a dark yellow color, and those that came from offshore were a bright silver. Some were almost black, a blackish-silver, according to the bottom they were on.

"And they would mix on the beach. It took a day or two for 'em all to become the same color. You do get a mixture here, but it's not as pronounced. Down there, there were so many of those mangrove swamps, with a lot of tannic acid. The fish would turn a dark yellow."

Trout are best fished with a gill net from a Florida-style well-skiff. With the net stacked aft and the outboard mounted in a motor well near the bow, this unusual boat runs fast and shallow. The speed is needed to beat the competition to distant sets, and the shallow draft lets the boat get right up on the beach and sand bars where the trout lie.

Roy Lee Yeomans has fished the specks in Louisiana every spring

LOUISIANA SPOTTED SEATROUT
Historical commercial landings [a]

YEAR	POUNDS	YEAR	POUNDS
1887	524,000	1960	467,000
1888	522,000	1961	619,000
1889	619,000	1962	424,000
1890	656,000	1963	460,000
1897	675,000	1964	356,000
1902	1,078,000	1965	458,000
1908	1,103,000	1966	647,000 [b]
1918	1,190,000	1967	621,000
1923	783,000	1968	619,000
1927	822,000	1969	720,000
1928	885,000	1970	786,000
1929	513,000	1971	1,122,000
1930	710,000	1972	1,700,000
1931	767,000	1973	2,527,000
1932	633,000	1974	2,124,000
1934	1,518,000	1975	1,897,000
1936	1,037,000	1976	1,611,000
1937	987,000	1977	1,084,000
1938	539,000	1978	680,000
1939	716,000	1979	798,000
1940	262,000	1980	604,000
1945	917,000	1981	587,000
1948	503,000	1982	728,000
1949	886,000	1983	1,341,000
1950	882,000	1984	973,000
1951	602,000	1985	1,162,000
1952	602,000	1986	1,868,000
1953	535,000	1987	1,802,000
1954	437,000	1988	1,433,000
1955	510,000	1989	1,489,000
1956	612,000	1990	658,692
1957	641,000	1991	1,255,713
1958	654,000	1992	971,481
1959	691,000	1993	not available

[a] *Includes some white trout through 1965*
[b] *Spotted seatrout only from 1966 through 1992*

since he moved here from Florida in the early 1970s. We made a trip together one day in early May; the weather was still cool, but the fishing was hot. With the boat barely on plane, in the lee of a small, sandy barrier island, we scanned the water's surface for signs of bait.

With Roy's experience, it wasn't long before we came upon a large area where the water's glassy surface was marred by thousands of shimmering little streaks and wrinkles, like frost on a windowpane— glass minnows, a small, delicate baitfish of which trout are particularly fond. Just as they were betrayed by their miniature wakes, we hoped their presence would indicate great numbers of fat trout lying beneath them.

As we approached to make the set, Roy squinted in concentration, asking himself: "How much water? Which way's the tide goin'? Which way will they run?"

"Stand by!" he shouted.

I grabbed the let-go, a sash weight hung from a large red buoy tied to the end of the net. Roy put the hammer down, headed straight for land and, just before running aground, veered off.

"Let 'er go!" he cried and I heaved weight and buoy toward the shore and quickly grabbed the gunwale so as not to be thrown overboard as he kicked the skiff around in a sliding 180-degree turn.

Roy, still on a plane, headed out and then turned to parallel the shoreline, taking in as many of the baitfish as he could. The net looked a little sinister as its leadline bored into the water, each weight— spaced less than a foot apart—solidly rapping the transom on its way out. Sounding a staccato toc-toc-toc-toc, it's like a semiautomatic weapon, but a little faster than you can pull the trigger.

When we were almost out of webbing, Roy cut back in toward shore and then turned into the "compass"—the area that is encircled by the net—dropping the end of the net near the bank. Then we started to "beat it down," rapping on the sides of the boat with a short length of 2 x 2 to scare the trout into the net.

As we sped back and forth within the compass, the surface occasionally erupted in a splash as a medium-sized fish hit the net near the corkline.

"Trout!" cheered Roy.

"How's he know?" I wondered. But then the telltale signs of success appeared. Popping up all around the net and inside the circle too, were clear little oil slicks that slowly grew in diameter. And then there was the odor—a clean, fresh fragrance like a just-cut watermelon. On the cool breeze, it filled your head and smelled wonderful. You'd never guess it came from the fish oils that the trout literally vomit as they bolt, sort of like a heron's dumping ballast as he takes off.

Encouraged now, we made another pass close to the net, rapping harder with the wooden club, and as we approached a curve, a school of small trout showered through the net. Too small to stick in our 3 1/2-inch mesh, they rammed the webbing, popped through the meshes like bananas from a peel, cleared the water headfirst and were gone.

Finally, it was time to go to work as Roy backed the skiff up to the end of the net, trimmed up the engine and shut her down. I caught the corkline, and we hauled back by hand. They weren't all too small.

If that set made trout fishing sound easy, well, it was one of the rare perfect ones. It doesn't often go that way. I remember a more typical day, when I was out with Pagaie Cheramie and we'd brought along "Chaz" Willyard, our mechanic and friend, who was just looking for a boat ride and enough cash to pay his light bill.

It was late July, and it was hot, Lou'siana full-sun-on-the-beach

Running out the net

Soaking the net in the swash behind a bar

Crabs, catfish and stingrays mean lost time, holes in the net and possible injury.

Trout caught in 3 1/2-inch webbing average nearly two pounds and have spawned at least once.

Back at the dock

hot. Even the mangroves were wilting. And those big, nasty, green-headed sandflies wouldn't leave us alone, diving in to make a searing little slash and then sneaking back to lap up the blood as it ran down our ankles. We were all sweating and low in spirits, thinking about the bills that, once again, probably wouldn't get paid.

The trout, of course, were out in the cooler, deeper water. They're not stupid. And it was between moons—there wasn't much, if any, run to the tide. In other words, it was a stinking, lousy day to fish. We were only there because we were fishermen and, since the boat wasn't broken, we had to go try. But as we painfully hauled in the net, it held little more than saltwater catfish, each one requiring our undivided attention to prevent taking a venomous barbed fin in the hand. We really didn't think the situation could get much worse. We were wrong.

In the distance, fishing off a point, was a rod-and-reeler and his wife in a little fiberglass runabout. Of course, he wasn't catching anything either, but unbeknownst to us, this sportsman was becoming

After the trout are dressed they're packed in ice and trucked to New Orleans and other urban areas.

more furious with every catfish we took out of the net. As we chucked each slimy two- to three-pounder into a crate that we'd later donate to a crabber friend who needed bait, the guy in the runabout simmered, boiled and finally blew up.

Suddenly he was bearing down on us at full speed and got close enough for us to count the freckles on his wife's bare shoulders—the high point of our day. At the last second, he turned hard, throwing his wake all over us and, as he sped away, he flipped us the finger. "Damned gill netters!" he screamed. "That's why we can't catch any trout!"

These days, Louisiana's commercial trout fishermen are increasingly taking the blame for the inevitable fishless days of the angling fraternity. The two user groups used to get along. They'd greet each other with a wave as they passed on the water and, well, at least stayed out of one another's way. But much has changed in the last 25 years.

Coastal erosion has taken a terrible toll on Louisiana, erasing as much as 50 square miles of the state in a single year. To ride with an old trout fishermen is to receive a depressing blow-by-blow litany of this loss: "There used to be an island here somewhere...a shell bar there...this little sandbar used to be an island with trees on it...this bay used to be full of grass...."

As coastal erosion accelerated, the number of commercial finfishermen increased by several hundred and that of sport fishermen escalated from thousands to hundreds of thousands, heightening the competition for speckled trout, whose numbers—through it all—have held up amazingly well.

A showdown was inevitable and, in the early 1970s, the battle line between sports and commercials was drawn, precipitated by the influx of out-of-state netters and fish dealers from Florida.

Unlike in Louisiana, where shrimp was king, finfishing in Florida had long been big business. Dealers who moved into Louisiana knew how to move more fish and more kinds of fish than did the relatively few local buyers, most of whom specialized in shrimp and dealt in trout and redfish only as a sideline.

Like the Slavic fishermen, who brought their knowledge of oyster culture to Louisiana in the early 1800s, the Floridians greatly enhanced the overall value of the state's seafood industry.[1] But the rapid expansion of the finfish sector led to the polarization of the state's commercial and recreational fishermen.

The dealers needed fish in quantities greater than the traditional Louisiana fishermen could supply. Soon, each fishhouse was surrounded with a fleet of oddly configured boats. In the net compartment of each was a billowing pile of a brand-new kind of net.

SPOTTED SEATROUT

With their fast well-skiffs and monofilament gill nets, the Florida fishermen were preceded by their reputation as perhaps the best all-round finfish harvesters on the Gulf Coast. They were welcomed neither by local sport fishermen nor by the local finfishermen who—for the most part—were fishing with small inboard-powered boats and heavy-twined trammel nets.

Because of their newfangled gear, the Floridians were highly visible and much resented. Although some settled down in Louisiana to become resident fishermen, their numbers were noticeably swollen each spring by a couple of hundred of the boys from back home, who came over just to cash in on the trout run.

Trout landings climbed steadily, from 786,000 pounds in 1970, to 1.1 million pounds in 1971, to 1.7 million pounds in 1972. In 1973, trout fishermen landed an all-time high of 2.5 million pounds, followed by 2.1 million pounds the next year.

The first statewide anti-commercial fishing group coalesced out of fears about overexploitation of the trout by the annual migration of Floridians and their use of the monofilament net.

Save Our Specks (SOS) was started by Gerry Waguesback, owner of Bonita Boats; Baton Rouge printer Albert Bankson, who would later help develop one of the state's first coastal recreational fishing communities; and other outboard motor, boat and marine supply dealers. An SOS brochure, prepared for the 1977 legislative session, contained excerpts from a letter written to the organization in 1975 by New Orleans *Times-Picayune* outdoor editor Dan Greene:

> Even more noticeable than the relatively piecemeal operations by local fishermen, however, has been the rapid influx of out-of-state gill net operations.
>
> During a trip to the Leeville area this past week, I saw

197

another large new Florida operation that sport fishermen inform me was installed just this past April for the purpose of fishing the barrier islands in and around Grand Isle.

I counted 18 small specially-equipped gill net runabouts, 1 large tender craft, conveyer belts and a fleet of five one-ton trucks and a semi-trailer presumably used to haul fish out of state. In addition, I was told that there were at least another half dozen vessels away from the area.

ALL VESSELS ON THE SCENE BORE FLORIDA REGISTRATIONS, AND THE TRUCKS HAD FLORIDA LICENSE PLATES.

Needless to say, it is this so-called invasion by out-of-state netters that has gone the longest way toward inciting the sport fishermen, and creating the battle that we have witnessed in recent months. In all that I have heard, it has been the out-of-state operations that have been the main bone of contention, not the operations by local commercial fishermen.

SOS was, at first, concerned mainly with eliminating the dreaded monofilament gill net. The group's brochure commenced with the statement: "The monofilament gill net is a deadly effective weapon that is threatening to wipe out Louisiana's population of Speckled Trout."

Members of SOS went up to Baton Rouge to try their luck, and they won. The Legislature banned the use of monofilament gill nets. Though SOS had at first targeted only the out-of-state fishermen and their monofilament nets, the group's initial success encouraged its members to return each subsequent year to try to further restrict or eliminate the commercial trout fishery.

In what had become one of the rites of spring, commercial fishermen were forced to forfeit valuable fishing time—always during the peak of the trout run—to make the long drive to Baton Rouge and attempt to fend off the latest attacks by those who had become obsessed with the notion that Louisiana could not truly be "Sportsman's Paradise" until all commercial fishing was eliminated.

Some years the "antis" succeeded and, once in a while, the netters prevailed. Over the years, however, the commercial fishermen have been losing the war.

The recreational lobby believed that monofilament nets were so popular—and so deadly—because they are difficult for the fish to detect. Indeed, there are occasions, such as when the water is extremely still and clear, when trout are more likely to hit a net made of clear plastic material than one comprised of more coarse and opaque nylon twine. But, in actuality, most commercial fishermen favored mono because of its light weight and the ease with which it cleared.

Monofilament webbing doesn't absorb water like a braided nylon net, and that makes it a lot lighter. It's easier to carry around in a small boat and easier to pick up. Inshore trout fishing is a low-tech operation—the webbing is picked up by hand—and, when you're making 15 or 18 sets daily with a 400-yard net, the lighter the better.

But, by far, the biggest advantage of the stiff monofilament over the more limp nylon is the relative ease with which unwanted species such as blue crabs, saltwater catfish, stingrays or baitfish like menhaden can be cleared. At times, the crabs or catfish can get so thick that they'll totally foul and roll up a net.

A misplaced set can cost a fisherman most of his day as he tries to pick his way through a tangled mess of pinching claws and barbed stingers. With a mono net, this lost time is minimized because most of these unwanted animals can merely be shaken out.

Monofilament nets enabled the fisherman to fish more efficiently and therefore catch more fish. But just as the recreational lobby considered wintertime trawling for trout in Texas, and purse-seining for bull redfish in the Gulf, to be "too efficient," they deemed monofilament too effective and, through "legislation for inefficiency," had it taken away.

After the ban on mono, Louisiana netters reverted to braided nylon and, even after a heavy dipping in tar or plastic, it wasn't easy to handle. Then, however, the new "multistrand" monofilament was introduced, and it quickly became the material of choice. The twine of a multistrand net is composed of at least three fine strands of monofilament which results in a light net that doesn't clear as easily as mono but is far better than braided nylon.

Initially, anti-commercial interests pushed restrictions on the composition of nets to regulate trout netters; later, they supported mesh-size limitations to further control harvest of the species.

The coastal trout fisherman's net of choice employed a 3 1/4-inch stretched mesh. With a relatively small, slender and tapered fish like the trout, a slight change in mesh size can make a big difference in the catch composition. A 1/4-inch variation up or down determines whether a particular year-class of fish will be caught or missed.

In the early 1980s, at the prompting of SOS, legislators passed a bill making the minimum mesh size on gill nets 4 inches, a hopelessly large size for trout fishermen in most regions of the state. There was, however, a "loophole" that allowed a *maximum* mesh size on trammel nets of 2 inches. So, as spring approached, fishermen were confronted with two choices: They could hang in a gill net with a mesh so large that it would only occasionally stop a very big trout. Or they could use the small-meshed three-walled trammel, which would stop everything from a 6-inch trout on up, and snare anything else that got near it.

The antis' strategy was to so handicap the fishermen that they would just give up.

And do what?

Because the netters couldn't afford to use gear that would catch no trout, they opted for the trammel—with predictable results. They fought catfish, crabs, stingrays and baitfish. And they killed a sickening number of small trout. Disgusted by this enforced slaughter, the netters called local TV stations, which reported on the situation.

Then, in an uncharacteristic move, some of the commercial fishermen united. In 1982, several Lafourche Parish netters formed their own advocacy group, the Organization of Louisiana Fishermen. OLF members agreed to chip in a fixed percentage of their landings toward the hiring of a polished lobbyist and their sacrifice was rewarded when the Legislature approved a 3-inch minimum mesh size on gill nets that year.

Most fishermen conceded that 3-inch webbing was a trifle too small for most trout fishing. Such gear produced two grades of fish: commercially valuable "large"—one pound and over—and small fish for which the fisherman received about half as much money and which were better off being left in the water until the following season.

A 3 1/4-inch net, on the other hand, strained out only the larger fish, allowing most of the "smalls" to pass through. Fishermen who had hung in the larger webbing to start with were rewarded in the spring of 1983, when the Legislature bumped up the legal minimum to 3 1/4 inches, making the hard-won 3-inch nets of the previous season illegal. Those who had chosen to hang 3-inch webbing after the trammel net fiasco now had to build new nets, at around $1,000 apiece.

Working with their 3 1/4-inch nets, fishermen supplied the market with trout for several years, and no biologist suggested that the species was overfished. But in the meantime, GCCA had absorbed SOS, taking over as the major "anti" group in the state. In the spring of 1987, GCCA pushed for a ban on all entanglement nets. The Legislature refused but, as part of a compromise, raised the minimum mesh size another 1/4-inch, to 3 1/2 inches. Now everyone's gear was undersized, and in order to fish the 1988 run, each fisherman had to hang in a new net.

Fishermen were extremely apprehensive about this new regulation, fearing that 3 1/2-inch webbing was just too large to make a living with. "If you have to go to a 3 1/2-inch net you're going to starve to death," warned veteran Claude McCall. "You average two-pound fish, and there just ain't enough of 'em."

Biologists claimed, however, that in time, use of the bigger webbing would allow the average size of the trout to increase. Indeed, they reported a measurable increase since fishermen began using the 3 1/4-inch nets. As it turned out, fishermen did adapt to the increased mesh size, which produced a lovely grade of fish, averaging slightly over two pounds. But what pushed many of them over the brink was the accompanying quota.

In addition to the 3 1/2-inch minimum mesh law, the 1987 Legislature imposed first-ever annual quotas on both redfish and speckled trout. Although biologists for LDWF testified that the trout population was in fine shape, they recommended the quota in anticipation of a shift in fishing effort to this species when the quota on the much-in-demand redfish was filled.

The ceiling was one million pounds (the average annual harvest over the past ten years, excluding the highest and lowest years), and the tally commenced September 1, 1987, when the law went into effect. Fishermen whittled away at inside fish all winter, and in early May 1988, just as the trout started to come in strong from the Gulf, the quota was exhausted and the commercial harvest of the fish halted.

"That's when they got me," related the netter who opened this chapter. "They'd already taken my wintertime fish and when they took the trout run from me, they put me in too much of a squeeze. That's when I lost everything I had."

This regulatory debacle has left those in the industry with a big question: Shouldn't it be possible to settle on one net that would enable fishermen to make a living and, at the same time, ensure a sustainable fishery for sports and commercials alike?

"No problem," say the biologists, "if you consider the facts." Trout, they explain, become sexually mature at about two years of age. At two years, a typical trout measures about 10 inches and weighs 1/3 pound; at three years, it's 13 inches and 3/4 pound; at four years, 17 1/2 inches and 1 3/4 pounds; at five years, 19 1/2 inches and 2 1/4 pounds; at six years, 22 inches and four pounds. By age six, most males have died, leaving a population of this age group consisting mainly of females.

Fecundity, the ability of fish to produce eggs, increases as the trout mature, with a 12-inch fish producing roughly 155,000 eggs and a 27-incher about 2,615,000. Larger females, however, do tend to have fewer viable eggs than younger, more vigorous females.

According to the biologists, three-year-old fish are the primary contributors of eggs in the seatrout population. This group has greater spawning potential than all four- and five-year-old fish combined. Two-year-old fish contribute a smaller amount of spawn because many of these fish are not sexually mature, and because those that are produce relatively few eggs. Three-year-old trout are nearly all sexually mature, their eggs are viable and they are plentiful.

Many in the industry argue, therefore, that if this age group was allowed to spawn each year, and there was decent habitat left to support their young, a perpetually renewable population of speckled trout could be maintained. This, commercial representatives point out, is easily achieved from the netters' perspective.

The advantage of a gill net as a fisheries management tool is that it is extremely selective. Undersized fish swim through undaunted while fish that are too large to enter the meshes back off and either sulk on the bottom or lie against the net until it's picked up, whereupon they ease off to safety. (That said, however, some very large trout are taken in gill nets, usually entangled by their two prominent canines.)

What, then, *is* the magic mesh size that would miss most of the biologically productive three-year-old fish and take only four-year-old (and older) trout that have spawned at least once and perhaps twice? "Three-and-one-half inches," say the biologists. Ironically, that's the same size that they have recommended for years and the same one that, after nearly 20 years of haphazard fishery regulation, is currently in effect in Louisiana.

In 1988, GCCA and the Louisiana Wildlife Federation attempted to have both trout and redfish declared gamefish permanently. The Legislature approved a three-year moratorium on the commercial harvest of redfish but, as a concession to the fishermen, raised the trout quota to 1.25 million pounds.

"At this time there is no indication that we have any problem with speckled trout," said Joey Shepard, a biologist with the finfish section of LDWF. "This year will probably be at least as good as last year. And, 1987 and the year before that were the best in the past five or six."

Subsequent landings data proved that Shepard's predictions were not far off. In 1986, total landings reached a high for the decade, topping 14.5 million pounds; commercial fishermen brought in nearly 2 million pounds of these trout while sport fishermen landed 12.5 million pounds. Total landings in 1987 reached 9.3 million pounds with commercials putting 1.8 million pounds of trout on the market and sport fishermen landing 7.5 million pounds. Landings in 1988 did fall off somewhat, but not substantially: Of the total 8.5 million pounds of trout harvested, commercials brought in 1.4 million pounds and recreational fishermen 7.1 million pounds. These figures might be compared to those of 1981 when commercial fishermen netted less than 600,000 pounds and rod-and-reelers brought in 2.3 million pounds, for a decade-low total of 2.9 million pounds.

In 1989, the 1988-1989 trout quota was met on April 9 and the harvest of this species curtailed until September 1989. "The timing is unfortunate," said LDWF Secretary Virginia Van Sickle in a New Orleans *Times-Picayune* article. Traditionally, demand for fish, particularly trout, plummets during the winter months, remaining depressed until Lent, when prices begin to rise. But for the second straight year, fishermen had to sit on the sidelines during the profitable spring trout run.

Since the trout quota was set up to commence in September, fishermen were stuck harvesting most of their allotment when prices were at their lowest. By harvesting the species throughout spring and summer, fishermen would receive a better price for their product, a point that was not lost on Van Sickle.

"Although we cannot do anything about it this session, we may in the future make a change, perhaps start the season in January," she said. "Then, when the spring market opens up, the netters could fish and get the most for their trout. By maximizing the value of the fish, both the fishermen and the state would benefit. This would be subject to legislative approval and hopefully not be objectionable to the recreational industry."

Van Sickle added that LDWF did an assessment of the trout population in 1988 to determine an allowable rate of harvest. "We found that the fish are doing well and that a 25-fish-per-day bag limit for the recreationals and a 1.25 million pound quota for commercials is not too liberal an allocation."

CLAUDE McCALL

Claude McCall marches to a different beat. At 70, his only means of transportation is a Kawasaki 440. Is his idea of home a brick house on a sycamore-lined avenue? Hardly. Claude likes his 20-foot Gi-Gi travel trailer. He keeps it looking brand new and parks it out of the weather, tucked inside a boatshed at Wayland Demere's fishhouse/marina in Leeville.

You'd hardly know Claude was there if you weren't looking for him. But he gets looked up, plenty. If you've got a bewildering mechanical problem, be it with an inboard or outboard engine; a design question, as you try to build that perfect skiff; or maybe some doubts about the chemical composition of the latest adhesives—go find Claude. He knows. The fishermen here call him the Wizard. The Wizard at Wayland's.

Claude knows because he's never been afraid to experiment and because he has lived and breathed fishing for more than 40 years. As we sat in the fishhouse office on a blustery day in February 1988, Claude told me his story:

I always did like to play around with electronics—I built my first short-wave receiver when I was nine. After I finished the first semester of my senior year I quit school to go into radio electronics full time. But I got tired of the snow and ice in North Carolina and headed to Florida. That was in 1941. I worked in radio repair until 1946 and then went fishin'.

I started in hook-and-line trout fishing, commercially, out of Pass-a-Grille in lower Tampa Bay and Boca Ciega Bay. I used live bait—shrimp when I couldn't get either small pinfish or what we called whitebait, a little herring. I did real well, until they started all that dredging and filling and so forth.

That was the end of that. I had to start guiding because there wasn't enough fish to make a living with. I guided for four years but then it got so bad you couldn't even keep a party happy. Water just like soup. It got muddy and stayed muddy. The grass started dying out. And fishing, it just played out.

Boca Ciega used to be a big, wide-open bay with a lot of grass flats. Shallow water, grassy bottom. When they got through, all that was gone. They even filled in the main channel. They filled in places that the developers never even bought. It wound up on Boca Ciega that there were just channels between the real estate developments.

The fishing had to fall off. The fish didn't have anywhere to go. But, of course, we got the blame.

I remember the newspaper interviewed one sport who'd been sold a bill of goods about how good the fishin' was. He moved down from up North somewhere and then couldn't catch any fish. He was really comin' down on the commercial fishermen but never mentioned that his new waterfront home was built on top of what had been some of the best grass flats out there.

A few years after World War II, water traffic got real bad at Pass-a-Grille Beach. Sports, you know. When you did manage to find a bunch of trout, you'd work 'em up to where you weren't casting any

CLAUDE McCALL

Claude McCall

McCall relocated to Louisiana after his territory in Florida became overdeveloped.

farther than about 10 feet. Just about the time you got 'em started, here'd come four or five boats. They'd see you pull a fish, and they'd come right in on top of you. And that'd be the end of it.

There was a buddy of mine, William Rocco, I never will forget him. Right out the south pass there at Pass-a-Grille, the grass was disappearin', but there was this one little spot of it, about as big around as his boat. He had drifted down to it, and there was a bunch of trout on it. And he was settin' there, pullin' trout.

It was one of those days when there was a misty rain, blowin' a bit, a mixture of rain and fog, and he figured, "Well, I got these, nobody's gonna screw me up here." Then, he heard a noise off in the distance. A roaring. And he was wonderin' what the hell it was.

Next thing he knew, there was boats coming at 'im full throttle! Throwin' water in his boat! Just shearin' this way and that to keep from hittin' 'im. Couldn't see any distance in that weather, you know. And he said he was sittin' there holdin' on t' both sides of his boat with his eyes closed and just hopin' that nobody'd hit 'im.

What it was, they had that Gasparilla Festival to celebrate the pirate days—a promotion for the area—and they had a so-called treasure hunt where they had clues here, there and yonder. When you found one it'd give you a clue to where to find the next one. The treasure was in the last one; I think it was a certificate for a new car. There were about 200 boats, full o' wild-eyed sports, trying to find that last one. And he was right in the middle of it!

Boat traffic's something a lot of people don't consider, but it'll hurt fishing. I learned that, fishin' snook.[1] With snook, boat traffic hurts bad because, in the wintertime, they'll huddle up under a dock, and you can see 'em just stacked up like cordwood. Just once in a great while, it'll get quiet enough that they'll start feeding. But anything goin' on—people walkin' on the dock, boat traffic and so forth—they'll stay there, and you can't get 'em to bite, no way.

I was still fishin' snook the last year we got to fish 'em commercially, around the Skyway Bridge, which crosses Tampa Bay from St. Petersburg. I was out next to the ship channel and divin', just lookin' around, and there were snook there.

I'd dive down, and about 10 feet below the surface there was a layer of snook. You'd dive down through them, and they'd close in over top of you and it was just black. You couldn't see, they blocked out the sunlight. I have yet to catch even one snook around that ship channel where I saw all those fish. But at each end of the bridge, when that tide started out and ran strongly, they'd hit. If it was quiet— no boat traffic and so forth—you could shut your motor off and drift downtide, ease your anchor over and fish back towards or under the bridge, and those things would hit just as fast as you could get a bait out. But if one outboard motor came by, that was it.

It hurts over here too, especially with trout on the beach, but it doesn't hurt as much in Louisiana as it used to down there because the water's not as clear. They'll spook but they'll calm down and start feedin' again a lot quicker if the water's not clear. Of course, the more traffic there is, the worse it hurts.

I've been diving and heard outboards go by. You could hear the gears whining. Surprisingly, you wouldn't hear the explosion of the exhaust. You'd hear the whine, though. Some inboards are quieter, but if you've got a rattle in the shaft, the stuffing box, the rudder or anything, it can hurt your fishin'.

I rigged one little boat with an inboard, a Studebaker Champion, and was real careful with the shaft and everything so it wouldn't rattle. Even so, I couldn't catch a trout with it. This was when trout were still real good at Pass-a-Grille Beach. Hook-and-line you could average, oh, 250 pounds a day, and all the rest of the fishermen were knockin' 'em loose.

Then I found that every time I moved around in the boat, the rudder would make a certain click. The trout didn't like that noise. I got rid of the click and started catchin' trout right away. Now, some noises seemed to attract them. But not that one. And not a rattlin' shaft. Outboards don't attract 'em either, I'll guarantee that.

Besides the noise, an outboard puts out a lot more pollution than an inboard. A two-cycle engine's a lot worse than an automobile. There's all kinds of stuff in the exhaust and you know that the water absorbs a lot of that. How much I don't know.

When the situation got too bad in Florida, I came to Louisiana. I'd been livin' with a gal in a houseboat, and when I decided to come over, she said she'd come too, but only if I brought the houseboat. I didn't want to tow that thing over here, so I just gave it to her and left.

I got here March 2, 1971—on my birthday. Fred Shiver came over, he and Wayland Demere. They were the first people to come over from Florida. They started that fishhouse in Golden Meadow. Then I came in, and a few others. It wasn't a great big operation. And still isn't, of course.

The locals, before Wayland came, were paying 15 cents a pound for trout and they didn't want anything under a pound and a half. They were gettin' a good price for it, too. When Wayland and Fred came in, they started off at 22 cents, and in a little while they started going up as they got their markets squared away. Some of these local buyers were raisin' hell, threatenin' to run 'em clean out of the country!

For several years, Wayland's son Delton and I were the only ones fishin'. Even during a real good year, you'd have periods when you couldn't catch enough to eat. But the good times were a whole lot better than they are now.

In late summer, back then, you just couldn't catch any trout. But in the fall, it'd pick up, be good all winter and get real fancy in the spring and early summer. But late last summer, you could catch trout. It wasn't good, but there was more during July and August than I've ever seen before here. But last spring was about as poor as I've seen it. Now, what would make that difference, I don't know.

This year? It won't matter much. If I could fish 'em, I'd fish 'em, but I'd bet real money that just as soon as they start comin' in they're gonna shut it off.

In the 17 years I've been in Louisiana, I've seen it change a lot. When I first came over, all in behind West Timbalier [a barrier island] it was grassy flats. The island was longer than it is now, and for quite a ways it was just solid grass along the inside. It was a broad-leafed grass that I always called turtle grass and it extended way out into the bay.

Now I never could take cold weather but, during the wintertime, Delton used to fish the inside of West Timbalier. And he'd fish in a norther, blowin' like a hurricane, and knock 'em loose right in the coldest part of the winter. He didn't fish right in the grass, but on the edge of the shelf, where it dropped off into deeper water. And that just hasn't produced anything at all since that grass left.

I'm not sure what knocked out the grass. Saltwater intrusion, probably. And, anything that stirs up the water will hurt the grass. There's been a whole lot of dredging over there, canal dredging. The oil companies are always changing something. If that grass can't get sunlight, it doesn't grow. Now, it could be that pollution did

Promotion of recreational fishing, such as this early 1950s ad from a national outdoor magazine, helped spur coastal development that destroyed fishery habitat.

By the 1970s, coastal developments virtually carpeted the salt marsh for 50 miles north of St. Petersburg.

something too—they had some oil spills out there. But anyway, when the grass left, the fish thinned out quite a bit.

A lot of those places that we used to fish aren't there any more. They're all washed out and gone—they've just eroded away.

A lot of things happened to hurt the fishing, but one thing is for sure, commercial fishermen got the blame. Fishing, no matter where you are, or however things are handled, has good years and poor years. It's cyclical. All this stuff is.

Now, when they have a good shrimp season, they attribute it to good weather conditions. And when they have a bad season, they blame it on the same thing. But, when we have a good year, the sport fishermen say we're taking too much, that we're destroyin' everything. And when we have a poor year, they say we've already destroyed it! No matter what the figures are, they're used against us.

Some sports fish full time—like the retired ones. And some of 'em work at it pretty hard. But, we're blamed for killin' all the fish out. It's been conceded all along that sportsmen kill a lot more fish than commercial fishermen, yet no one really bears down on those figures. I don't know why.

They always say that the recreationals spend so much more money than we do. But the commercial fisherman spends all he makes locally—and he spends it right quick. He's probably got it spent before he makes it! All they figure is the value of our dockside landings. But look at the markup every time the fish changes hands, the fishhouse workers, the fish companies, the truckers and the consumers—the restaurants and the general public that want fish to eat. That's all part of it.

We're up against such big money that we can't possibly win. There's no way we can meet the kind of money that the GCCA has.

The fisherman is just not any good at propaganda. And all the truth does is confuse the issue. Nobody wants the truth. Especially politicians. All it boils down to is the impression you make on the politicians.

We're not unique in Louisiana. The commercial fisherman is in trouble everywhere you look.

What gets me is, this country now eats an awful lot of seafood. If things were handled properly, this country could be a net exporter of seafood without hurting the resource. Just through proper management. There needs to be regulation, but not the kind we have now. The management that's being used now just tries to knock the commercial fisherman down. We'll wind up with almost no domestic production of seafood; it'll all be imported.

How about if we get in a war and can't get imports? We'll have to eat steak, I guess.

Fish farms? It'll be a long time before they can supply even a small percentage of the seafood used in this country.

There's room for both the sport-fishing industry and the commercial industry if it's handled properly. Both need regulation.

For an area that's overfished, they should limit the number of commercial licenses, like they do in Alaska. Limited entry.

Regulation of mesh sizes will determine the size fish you're gonna catch. A 3 1/2-inch minimum on trout is about right. The fish you take with that have all spawned at least once, maybe twice. And on redfish, all you've got to do is regulate the mesh size, with a window, for the sizes that can be taken. In other words, you only keep fish between one size and the next size.

But, most people have already made up their minds, and no matter what you say they won't change it.

Now you take Florida. Way back in, oh, it was sometime in the

1950s, they made a gamefish out of the snook. Well, the last day I got to fish 'em legally I put over 600 pounds in the fishhouse. That's hook-and-line, just like a sportsman would fish. The sportsmen weren't catchin' any—they didn't know how to fish 'em. But I was fishin' 'em.

That last day, I spent the incoming tide catching bait, and the outgoing tide fishin'. I ran out of bait with them still bitin'!

According to the propaganda at the time, the snook was, you might say, extinct. Now it's the same thing with the redfish. The GCCA comes on TV every hour with an ad saying the red is "endangered." They've got billboards up everywhere, with just a redfish skeleton on them, saying "Going, going...." And they say it's all our fault.

How do you counteract that? Commercial fishermen can't do it, they don't have the money or the time. Or the ability, the propaganda ability. The sports want the fish, they outnumber us, they've got the money for political campaigns and propaganda, and we can't match it.

Louisiana has an automobile license plate slogan, "Sportsman's Paradise." And when a sportsman's in paradise, he don't want to see anybody tryin' to make a livin' there. He wants it to be all sport. I don't think there's a whole lot the commercial fisherman can or will do about it.

If the sports put us out of business, I don't know who they'll blame when they don't catch any fish. They'll be in bad shape!

I know from experience that the fish aren't as plentiful as they used to be. But they'll never be that plentiful again, no matter what is done. The bottom has changed too much, the habitat has changed too much. No matter how much they change the take on 'em, there'll never be the fish there used to be. There just isn't the habitat to support 'em. Too many things have changed.

PART III

Many are coming to the conclusion that the ultimate goal of the recreational lobby is to eliminate every aspect of the commercial fishing industry from the Gulf.

—Jane Barnett, "Sport Group Uses
   Conservation to Fight Commercial
   Fishermen," *National Fisherman*, 1987

MULLET

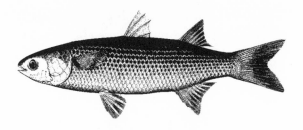

Louisiana's coastal fishermen have traditionally depended upon redfish and speckled trout for their livelihoods. But now, with reds off-limits and specks under a quota, Bayou State fishermen must look to other species to pay their bills.

The autumn spawning run of striped mullet is one fishery that netters can count on. Mullet are fished all along the South Atlantic and Gulf coasts, with the fishery's epicenter in Florida. There, annual landings over the past 10 years have averaged 24.2 million pounds. A record of 55.9 million pounds was landed in that state in 1943, due to heightened demand during the war.

Hank McAvoy, seafood marketing specialist with the Florida Bureau of Seafood Marketing, explained that during World War II, "Many foods such as red meat were rationed. They were probably looking for substitutes for the other foods that weren't available."

In Louisiana, where mullet fishing and processing are not fully developed, landings have been considerably lower. In 1980, a meager 204,310 pounds with a dockside value of $23,931 were reported. In 1991, fishermen landed 3.6 million pounds, worth $2.2 million.

The striped, or black mullet, *Mugil cephalis*, is a classic estuarine/ marine fish. The males mature in one to two years; the females in two to three. As autumn approaches, the mature fish cease feeding, their gonads ripen and they depart the wetlands for their seaward spawning run. Spawning occurs up to 50 miles offshore; when completed the adult fish return to the estuary. The eggs hatch and, by January and February, the larvae too are making their way landward. By late spring, they are two to four inches long and dispersed throughout the coastal wetlands, from the salt marshes to the freshwater cypress swamps.

The small mullet grow rapidly as they gorge upon the abundant vegetative matter in these nursery grounds.

Although some mullet are landed during the summer months, the bulk of the annual harvest is made up of roe-laden fish. Managers can easily maintain a stable population, however, thanks to the selectivity of the gill net, which enables fishermen to target a specific year-class.

"Larger-meshed gill nets of, say, four inches allow you to harvest only fish that have spawned at least once, possibly twice," said Dr. Bruce Thompson. He is assistant professor at the LSU Coastal Fisheries Institute and chairman of the state's Technical Working Group Subcommittee on Striped Mullet. "Since a mature adult will make from two to five spawning runs and the market does not want the smaller roe mullet," said Thompson, "I see this as a model example of a fishery that can be self-regulating."

"We try to get most of our fishermen to use 4-inch mesh," said processor Debby Black. "And usually, the fish in the first run are so big that they bounce right off it—they're more like 4 1/2-inch-mesh fish."

Black noted, "You catch some, though. And the second run is 4-

inch fish. Then, toward the end of the season, most of the fishermen go to 3 3/4-inch mesh. But we don't cut anything from a net smaller than that. That way, the small fish have a chance to get big. And then you get that crop every year."

Commercial fishermen obviously wish to maintain a stable population of mullet, to be assured of a profitable harvest of the larger fish each autumn. But there are other considerations. Smaller mullet are fodder for nearly every other commercially and recreationally important fish in Louisiana's waters.

Managers, therefore, strive to maintain not just a population abundant enough to produce an annual crop for the fishermen, but a "forage reserve"—enough smaller fish to provide adequate forage for the other species.

This consideration of the impact of management of one species of fish upon other species is just the beginning of a new wave of management which attempts to include the entire system. As the science of fishery management advances into the next century, decisions will no longer be based simply on the maximum immediate benefit to man; pelicans, otters and other fish species will be plugged into the equations as well.

DEBBY BLACK

Debby Black married into a family of Florida fishermen who later emigrated from that state to Louisiana during the late 1970s. Initially, the Blacks came to fish; later, they opened a fishhouse that has evolved into a large-scale mullet-processing facility in Hopedale. Here, Black describes the evolution and workings of the family's processing operation:

My husband, his twin brother, their dad and my sister-in-law, we all came over here about 15 years ago from Port Salerno. We came because we could catch Spanish mackerel in the summertime off Grand Isle.

Then we figured out that mackerel wasn't the money fish. The money was in trout and reds. We had one outstanding year with the trout, and that's when we got into the fish business. We built a fishhouse in Leeville, and then Ira, my father-in-law, decided to move over here to Hopedale.

About 1983, we decided to try mullet. See, they used to send 'em all to Florida. They'd purse seine them and just put them on semis and truck 'em out of here as fast as they could go. My father-in-law said, "This is stupid. There's plenty of people around here who need

Debby Black

work. I mean, we can put in our own freezers."

And that's what we did.

Some years we have a lot more boats fishing here than others. We have about 20 locals and the rest come over from Florida for the season. Plus, several of my Florida fishermen have settled down here.

The guys who catch the most fish are the ones who do it in Florida. They've been doing it their whole lives, and they know how to fish mullet. They take several of the local people along, though. They're willing to share their knowledge.

We don't have much conflict between the Florida fishermen and the local fishermen, because everybody's in the same boat. Everybody's got to try to make it. And they're like brothers: "If you can help each other, help 'em. If you can't help 'em, don't hurt 'em."

The local people look forward to mullet season every year because the fishermen spend a lot of money here—money that I'm bringing

Gravid mullet with roe and gizzard

into Louisiana. When my fishermen come over here, they all rent places to live. They all buy new slicker suits, they buy all their boat groceries here, and they probably spend about $80 to $100 a day on fuel.

They buy their nets here, and not a year goes by that there aren't four or five outboard motors bought here at around $5,000 apiece. If they blow one up, they're making enough money that they'll just run out and buy another one. They can pay for that in just a little while. Some fishermen buy boats when they come over, if it looks like it's going to be a good season. Others buy vehicles when they're here, say, a new truck.

When they're having a good run of fish, they'll pay local people to pick fish for them. "Here, I'll give you $100 to pick my fish," they'll say. People jump on that 'cause it's only a few hours' work. The fisherman just ropes in the net full of fish and pays somebody to unload the boat while he goes to sleep. He's been up all night, so it's

The cutting line

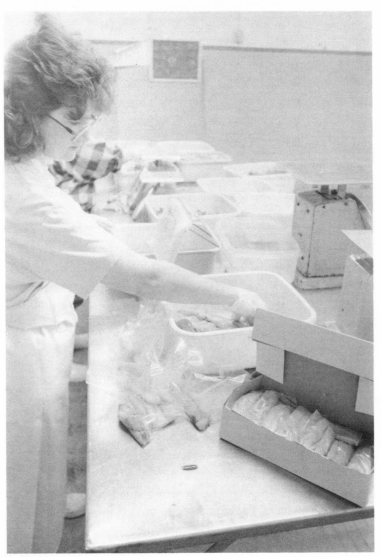

Packaging roe for export

worth his while.

A lot of the fishermen are like tourists—if they make a little money, they go down to Bourbon Street and all that, you know. They go back home with a little money, but they drop a lot of it here. Some of their wives get a little upset. They say, "I'm coming over next year. My husband makes a lot of money, but he doesn't come home with too much!"

The years we've had the best fish, we've had the crummiest weather. If you're cold, wet and miserable, you're going to be making money. In the past years, the bumper seasons have been when we've had nasty weather.

The mullet run only lasts six to eight weeks. It starts around the end of October, but the fishermen are all here and ready to go by the middle of the month. They push you and push you to open early. You can't blame them. They can't catch anything all year long, so when they've got a chance, they want to make some money.

During the season, we employ about 100 to 125 people. We usually run two conveyor lines. As the fish come out of the tank, we have people sorting out the males and females, and then we have two or three cutters on each line. They just cut, and then the people after that pull the roe, and the next people pull gizzards. And at the end of the line they pack the "splits"—the eviscerated fish—for crab bait and put them in the freezers.

We freeze the roe, put it in cartons and send it to Los Angeles or San Diego, wherever the ship's going to leave from.

Roe's a luxury product in the Orient. They very fastidiously clean it, dry it, put it in some pretty little packages and sell it for big bucks. The least I ever got for it, for two-to-four-ounce roe, was $4 per pound; four-to-six-ounce, $6; six-to-eight-ounce, $7. Over here, you get very little eight-ounce-and-up roe—they get a lot bigger in Florida and North Carolina.

We freeze the gizzards also and get about $2 to $2.50 a pound. The Taiwanese are very fond of the gizzards. I don't know what they do with them, but the buyers don't want to take our roe unless they can get the gizzards, too. [The mullet's muscular, gizzardlike stomach aids the fish in digesting vegetable matter.]

We don't cut the males, we leave them whole. We pack them in boxes and they go to Egypt. We also send the Egyptians some summer mullet—you know, just something to get my fishermen by. We didn't feel that fishing 150,000 to 200,000 pounds would hurt our season, because in years before they'd caught millions of summer mullet with the purse seines and then had bang-up roe seasons.

BUD HAWORTH

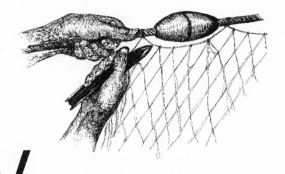

W.A. "Bud" Haworth, who moved to Louisiana several years ago from Mayport, Florida, fishes out of a 28-foot well-skiff. The boat is rigged with a tuna tower, and a picking light over the stern for clearing the net after dark.

Most mullet fishermen come out only at night. "They won't hit that net in the daytime," explained Haworth. "Maybe early in the season, but after that, you can forget it. The water's so dirty right now that you need a spotlight. When you shine that over the water, you see the mullet jump. But that's not the best way to do it 'cause you scare 'em with a light. And they're fast—they get out of there!

"It's better if, when the water's clear, you see 'em 'fire.' [As they flee, the fish disturb millions of minute phosphorescent organisms which light up to produce comet-like streaks.] When you see plenty of fire, you put your net down around that."

Haworth recalled the days back on the East Coast of Florida when, as a younger man, "If it hadn't been for mullet and grits, we wouldn't have made it."

He added, wryly, "I've fished mullet my whole life but I'll tell you, when I make my first million, I'm gettin' out o' this business!"

Bud Haworth: "When I make my first million, I'm gettin' out o' this business!"

Checking a small late-season catch for the presence of roe

BLACK DRUM

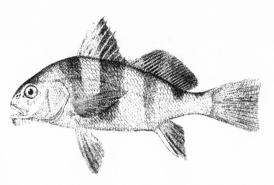

Mr. B's is a tasteful restaurant on stylish Royal Street in the French Quarter of New Orleans. The building's exterior is understated; the menu posted outside proclaims the delights to be sampled within.

Among the appetizers listed, you find, "Black Drum Beignets, bite-sized pieces of fresh drum marinated in Creole seasoning, deep fried and served with beignet sauce." And, adjacent to the "Quail Ridge 1985 Chardonnay," is "Grilled Black Drum, fresh fillet of drum grilled over hickory, with lemon butter; served with fresh vegetables and boiled new potatoes."

Black drum has finally come of age.

Except among a few local initiates, black drum was never a desirable item. Indeed, the fish was generally regarded as little more than a pest by oyster fishermen, who claimed that a school of the powerfully jawed fish could, by crushing and eating the shellfish, destroy an oyster bed overnight. Oystermen used to discourage such predation by staking dead drum around their reefs.

By 1988, regard for the fish had improved dramatically. "Drum is a really good fish," said Paul Crout, chef at Mr. B's. "I prefer it to redfish—and it's much more available."

The Cajun-cuisine rage of the mid-1980s created unprecedented demand for red drum. Although not as handsome a fish, the black drum's flesh is very similar in flavor to that of redfish—it is firm and moist, and grills and blackens just as well. So it's not surprising that demand for the red's humble cousin should also have skyrocketed. Fishermen, reeling from the ban on redfish, wasted no time gearing up to meet this demand.

The Underutilized Species Act of 1978 was designed to encourage diversification of Louisiana's fisheries. Under this act, a few fishermen were issued special permits to purse seine black drum within state waters, which extend three miles out from the shoreline. The deep, $20,000 purse seines, operated from $400,000 vessels, facilitated the landing of large quantities of black drum—enough to establish a market which, at the time, was centered in Nigeria. The "redfish crisis," however, led to the banning of all purse seines (except those used for menhaden) within state waters.

Fishermen now harvest black drum by a variety of methods. Shrimp trawlers catch some as they drag offshore during the winter and early spring. Some inshore fishermen found that drum could be taken over oyster reefs with trotlines. But most turned to gill nets. Large-meshed nets are either anchored out as set nets or used to strike tight schools of the large fish.

I was one of the many who, after the redfish closure, was forced to switch over to drum. With an 18-foot, Cajun-style inboard, I'd been perfectly equipped for working the sheltered waters of the marsh and hauling the comparatively high-valued redfish. But, not only were the drum out in much bigger waters, I couldn't even carry a deep, heavily weighted drum *net* in my little boat, not to mention the large,

BLACK DRUM

Landings from 1980 through 1991

Year	Landings (Pounds) [a]	Dockside Value
1980	471,656	$92,910
1981	2,888,988	$612,204
1982	1,690,712	$572,882
1983	1,858,879	$703,453
1984	1,975,626	$1,042,759
1985	3,421,325	$1,018,687
1986	5,225,976	$1,836,960
1987	8,020,901	$2,670,319
1988	8,756,913	$2,347,834
1989 [b]	4,405,849	$1,831,936
1990	2,875,627	$1,115,212
1991	1,914,090	$1,170,134

[a] *The landings increase much more dramatically than the dollar values because larger drum, which comprise the majority of the increase in harvest, are priced much lower than smaller fish.*

[b] *The first controls are put on the fishery .*

Source: *National Marine Fisheries Service, Washington, D.C.*

undervalued fish.

So, in early April, a few months after the closure, I jumped aboard as a deckhand with old-timer Roy Lee Yeomans.

Roy, his stepson Carl Cheramie and I left Leeville at sunup. There was no need to head out too early; we were only running to one of the near passes, about 12 miles away. I drove the Lady Gail, Roy's gas-powered, 30-foot Lafitte skiff, taking my time while Roy and Carl ran ahead in a 24-foot well-skiff in search of some fish.

When I reached the pass, Roy had already tied up to another boat, a 24-foot fiberglass T-Craft that had been converted to a net boat. Lonnie Black, another Florida veteran, and his son Russell were comparing notes with Roy. Lonnie, with polarized dark glasses, never took his eyes off the water.

"Still too early," he said, as I dropped anchor beside him. According to Lonnie, the drum would hang well off the pass in deep water. "As the tide comes in, they'll come in with it."

As the morning wore on and the tide slowly rose, we occasionally broke loose and rode, scanning the water for the telltale "muds," the turbid plumes that the big drum create as they dredge the bottom for food.

Roy spotted some muds in the distance but they were, he said, poorly organized. I took his word for it—you sure couldn't prove it by me. Even after eight years of inshore fishing I couldn't make out any muds. The water looked uniformly green and pretty to me. I guess that's why I was riding in his boat instead of he in mine.

When we came back together, Lonnie confirmed Roy's observations. "Some muds startin' to form, but it's not quite right yet." So we tied up again and waited.

While waiting, the two captains plotted their strategy for the imminent set. Since Louisiana law limits the length of our nets to

BLACK DRUM

Lonnie Black

Roy Lee Yeomans

Hauling back

1,200 feet, Roy and Lonnie decided that, when things got right, they'd strike simultaneously, doubling the amount of area that either boat could take in separately. And that's what we did.

The whole time we were anchored up, black drum were slipping past us, gathering on the shallow and sandy flats to the inside. Finally, the tide had brought in enough fish and, according to Lonnie, the thin cirrus puffs of muddy water had coalesced into one huge cumulonimbus. Again, damned if I could see it.

We each cranked up our engines and moved out. Barely on plane, the growling outboards sounded particularly menacing.

We kept ourselves between the fish and the deep water of the pass because that's the way they'd run. When we reached the near edge of the great oblong mud, Russell threw their strike-buoy out over the transom. I threw ours over theirs, overlapping the nets, and we spread out. Running parallel to each other, one on each side of the cloudy water, we started to pay out the nets.

BLACK DRUM

Icing down the catch

I still didn't see any sign of fish and was beginning to imagine how very unexciting it was going to be to haul back 1,200 feet of sopping, empty webbing.

But then there was a shout, "Pompano!" as one pompano and then another cleared water by the boat and skipped across the surface, flashing banana yellow in the sunlight. Pompano follow the schools of spawning drum, feeding either on the freshly laid eggs or on small shellfish uncovered as the large fish roil the water.

"Maybe there is something around here," I began to think when, suddenly up ahead, I couldn't believe what I saw.

The drum heard us coming and stampeded.

"Thar they are! Yonder they are!" cried out Roy who, at 62 and after a lifetime of fishing, was as excited as a 12-year-old.

The water was maybe six feet deep, and it was solid drum from top to bottom. As the school panicked, the fish below forced those at the top clear out of the water. For nearly an acre the blackish forms, only half submerged, launched like torpedoes for the pass. You could hear the roar above the engines as the fish cut the surface.

Most of them were beyond us—we'd struck a little too soon—but we continued our set, taking in what we could. Nearing the end of his net, Lonnie cut to port and turned into the circle. We cut to starboard, running outside him. We had the fish—or, at least, some of them. But they didn't like the idea.

The drum were racing to get back to deep water, right down the alleyway between our nets. When that mass of big fish hit the wall of webbing back at the strike-buoys, they lifted if half out of the water and then sunk it. They piled out over it and some plowed under it. But the eight-inch net grabbed a bunch of 'em too.

"They're gettin' on it now!" shouted Roy excitedly. "Look at 'em goin' on up it!" As the drum worked their way around the circle, testing and ramming the net, even I couldn't miss their wild thrashing along the corkline.

Lonnie slowly swept his net through the inside of the circle until he reached his strike-buoy; he tied that to his boat and started to haul back. After several hours, his circle was small enough that his net was totally loaded; it couldn't hold any more fish. Still, the water within his circle was a deep gun-metal gray—solid drum. When they realized that they were penned up, the fish settled down, avoiding the net and waiting. But, as Lonnie opened up his net, the drum inside charged to what they thought was freedom. Instead they met our backup net, fresh and clean. We dragged down, and then it was our turn to clear.

Once the fish have hit and the splashing dies down, drum fishing ceases to be fun—it quickly turns into a punishing contact sport. With Roy on the corkline, hefty Carl on the leadline and I in the center, "scratchin' bunt," we started to haul the net back in over the stern.

BLACK DRUM

The drum ranged in size from around six to 30 pounds and averaged about 12 pounds. That may not sound heavy but if you multiply this figure by 500 or 1,000 head of fish—we had 875 that day—it adds up fast.

We stood up and, bracing our knees against the transom, strained to heave in a short piece of net, tangled with fish. Then we dropped to our knees to clear them out of the twine. With a grunt, we heaved each one forward, where it landed with a heavy thud in the bottom of the skiff. Each fish solidly slapped the deck with its tail and then, as its thrashing lessened, drummed mournfully—boom... boommm...boom...boommm—deeper than the lowest notes on a string bass.

The hours passed with only the sounds of water lapping against the sides of the boat, we grunting and the fish splashing and drumming, until the skiff was nearly loaded. We anxiously checked our freeboard more and more frequently until, with a load of nearly 500 fish, we cranked up and gently idled over to the Lady Gail, watching for any freak wave that might swamp our half-sunk craft.

Then Carl and I heaved the fish, one by one, over to the big skiff while Roy, with a shovel, iced them down. When we had the well-skiff offloaded, we took a short breather while Roy covered the mountain of fish with more ice and then a tarp to shade them. We grabbed a quick sandwich and Coke and went back for more.

As the sun set, we realized that we had our hands full, and untied the end of the net, opening up a gateway about six feet wide. The remaining fish didn't need prompting to stream out through it. After we finally got the net up, transferred all the fish to the Lady Gail and got them iced down, we idled back toward town. It was after dark by the time we arrived at the fishhouse, but we had to handle those damned fish one more time as we gutted them onboard and slung them across the dock to the boys at the scales.

That made at least three times we'd handled more than 10,000 pounds of fish that day.

And then the boys at the fishhouse had to handle them as they graded them into two classes: the more valuable six- to 10-pounders, which went mostly to local markets, and the bulls, over 10 pounds. These were destined for cutting houses where they would be filleted, packaged and shipped to out-of-state markets in Texas, New York and the West Coast.

After grading, the fish were dragged to the cooler, stacked and generously iced down until a buyer could be located, which wasn't always easy. With everyone loading up on drum, every shed had a cooler-full. So it wasn't really a seller's market. When a truck did show up, the boys had to dig the big fish out of the ice and, slinging them one at a time, load it up.

Most everyone involved in the spring run of black drum would agree that the fishery is no picnic. The fishermen get bad backs, the dock workers severe cases of fishhouse blues and the owners of the sheds bad nerves as they worry over whether they'll find a buyer before their fish sour. But, rough as it is, it helps to keep the bill collectors at bay.

FISHING UNDER THE PLANE

Afine spring day, clear and calm, on Timbalier Bay. Heard over the VHF:

"OK, Roy, come straight ahead. Toward the last boat I just set. Over toward Gordon's boat. Come toward the southeast," said Matt, our spotter pilot.

"You talkin' to me, Matt?" asked Roy as he cranked up his 135-horse Evinrude.

"Roger, Roy. Come to the southeast. Come to your right. It's about a mile or so."

Roy accelerated. The outboard whined.

"Keep coming to the right. Keep coming around to the right. Come around some more. You need to go to the right of that oil rig up there. Would you prefer to set to the right or the left? Which way do you have your leads?"

Fishermen prefer to set large schools of fish with the leadline to the inside of the circle. It makes the net a little harder to "blow" when the fish rush it.

"Yea, Matt, to the right, that's OK."

"OK, Fritchey," said Roy, "stand by. I think I see 'em up ahead. See 'em right yonder?"

"OK, Roy, come up slow to the left. Come around to your left some. Now speed up a little but don't turn hard. All right, keep comin' around to the left. A beautiful blaze o' fish here. They're on your left side. Keep comin' around slow. Come around kind o' hard now. Come around hard left."

"See 'em yet?" I asked. "Do you see 'em?"

"Yeah, yeah!" shouted Roy. "I see 'em. Right there!"

"Come around hard. Hard. Come around...come around hard left. Keep comin' left. Come left...come left. All right, straighten up. Drop it, drop it," said Matt, very calmly from overhead. "Go straight."

I threw over the buoy, tied to the tag end of the net.

"Try to hold it, now," said Roy, glancing at the net leaping overboard, "to keep it from comin' off in a pile."

"Go straight for a little while, Roy. All right, put a little right cup. Not much, just a little bit o' right cup."

We heard the "toc-toc-toc" of the net leads as they struck the transom on their way out.

"All right, come around hard. Hard to the right. Don't mess your net up but come around. Come around as hard as you can without messin' up your net."

"Toc-toc-toc...."

"Don't worry about makin' a circle—I'll have to stretch you out. Come around. Come around hard. All right, straighten up right there. Go straight. Gonna come out good. Don't turn back now. They're in between you and the strike buoy...some of 'em. You need to get a little farther out. OK. Go ahead. Come on back now whenever you're ready...you got 'em."

"Toc-toc-toc."

"OK, Percy, come on over here toward the last boat I just set. Where Roy's at. There's a pretty good bunch o' fish just to the west o' him."

"We're on our way, Matt."

"OK, Percy, come straight ahead...."

Increasingly denied access to trout and redfish, fishermen have been forced to turn to heretofore underutilized species such as black drum and sheepshead. Prices for these species are relatively low. To produce the higher volume they need in order to turn a profit, fishermen must use larger boats, nets and crews. And when they take these rigs out, they need to catch fish.

Enter airplane-assisted fishing.

The drum school up in Lake Pontchartrain, Breton Sound, Barataria Bay, Timbalier Bay. Locating a school of fish in these big waters puts a strain on the eyes. And the nerves. It's a heck of a lot easier to let the pilot do the shopping while you wait on anchor, swapping lies and saving fuel. And if your competition is using airborne eyes, you're pretty much forced to do the same.

So, each calm morning during late spring and early summer, those fishermen who were able to refit to strike for black drum would fan out over coastal waters and wait for the plane to show up. From above, the experienced pilot could easily spot the muddy telltales of fish. As he made his sweep across the coast, he successively put each of the netters onto his own school of fish, which usually took the remainder of the day to get into the boat.

By sundown, the fishermen would be unloading their drum; the cumulative haul sent a huge pulse of product into the market. As the buyers overloaded with fish, prices plummeted.

Without the airplane, said many of the fishermen, they might catch less fish, but they would still come out ahead, handling less fish for more money and keeping that 15 percent that goes to the pilot in their own pockets.

But no one could say anything for fear of being cut off. A pilot is strictly a freelance worker and can set whomever he chooses. Antagonize him and he can just as readily set you on a thundering herd of devilfish. Or simply blackball you, forcing you to fend for yourself in this low-valued, high-quantity fishery.

The fishermen were not happy about the plane but, nevertheless, seemed resigned to its use. Until Cliff Glockner came along.

Glockner, fishing out of Lacombe, on the North Shore of Lake Pontchartrain, spearheaded a drive to ban the plane.

"At first, I asked some of the fishermen in the Lake to stop usin' the plane, but they refused. Then we had a meeting of fishermen from all over the state, the dealers and the pilots. We took a vote and 90 percent came out against the plane. So I went to Representative Ed Deano to have the legislation drawn up."

Glockner cited two reasons for banning airplane-assisted fishing: "The main reason, the plane put 90 percent of the fishermen out of business. You can't sell high-priced fish when you've got a guy dumpin' a lot of cheap fish. I need to make at least $2.50 a head for a bull to show a profit, but I've seen it get as low as $1.25.

"Second, we're goin' under a quota. We're all allowed 300,000 head of bulls, but the airplane will fill the quota for us. He'll get the gold mine and we'll get the shaft!"

"He" refers to independent spotter pilot Matt Raigan. In addition to spotting for fishermen on a commission basis, Raigan owns three boats and half a share in another.

"We have so much invested in equipment, we have to deal in volume," declared Raigan. He admitted that "us catching in volume puts a hardship on the little guys, but they have to change their way. No offense to them, but they've been fishin' the same way for years—

it's primitive. If I'm gonna go into farmin', I'm not gonna get a plowshare, I'm gonna get a combine."

"Technology's fine," countered Glockner, "but you can go too far with somethin'. They told the farmers, 'We'll use technology to produce all the food the world needs.' But people are still starvin' and grain's rottin' in the silos. It's the same thing with bull drum— they can lay up in the boat and rot because of overproduction."

Glockner and his supporters succeeded in grounding the plane by convincing the 1990 Legislature to outlaw the use of spotter planes in fishing for any fish "except menhaden and herring-like fish." By limiting their own efficiency, the fishermen succeeded in raising the overall value of the wetland-dependent black drum.

That may be so, admitted Raigan, but he cautioned that choking down the rate of production may come back to haunt them. The market for this fish—and most others—demands stability, he explained. "Those people in Texas and New York are buyin' drum because of its availability. If we can't supply enough, they'll go to another fish."

AHEAD OF THE GAME ON DRUM

Both black drum and redfish are members of the croaker family (Sciaenidae), and their life cycles are very similar. The brood stock of both species congregate in large schools and spend much of their lives in offshore waters. Each year they migrate to the beaches and passes to spawn. Though they share the same spawning territories, the two species seem to have worked out a time-sharing plan whereby the bull reds come ashore in late summer and autumn while the bull drum arrive in late winter and early spring.

Mature drum can exceed 50 pounds in weight and may live to be more than 40 years old. This longevity of the breeders is the species' hedge against those seasons when adverse environmental conditions may cause a poor spawn. As the eggs hatch, the larvae and fingerlings make their way toward the fertile grassy marshlands far to the inside. The small drum remain in these shallow nursery grounds, often in close association with immature redfish, for about five years, when they drop back down to the outside waters to join the sexually mature brood stock.

Traditionally, the juvenile fish were harvested incidentally in the marsh by inshore redfishermen. Cajun trammel netters have caught and sold these small, one- to six-pound *tambours* since the 1800s. These small fish, which yield a firm, mild-flavored meat, command a solid price and have always been sought by fishermen. Bull drum, the flesh of which was considered coarse and strong, even wormy, were ignored.

This had been the structure of the redfish market, as well. But a rapidly expanding fishery based on the adult spawners led, eventually, to a total shutdown on the redfishing industry. Could the same thing happen to drum?

"I don't think so," said John Roussel, chief of the LDWF Finfish Section, Seafood Division. "We have taken a preliminary look at the available data and no problem is evident right now," said Roussel, as the fishermen worked the bulls during the late 1980s. "We are developing a management plan and it will be preventative rather than reactive as with the redfish. We're ahead of the ball game on drum."

Except for the short time when sexually mature redfish were purse seined in the Gulf, that species has always been managed by harvesting the juvenile inshore fish only, with a certain portion allowed to escape to be recruited into the brood stock.

But, said Roussel, "I'm not saying that you can't harvest bull drum because we don't harvest bull reds. Whenever you have a surplus, you can take from any of several different areas. Theoretically, with redfish, you could protect all the juveniles and harvest a certain number of bulls.

"We're not really advocating quotas at this time and I'm not saying that we can't continue to fish bull drum," he said. "We've only just begun looking real close at drum. Reds and trout have been taking all our attention. We should be well on our way to developing a management plan by next spring."

Designing a management plan in order to establish a sustainable fishery is, in theory, simple. First, you determine just how many fish are out there in the Magic Kingdom. Then, you estimate how many die off each year through natural causes. And then you calculate the "total allowable catch" (TAC)—the number of additional fish that can be withdrawn by commercial and recreational fishermen without impairing the species' ability to sustain itself. Biologically, the TAC should coincide with the "maximum sustainable yield," the largest average catch that can continuously be taken from a stock.

Finally, the TAC is divided up each year between the two "user groups"—the recreationals, who fish for fun and who take their catch home for their own personal consumption, and the commercials, whose fish are distributed to consumers via markets and restaurants. Since the fish are a common property resource—owned by all the people—they are to be allocated in a manner that satisfies the democratic principle, "the greatest good to the greatest number of people."

Allowing a new commercial fishery to proceed without restraint for a few years is one of the best ways to begin to get a handle on how many fish are out there. And on how many can safely be harvested.

Each commercial fisherman is licensed, there are relatively few of them and communications are good as to what type of gear they are using. The ultimate field men, the fishermen are on the water every day; they know best when and where to find the fish. Commercial fishermen sell their catch to dockside dealers who report these purchases to state or federal agencies. Managers can then correlate the total number of fish landed each year with the amount of effort expended to catch it, in order to monitor population status. While fluctuations in landings from year to year are normal, when trends develop that show, for instance, a declining harvest at the same time fishing effort is increasing, managers are alerted that a problem may be developing.

In addition to tracking the commercial harvest, scientists employ a variety of "fishery independent" methods to estimate stocks of fish. During the spawning season, waters may be sampled with nets fine-meshed enough to collect the eggs suspended in the water. Scientists know the "fecundity"—the number of eggs that females are capable of laying—so they can relate the concentration of eggs found in the water to the number of fish that are spawning. Overflight surveys are also utilized, where schools of fish are spotted from the air, the size of each school is estimated and total populations are extrapolated. Biologists also sample regularly with nets placed in fixed locations.

Taking a census on a highly mobile animal, living in an unseen environment, is imprecise, to say the least. The best estimates result from the integration of a variety of techniques. This was LDWF Secretary Virginia Van Sickle's approach when she set up the Ad Hoc Black Drum Committee to design the black drum management plan. In addition to department representatives, the committee included representatives of both the commercial and recreational fishing industries.

For the hard data on which to formulate its plan, this committee relied on a Black Drum Stock Assessment Subcommittee, comprised of fishery biologists and statisticians from several Louisiana universities and from Van Sickle's department. While these academic and LDWF biologists worked independently to arrive at their best estimates of the black drum population and at the number of fish that could safely be harvested, it was up to the full committee to decide how best to allocate these fish.

Van Sickle had been appointed department secretary by reformist

Gov. Roemer. A marine biologist, she sought to maximize the value of the state's fishery harvest, at the same time protecting each species with a scientifically based management strategy. The black drum management plan marked her first accomplishment in this direction.

This terse chronology of the management plan's evolution illustrates how the new and untrammeled black drum fishery was successfully transformed into a tightly controlled and sustainable one. Though tailored to the life history of this particular species, the plan serves as a model for the sustainable management of all other species.

OCTOBER 12, 1989—Concerned with the rapidly escalating catch of bull drum, the Louisiana Wildlife and Fisheries Commission enacted interim measures for a period of six months while biologists worked on the management plan.

A first-time minimum size limit of 14-inches was imposed on recreational fishermen, with no bag limit. For the commercial harvest, a six-month, 300,000-fish quota, 18-inch minimum, was imposed.

APRIL 12, 1990—The same interim measures were extended for another six months or until the permanent plan was approved, whichever happened first.

MAY 1990—The permanent management plan was completed. The department recommended a daily bag limit for recreational fishermen identical to that for redfish: five fish per day which must be at least 16 inches long, with not more than one exceeding 27 inches.

"Although the recreational limits appear to be strict," explained LDWF Finfish Chief John Roussel, "the available data indicates that the daily bag limit will have very little effect on the total annual recreational harvest since relatively few recreational fishermen actively target black drum. And even fewer harvest more than five fish per day. Projections indicate that the size limit will reduce the recreational harvest initially since the bulk of the recreational harvest has traditionally consisted of fish less than 16 inches. However, in successive years, as the available fish grow into a larger size-class, the effect of the size restriction should be greatly reduced."

Under the permanent plan, commercial fishermen may harvest 3.25 million pounds of drum annually from 16 to 27 inches, plus an additional 300,000 fish longer than 27 inches (bulls). Fishermen must procure a special black drum permit to fish for bulls and each permit holder must report on a monthly basis the number of bulls caught the previous month. Failure to report regularly may result in forfeiture of the permit.

This constant flow of up-to-date landings data allows managers to respond quickly, adjusting quotas to accommodate fluctuations in populations.

SEPTEMBER 1, 1990—The department's black drum management plan was implemented.

BUCKTOWN: URBAN FISHING VILLAGE

*I guess I don't talk like a Coonass but I'm just as good a fisherman.
It's just that I live in the middle of a city. I guess we're unique that way.*
    —Stanley "Bubba" Rando,
    Bucktown fisherman

For nearly 150 years Bucktown was a picturesque, slightly funky fishing community. With galleried fishing camps built up on pilings, boatsheds, nets and trawl boards stowed on the bank, an occasional sunken boat sprouting elephant ears, and working skiffs docked throughout, Bucktown was typical of the many colorful South Louisiana fishing villages. But, with a difference—this little hub of commercial fishing activity was located within metropolitan New Orleans, a few miles from downtown.

In the late 1980s, after years of protest by fishermen and preservation-minded citizens, Old Bucktown was razed. Gone are the rustic camps and sheds, replaced by a waterside parking lot. The entrance is marked by a fancy new sign, "Bucktown Village Park." Much of the old-time character of Bucktown is gone but the skiffs remain—about 60 of them, lined up in a neat row.

The Bucktown fleet

Although Bucktown's a lot more hygienic in appearance these days, it still functions as a port for a group of New Orleans fishermen whose grandfathers paddled out into Lake Pontchartrain in pirogues to work their crab nets. Today these fishermen motor high-speed Lafitte skiffs onto this 600-square-mile lake which, according to a study by the National Marine Fisheries Service, yielded $8 million worth of blue crabs, shrimp and finfish in 1985. They also range over 100 miles into the Louisiana marshes as they follow the fish or shrimp, always returning to Bucktown and their suburban homes.

Maintaining the fishing tradition in New Orleans, however, hasn't been easy.

New Orleans and adjacent Jefferson Parish are surrounded by levees to prevent flooding by Lake Pontchartrain and the Mississippi River. Rainfall must therefore be pumped out of this gigantic below sea-level basin, into these waters.

Pumping Station No. 6, one of the largest in the world, delivers

Two generations of Bucktown fishermen: Bubba Rando and his father, Frank

8,000 cubic feet per second into the Seventeenth Street Canal. Bucktown is situated near the mouth of this canal, where it empties into the south shore of Lake Pontchartrain.

The New Orleans Sewerage and Water Board (S&WB) has never been happy about the Bucktown fishermen, whose only claim to the site was based on tradition. They docked their boats free of charge and used the land as squatters.

In 1963, the S&WB gave the boat owners one week to remove their vessels. Though a deal was struck that enabled the fishermen to remain, efforts to displace them continued to mount through the 1970s and 1980s. Finally, they organized the Lake Pontchartrain Fishermen's Association to negotiate a compromise with the S&WB.

The water board agreed to lease the organization an area large enough to moor 63 boats, grandfathering in those fishermen who qualified.

Although they did acquire a more secure base for their own

operations, Bucktowners fear that upcoming fishermen will be unable to land their catches in this urban fishing port. Said Nan Rembert, secretary/treasurer of their organization, "According to the lease, when you die or retire you can't pass your slip on to another family member. As the slips empty, we're supposed to chain them off."

FRANK RANDO

Stanley "Bubba" Rando, in his mid-40s, is a third-generation Bucktown fisherman. With a wife and young daughter, he hustles the year round, ranging from Lake Pontchartrain to Cocodrie, in pursuit of shrimp and finfish such as speckled trout, redfish, black drum and sheepshead.

"When I was a kid I spent all my summers on the boat with my pop," said Rando. "Weekends, anytime I didn't have to be in school, I was on the boat. But my momma begged me not to be a fisherman. So, you know, I tried to honor her. I went into the plumbers' union and worked for seven or eight years. But then, I had to go back fishin'. It was too much in my blood."

When Bubba went into the business full time, he built himself a bigger and stronger boat than his father's 28-footer. Frank Rando, Jr., in his mid-seventies, now does most of his fishing from his son's 32-foot fiberglass skiff; unless it's the opening day of shrimp season, when he unties his wooden skiff to take a couple of his old-time fishing buddies into the lake to try their luck.

Except for a few years during World War II, wiry Frank Rando pulled his living from the water, either crabbing, shrimping, finfishing, or fur trapping in the LaBranche wetlands, along the southwestern

shore of Lake Pontchartrain. As he, Bubba and I passed an afternoon
in his wood-frame house along the Seventeenth Street Canal, late in
the summer of 1990, Frank Rando described his life as a Bucktown
fisherman:

My daddy came over from Sicily. He fished until he got real old
and then he worked for the Jefferson Waterworks. He never had a
motorboat, just a pirogue. And he had a little skiff that he used to
row out in the lake and fish sheephead, you know, with a pole.
"Sheephead Frank" they called 'im. That's what everybody knew 'im
as.

I used to sell 'em, mostly to individual people. He wouldn't catch
that many, some days he'd catch two or three, some days it might
only be one. But I'd go sell 'em, get 30 or 40 cents. A big one, you'd
get 50 cents for.

The hard crabs wasn't worth nothin' when he was fishin'. Mostly
everybody was makin' soft crabs. They'd bring 'em in hard and keep
'em. Put 'em in boxes and shed 'em, you know. Everybody had boxes.
Most of 'em were four feet wide, maybe eight feet long and about a
foot deep. They'd keep 'em in the lake, maybe half a block off the
shore.

There used to be a big sand bar and shell pile out here along the
lake. And you could put the fish cars—that's what they called 'em—
inside the sand bar. And it wouldn't get too rough, you know.

The bar was about a block off the shore and a couple hundred
feet wide. From the mouth of the canal, it ran to the west. There was
a place where you could run right down the street and drive out on
the sandbar with a truck. I say a truck but it was a Model T Ford that
you'd take and make a truck out of. The shells used to wash in there
and pile up—we'd scoop 'em up and put 'em around the house.

Frank Rando

Right after I got out of school, in 1936, I started fishin' crabs. With a pirogue and nets. I was 16, 17 years old. I fished soft crabs for a couple o' years and then started runnin' nets out in the deeper water for hard crabs, with a row skiff.

We'd use round nets, with a single rim on 'em. We used to set 'em out in a circle, one here and another about 100 feet away. That way you'd go round and when you'd finish you'd be right back where you started from.

We'd bait with fish heads. We used to go down to the French Market and buy fish heads by the basket. Redfish heads, grouper, drum heads. And then you had to bring 'em home and cut 'em up, salt 'em down in a barrel. You could keep it if you salted it. We'd bait the nets every day or every other day—it depended on how much fishin' you did.

Before the war, we fished in the lake with a seine for buffalo and carp.[1] We'd just go out there and make a blind set—we wouldn't see the fish beforehand. We'd just run the net out in a circle and then pull it in. Sometime you'd catch plenty, sometime you'd only catch a couple.

The market'd buy 'em. A nickel a pound. Some of 'em were 25, 30 pounds. Man, they were big fish. You'd get plenty money for 'em—a dollar and a half!

But they don't have no more of 'em in the lake. That quit years ago. There was very little salt then. What I think really helped to make it salty...the ship channel. That really increased the salt in the lake. It used to be almost fresh—I guess that was good for the crabs.

It was probably good for the grass, too. They always used to have a little grass, on the other side the lake, like around Fontainbleau Park, the North Shore. They had grass on that side the lake, but this side, they never did. Not that I know of. If they did, it was way before my time.

And those grass beds over there, they wasn't all that big. A couple hundred feet wide, maybe, runnin' down along the shoreline. They never did have grass in the middle of the lake. The water wasn't no more than knee deep where the grass was. It'd be all the way to the top in that water.

We also used to fish with a line before the war. Croakers and trout. We used to sell 'em out at West End Park. Down in what they call "The Corner," towards the basin. Around that end of the park where the Southern Yacht Club is. We used to take the fish out there, like on a Thursday or Friday or Saturday night. Well, Thursday was the best night because people'd buy 'em for Friday, you know.

Everybody made a little table, and you'd lay 'em on display on that table. Same way with soft crabs, that's how they used to sell their soft crabs. Shrimp too, they used to do that with. A lot of 'em didn't have a table, they'd spread paper on the ground. And people'd come along and buy 'em.

We used to get by each light. Sometime there'd be two or three of us by one light, a couple by another light, all along the park there. People used to come out there, man. Always plenty people'd come out there. They'd pull up there and buy your fish, crabs or shrimp, whatever you had. Whatever they were lookin' for, they could get it. We used to sell it whole, no cleanin', uh uhh. They bought 'em as is.

At that time, the lake was closed to commercial fishing. They didn't open it until the '40s. I guess it was for everything—you just wasn't supposed to fish, you know, commercial. Some o' the sports from New Orleans, they wanted the lake to be like their own playground. But they never did try to stop you from fishin'. Nobody ever tried to stop you. I guess 'cause they knew they had enough of it, you know. Wildlife and Fisheries, they never bothered nobody. But up to now, you know, only certain parts of the lake are open. It used to be four miles off o' shore—you had to go four miles off the bank before you could fish. Now it's a mile and a quarter. In Jefferson Parish you can still fish in close, against the bank even. But it's so polluted you never get anything in there close. I haven't heard of anybody catchin' any shrimp or anything next to the bank over there for quite a while.

But, it used to be, like in the shrimp season—when the shrimp'd come in the lake—you could stand on the edge of the lake shore and throw a cast net and catch shrimp. You'd just walk down to the lake shore, throw a few clams in the water and you'd catch all you wanted to eat. I mean big shrimp too, right against the bank.

In 1941, things were rough—we couldn't hardly make a livin'. So I went and jernt the Merchant Marines. And I went to sea for a year and a half, until the middle o' '42. Things got kinda rough in the Merchant Marines too, so I come in. That was when Higgins was buildin' those landin' boats for the service. So I went to work for Higgins for six or eight months. Then I got drafted but, instead of goin' into the Army, I went into the Marines.

When I got out of the service after the war, I went right back fishin'. Oh yeah.

That's when I got my first motorboat. It was an 18-foot boat, a little V-bottom. It had a two-cylinder eight-horsepower engine...a Red Wing. It was a real good boat for crabbin', for runnin' crab nets.

We'd sell 'em to the restaurants out here. We used to get 20 cents a dozen, then they went up to 25, 30 cents. They had to be cherce crabs, yeah.

Two, three baskets, that was a fairly good day. A lot of days you'd go out and catch about a basket, half a basket. When they wasn't bitin' you wouldn't stay out too long, you know. If you were catchin' a few, you'd stay out.

It took me awhile to get a bigger boat. Things was rough! My wife and I both worked. In 1950, we built this house. My wife was workin' as a waitress, I was fishin' crabs and workin' in the gamblin' house at night. Between the two of us, we managed to get this house built. We built it ourselves. A man gave us the materials on credit. Couldn't pay for it cash so he said, "Well, I'll give you the stuff and when you get the money, pay me." You couldn't beat that, you know.

In the gamblin' house? I was a shill. You sit around the dice table and you roll the dice. They give you a handful of money, to play with, you know. They'd get three or four of us around the dice table and we'd entice the people that's in there. Like decoys. They think you're playin'—they don't know the difference. So they get there and start playin' it too. That was right out at West End Park.

I was makin' $35 a week there at the Pontchartrain Club and I'd make another $30 or $40 a week crabbin'. And my wife, she was makin' maybe $25, $30 a week waitress. Things was rough!

It was after the war when we started fishin' redfish. In 1946. We was trammel nettin'—"Junior" DeFreitas and me, we used to fish partners. And we used to row a skiff. Well, Junior had a motorboat—we used his motorboat to tow the skiff. When we got out in the lake, then we'd row. We'd just fish reds in the summertime—June, July and August—when they'd come ashore.

Mostly, we fished the north shore of Lake Borgne. We used to fish from, say, Bayou Bienvenue to the Rigolets. But, most of the time, our biggest fishin' was from the Rigolets to the Chef. In that section there.

You'd see the fish, you didn't just put out for nothin'. You could see 'em run or you could see 'em movin' along the shore. When they had a school, they'd make a pretty good size wave. If they're goin' that way, you'd get ahead of 'em a little bit, put one end of the net down and go around 'em. They don't even know they're in the net, 'till you start closin' it up.

Sometimes we'd go out and catch 600, 800 pounds. Once in a while we'd catch 1,000, 1,200 pounds in one school. If we caught one school we'd come in, we wouldn't go look for more. We'd be satisfied with that one school. Mostly we didn't carry no ice with us. We'd catch that one school and come on in with it, so they wouldn't get bad.

Sometimes we used to take the fish down to the French Market. If we caught some fish we'd call around and ask if they wanted 'em. Battistella or Ferrara, Christina, they all used to buy 'em. We used to go to all of 'em.

Our top price was generally about, oh, anywhere from 20 to 25 cents, sometimes 28 cents a pound. Twenty-eight, 30 cents a pound, that was a really good price.

We never had no trouble sellin' 'em. You could always sell redfish. People used to eat redfish, oh yeah, man. They always did serve 'em in the restaurants...up until they stopped it.

The freeze of 1989? I seen one worse than that. Back in the early '50s. I think it was 1951. In February. The whole lake had ice on it, all the way across. Oh, it wasn't thick but it was there. They had big old icicles hangin' off the bridge, almost hittin' the water. Boy, they had fish all over the lake, the whole lake was covered.

Everybody that had a motorboat was out there pickin' 'em up. My brother-in-law had borrowed a little outboard motor that he put on his skiff. We had two skiffs, the one he put the motor on and my little row skiff, and he'd tow me out there in the middle o' the lake and turn me loose. I'd go rowin' around pickin' up fish and he and my other brother-in-law'd go runnin' around scoopin' 'em up with a dip net. When we'd get a load we'd come on in.

The market was buyin' 'em. Some o' those guys with big boats, man, they'd load 'em down with fish. Sheephead, redfish, trout. The drums, they wouldn't pick 'em up—too big and they weren't worth that much. They wouldn't pick up too many sheephead either, mostly trout and redfish. Oh, they had plenty.

Parts o' the lake they never did go in. Like that part over there, where the fish would be the most, nobody even went. They had enough right out here in the middle.

That's the biggest fish kill I ever seen. It took a little while after, and we caught just like before.

Closin' the reds? I don't know if it did any good or not. But I really think they should open it again. Bubba can tell you, they got plenty o' redfish in the lake. Right before the freeze, some of the fishermen were catchin' a couple hundred in a day, right out here. They had to just throw 'em back and watch 'em swim away. Eight-, 10-, 12-pound fish. That's a lot o' redfish...they got 'em.

PART IV

Bold headlines sickened us as they told of the bestial slaughter of helpless men, women and children at My Lai in South Vietnam. During World War II, we were equally horrified by the savagery of Nazis in the town of Lidice, which was razed, all its male inhabitants shot to death, and its women and children sent to starve in a concentration camp.

These outrages, only two of many that occurred in recent years, were not without numerous precedents much closer to the American scene than Europe and Southeast Asia. There were in the western United States scores of My Lais and Lidices, some of them perpetrated almost within the memory of the living.

They were carried out by uniformed American troops under the guise of "civilizing actions," by lawless bands of settlers and tradesmen who advocated extermination of the Indians as the simplest means by which they could confiscate land and other natural resources for their own enrichment.

To their credit, many Americans vigorously condemned the injustices and atrocities, but a far greater number approved and applauded them. As late as the eighteen seventies and eighties, numerous newspapers, and especially those in the West, called the fiendish acts commendable and justified, and hailed the perpetrators of them as worthy citizens and heroes.

—John Upton Terrell, "Land Grab: The Truth
About 'The Winning of the West,'" 1972

THE "CON" IN CONSERVATION

*The catch word of "conservation" is employed to give respectability
to what really is a bold attempt to seize...a fishing preserve.*
        —*Oregon Voter,*
            November 2, 1928

In 1928, sport-fishing interests petitioned for statewide referendums
calling for the exclusion of commercial salmon fishermen from four
major Oregon rivers. As the recreationals tried to elicit broadened
support for their initiatives among the non-angling public they
claimed that the measures were warranted on the basis of
"conservation." A particularly astute journalist spotted the difference
between the conservation and the monopolization of a public resource
and, a few days before the vote, wrote an article that included the
above excerpt. The public soundly defeated the four referendums.

Nowadays, operating behind the honorable façade of
"conservation" is proving much more successful for the sophisticated
and almost unimaginably diverse recreational fishing industry.

Recreational fishermen far outnumber commercial fishermen in
nearshore waters. During the 1988-1989 season, for instance,

residents in relatively unpopulated Louisiana purchased nearly 220,000 recreational saltwater fishing licenses; including nonresidents and anglers under 16 and over 60 years of age, who are exempted from the purchase of a license, the National Marine Fisheries Service estimated that the total number of saltwater anglers may have approached 600,000. There are fewer than 2,000 coastal netters.

Even with moderate daily bag limits, the vastly greater number of recreational anglers harvests the lion's share of those special fish that both the recreational and commercial industries have come to depend upon the most. From 1980 through 1988, according to NMFS statistics, recreational fishermen killed an estimated 89 out of every 100 spotted seatrout harvested from Louisiana waters; recreationals also hooked an average 72 percent of the redfish landed during the same period.

Yet, in a nationally coordinated effort, the recreational industry is making an aggressive, almost desperate, grab for that small share of fish that remains to both coastal finfishermen and consumers.

In 1981, Texas declared redfish and speckled trout gamefish. Alabama made the two species gamefish in 1984, and in 1987 South Carolina followed suit. In 1988, both Florida and Louisiana went "all sport" on redfish, ostensibly for only three years, yet the commercial fishery remains closed in both states. GCCA or one of the other divisions of the Coastal Conservation Association—the Florida Conservation Association or the Atlantic Coast Conservation Association—spearheaded each of the political fights that led to the monopolization of these valued species by the recreational industry.

Clearly, operating as a "conservation association" works. "But," asks St. Mary Parish fisherman Daniel Edgar, who also buys fish dockside and operates a boat launch for recreational fishermen, "if they're conservationists, why are they going after the guys who catch the 11 trout instead of the guys who are killing the 89?"

The answer to Edgar's question is provided by the Sport Fishing Institute (SFI), located in Washington, D.C. SFI is well-funded by nearly 100 members including Ford Motor Company, K Mart, ITT Commercial Finance, Bertram Yachts and the Outboard Marine and Yamaha Motor corporations.

SFI economists produce state-by-state profiles on the economic impact of recreational fishing, which are used in sport/commercial allocation battles. According to a pamphlet distributed by the organization, "In the Gulf of Mexico SFI played a pivotal role in having redfish declared a gamefish by testifying in court and before the Florida Marine Fisheries Commission on the economic benefits of sportfishing."

SFI studies are usually constructed to produce findings demonstrating that "recreational fishermen create up to three times more economic activity than that produced by commercial fishermen." An SFI study may also include the potential value of a fishery if commercial fishermen are excluded.

A recent study, to be used in an East Coast allocation battle, suggests that declaring the striped bass a gamefish "would produce an estimated $10.2 million in total economic activity in Maryland compared to $7.75 million generated by the current striper allocation" [which shares the fish equally among commercials and recreationals].

"The $2.45 million difference," explained SFI economist Tony Fedler, represents "increased angler expenditures."

In other words, the small quantities of fish that coastal fishermen are still permitted to harvest for the markets and restaurants are being identified by recreational industry members as a cap on the potential growth in profits for their own companies. The quickest and easiest way to increase "angler expenditures"? Get rid of the commercials.

Since the fish are a publicly owned resource, it helps immensely if the public perceives this expansion as the selfless achievement of "conservationists" rather than as a self-serving tactic by a competing industry—an industry heavily weighted with coastal developers; oil companies; outboard engine, boat and tackle manufacturers; and publishers of magazines and newspapers that depend upon these businesses for advertising revenues.

It's a cynical strategy, but it is proving so seductive that some well-intentioned citizens are not just staying out of the fight, they're earnestly assisting this consumption-oriented industry.

In September 1990, the Aquarium of the Americas opened on the riverfront of New Orleans. The city's taxpayers are financing $25 million of the $40 million price tag on this tourist attraction.

As a curious visitor toured the "eco-educational" facility, intently studying each exhibit, he soon found himself before a medium-sized tank containing a densely packed school of the hotly contested redfish. Beside the eye-catching tank of hapless reds, the visitor encountered a plug by the Gulf Coast Conservation Association; GCCA's statement warned the reader that it would definitely be inadvisable to reopen the fishery for this species to Louisiana's commercial fishermen.

According to a public relations assistant for the Audubon Institute, which operates the aquarium, 864,000 visitors toured the facility in its first four months.

The Louisiana Seafood Promotion and Marketing Board is affiliated with the Louisiana Department of Wildlife and Fisheries, and is funded mainly by a surcharge on the commercial fishermen's license fees. The board is comprised of industry members charged with developing, maintaining and expanding markets for the state's seafood harvest. For its September 1990 meeting, the group invited Liz McCarthy, deputy director of development at the Audubon Institute.

The Seafood Promotion Board was considering an exhibit of its own in the aquarium. Executive Director Karl Turner asked McCarthy, "About how much would we be talking for our group to place an exhibit in the aquarium?"

"They start at $25,000," she responded.

After a brief discussion among the board members, Turner hesitantly asked, "Uh, Liz, could you tell us how much GCCA paid for their display?"

"Oh, we let them do theirs for free," replied McCarthy, "as a favor for what they're trying to do."

Like a flock of pintails pitching straight into a corn-fed pond during a bitter Northwester, trusting Americans throw caution to the wind at the mere mention of the word "conservation," particularly during these times of environmental anxiety. Pulling the conservation con, like shooting ducks over a baited pond, is downright unsportsmanlike. Which, alas, has not prevented the publisher of three major outdoor magazines from adopting the tactic.

The Times Mirror Magazines Corporation of 2 Park Avenue, New York, publishes *Salt Water Sportsman*, *Field & Stream* and *Outdoor Life*. Times Mirror also publishes at least seven other magazines appealing to a broad range of audiences: *Yachting*, *Popular Science*, *Home Mechanix*, *Ski Magazine*, *Skiing*, *Skiing Trade News* and *Golf Magazine*. The estimated 30 million readers of all these magazines were targeted to receive the New York corporation's "Conservation Message."

According to one of its pamphlets, "Times Mirror Magazines has a responsibility—and a unique opportunity—to communicate with our readers on key environmental issues. Recently we translated this commitment and concern into action with the establishment of the Times Mirror Magazines Conservation Council."

Formed in the summer of 1990, the Times Mirror Magazines Conservation Council is headed by Dr. David Rockland, former director of economics at the Sport Fishing Institute.

"Under the direction of Dr. Rockland and the magazines' individual editors," the pamphlet continues, "the Washington office coordinates the selection of key environmental and conservation-oriented issues for editorial treatment in the magazines...Our magazines will be used to increase the awareness of important environmental issues and help initiate specific conservation programs."

The alert reader may automatically translate the seemingly innocent, "initiate specific conservation programs," into "grab all the fish from the commercial fishermen and the consumers so we can make more money." Indeed, in an editorial announcing the council, Times Mirror CEO Francis P. Pandolfi stated, the "commercial harvesters' take has long been in absurd disproportion to their numbers, as well as to sound economics."

The TMM Conservation Council has not yet publicized a "specific conservation program" for the redfish and spotted seatrout of Louisiana and Florida. Its first conservation program centered on the species closest to home for the New York-based corporation—the striped bass.

The striped bass is an estuarine-dependent species. Its natural

Times Mirror Magazines Corporation uses its publications to spread its version of fisheries "conservation" to 30 million readers.

range extends along the Atlantic Coast from the St. Lawrence River, south to the St. John's River in Florida, and into the Gulf of Mexico; most of the population hugs the coastline between North Carolina and Maine.

The striper is a popular sport fish—it strikes hard, fights well and is accessible to nearshore boaters and wading surfcasters.

The striped bass is also "a great eating fish," claimed Buddy Harrison who operates two of the better known seafood restaurants in the state of Maryland: Harrison's Pier 5 in the Clarion Hotel on Baltimore's Inner Harbor and Harrison's Chesapeake House at Tilghman's Island on the Eastern Shore.

"Striped bass tastes as good as snook," said Harrison. "It's far superior to anything else we have—weakfish, bluefish or channel bass [redfish]. On a scale of one to 10, I'd give the others a three to five and the striper? A 10. The taste is hard to describe unless you've eaten it—it's like the filet mignon of steaks. In texture and taste it's just the best fish going."

Needless to say, the striped bass—or "rockfish"—is to the coastal fishermen on the East Coast what the redfish and trout are to their brothers on the Gulf Coast—the money fish.

Commercial fishermen have harvested striped bass for over 300 years, making this, probably, the oldest American fishery. The Plymouth colonists supported themselves in 1623 by netting striped bass. In 1670, an act of the Plymouth Colony provided that all income from the striped bass, mackerel or herring fisheries at Cape Cod be used to establish a free school. As a result, the first public school in the New World was made possible through funds obtained largely from the sale of striped bass. In "Men's Lives," Peter Matthiessen describes the travails of the baymen whose families have haul seined stripers on Long Island beaches for centuries. "In the Chesapeake Bay," said Peter Jensen, Director of Fisheries at the Maryland Department of Natural Resources, "the fishery is as old as Captain John Smith."

A decline in the population of striped bass during the 1970s and early 1980s prompted either severe restrictions or closures on both the recreational and commercial fisheries. Jensen attributed the decline to "deteriorating water quality; loss of habitat through things like bulkheading,[1] coastal development and the loss of our bay grasses; and overfishing.

"Overfishing," he said, "is to be blamed on *all* of us—the recreational and commercial fishermen who did it, and the managers who let it happen."

Striped bass appear to be making a comeback and managers are

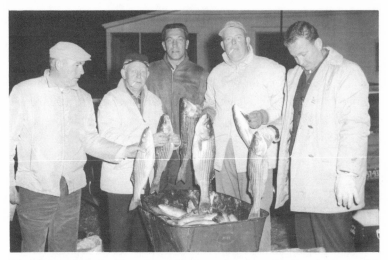

"Overfishing is to be blamed on *all* of us—the recreational and commercial fishermen who did it, and the managers who let it happen." Peter Jensen, Director of Fisheries, Maryland Department of Natural Resources.

now allowing both sport and commercial fishermen to, once again, retain some fish. It's alright to let the recreationals harvest stripers, but the commercials? "No way," said the Times Mirror Magazines Conservation Council, which doesn't want to see any commercial fisheries reopen and is trying to close those in Maryland and Virginia that have. The TMM Conservation Council "believes that prohibiting the sale of wild stocks of striped bass and instead having fresh striped bass fillets for restaurants come from aquaculture makes good conservation sense."

To enforce its beliefs, the TMM Conservation Council formed the Striped Bass Conservation Coalition which, in addition to tackle manufacturers such as Storm Lures and Lowrance Electronics, includes "conservation" and sport-fishing organizations from Virginia, Maryland, New Jersey, New York, Massachusetts and...Texas.

Times Mirror's Striped Bass Conservation Coalition drafted a bill to be introduced into the 1991 U.S. Congress to prohibit the sale of striped bass along the entire Atlantic coast.[2] While the advocacy groups within the coalition lobbied congressmen for passage of their anti-commercial bill, Times Mirror used its magazines to help create a political climate that would make it easier for lawmakers to side against the family fishermen.

Readers of Times Mirror's three outdoor magazines received even more of their usual fare of anti-commercial copy. (A *Salt Water Sportsman* editorial—wishfully perhaps—referred to the striped bass fishermen as "quaint relics of a bygone era.") But, in addition to targeting its sporting audience, the New York corporation also reached out to the readership of all its other magazines, from *Skiing* to *Home Mechanix* to *Golf Magazine*.

Each January 1991 issue contained a prominently placed, and convincing, "Conservation Agenda For The Outdoors," written by Conservation Council executive director David Rockland. Excerpts include:

> Uncontrolled commercial fisheries combined with water pollution and the loss of habitats caused East Coast striped bass populations to spiral downward in the late 1970s and early 1980s....State regulations are inconsistent. Connecticut and New Jersey have enacted regulations to protect striped bass through the prohibition of the sale of the fish; other critical states, such as Massachusetts and Maryland, must follow suit. Indeed, it may be time for Congress to apply the same remedy to the striped bass situation that it did to the indiscriminate killing of waterfowl a century ago—namely,

eliminating the incentive to harvest the fish commercially by making their sale illegal. Now ducks for market come from farms, a solution that will work for striped bass through aquaculture.

After encouraging readers to write to the chairmen of the two congressional committees with the greatest impact on marine fisheries management, the message concluded: "Remember, there are 30 million of us. Working together, we can make a difference."

By attempting to enlist the support of its readership against the traditional coastal finfishermen, Times Mirror took a calculated risk. It's safe to assume that few, if any readers of, say, *Popular Science*, are acquainted with either the intricacies of fishery management or the lifestyle of the coastal fisherman.

Scapegoating by a larger group against a smaller is always dependent on a lack of identification with the minority. Times Mirror's massive efforts to mobilize the public-at-large—the pearl in these expanding fish fights—could succeed in helping to establish and build the momentum leading to the extermination of the fishermen.

But, then again, when apprised of what he or she is being persuaded to assist, the objective Times Mirror magazine reader may recoil.

What if, for instance, a reader who is burdened with no preconceived opinions and armed only with common sense, should question the wisdom of Congress applying "the same remedy to the striped bass situation that it did to the indiscriminate killing of waterfowl a century ago"?

Wild ducks, like the fish, are a common property resource, owned by the public. The reader, of course, well knows that he is no longer permitted to savor the incomparable taste of a wild duck at his favorite restaurant. But, concerned less with his own pleasure than with the plight of our prized waterfowl, he may ask, "Well, what shape *are* the ducks in today?"

Commerce in wild ducks was banned somewhat less than a century ago with implementation of the Migratory Bird Treaty Act of 1918.[3] After less than 75 years of management by state and federal agencies, sportsmen and the recreational hunting industry, duck populations are, generally, at or approaching all-time lows. And so are sportsmen's bag limits. The numbers of ducks—which depend almost entirely on wetlands for their existence—may rebound somewhat since population levels are, as with fish, cyclic. Yet, some biologists believe that the decline is inexorable.

At least, by applying the "remedy" of banning the "indiscriminate killing" of wild ducks for the market, Congress did succeed in absolving the commercial harvesters of any blame for this decline.

Now wary, the objective TMM reader may next begin to question the continuing parallel with ducks within the Conservation Agenda: "Now ducks for market come from farms, a solution that will work for striped bass through aquaculture." The key words here are "*will* work."

In 1981, when GCCA and TPWD were in the midst of their push to ban commerce in speckled trout and redfish, they staved off possible opposition from fish dealers, the Texas Restaurant Association and other consumer-oriented groups by promising them unlimited quantities of farmed redfish—at prices far below what the fishermen could produce them for.

Salty Corpus Christi native Elizabeth Taylor, 78, didn't quite buy the line. Taylor, a hard-core sport fisherman, said, "I used to own a boat and I used to go out fishin' and catch all the fish I wanted. But I got too damned old. My legs couldn't take that bustin' from the waves.

"It was my feeling that older people and those that didn't go fishing should be able to go to the market to get their fish. And all you hear is how beneficial fish are to eat. So I went up to Austin to tell those landlubbers."

Taylor's efforts were rewarded with a polite letter from Gov. William Clements. Clements reassured Taylor that "there is today a dynamic fish farming industry in Texas that stands ready to use the technology already developed by the Parks and Wildlife Department, Texas A&M University, and University of Texas to produce these resources for Texas restaurants."

Aquaculture research and development kicked off in 1977 in Texas. In 1989—12 years and millions of dollars later—the aquaculture industry of the entire state of Texas produced, according to several of the state's experts, no spotted seatrout and "probably less than 10,000 pounds of redfish," about as much as a single family fisherman could harvest in a few months. A bitter freeze in December of 1989 wiped out most of the pond-raised redfish in Texas, delaying further the fulfillment of the promise to supply "all the farmed redfish you'll ever need."

When asked which fresh Texas-caught fish are currently available to her, Taylor grumped, "Nothin' but danged ol' drum. Shark. Flounder for about a month. No redfish and trout, for sure."

Aquaculture of striped bass may become as successful as it has been for catfish and rainbow trout. Indeed, "the striped bass has much better potential than the redfish," said Dr. Jim Avault, professor of aquaculture at the LSU School of Forestry, Wildlife and Fisheries. "It grows well, it winters well, and it takes a pellet well."

Actually, the aquacultured "striped bass" is a hybrid: the female is a striper, the male a smaller white bass. Aquaculturists in several states have already brought some hybrid stripers to market. Buddy Harrison served a few in his restaurants, "but it didn't go over that well. People just didn't care for the taste."

Many aquaculture-raised fish consistently fail taste tests when compared to wild-caught fish. As waste materials and unutilized feed decompose in their water, pond-raised fish often acquire a muddy "off-flavor" attributed to a compound called geosmin. Also, the texture of a fish raised in confinement is considerably mushier than that of one that has had to "earn its own way" in the wild. Some Louisiana restaurants still refuse to serve farm-raised catfish. Of course, prohibiting the harvest of the wild-caught variety would make it unavailable for comparison.

In addition to providing an enhanced dining experience, wild-caught fish, according to recent research, contain significantly higher levels of the "good" lipids than do fish raised on soy-based pellets. These lipids are rich in the healthful omega-3 fatty acids, believed to help reduce the risk of heart disease, the leading cause of death in this country.

Marine animals are rich in the omega-3 fatty acids while most vegetable oils and lipids of domestic land animals are rich in omega-6 fatty acids, which do not exhibit beneficial effects. Researchers at the LSU Human Nutrition Division of the School of Home Economics, working with both prawns and catfish, found that soy-based diets "cause a lipid fatty acid composition in the seafood that resembles that of land animals rather than marine animals."

"In other words," clarified an LSU marine advisory agent, "the pond-raised fish ain't nothin' but a swimmin' cow."

Rob Reigh, an assistant professor at LSU, specializes in fish and crustacean nutrition. Reigh said that efforts are now being made to raise the omega-3 levels in farmed fish. Menhaden oil, for instance, can be added to the soybean-based feed, but that affects the taste of the fish.

They'll get it right. Someday.

Some Times Mirror magazine readers may take the publisher's bait, contact their aforementioned congressmen and help allocate the entire annual crop of East Coast striped bass to the recreational industry. How about readers in Louisiana? Here, saltwater sportsmen and environmentalists may be appalled to learn that a New York corporation has asked 30 million people to help promote the culture of hybrid striped bass.

Louisiana, in 1987, issued 10 experimental mariculture permits. (Mariculture is the farming of marine finfish or shellfish.) Each permit holder is entitled to fence in or impound with earthen levees up to 8,000 acres of tidal marshland. Owners of these vast operations originally planned to raise redfish but a series of setbacks culminating in the freeze of 1989 dashed hopes of profitably raising this species. But a hardier species that the mariculturists were experimenting with did survive the freeze—the hybrid striped bass.

While only four of the permitted mariculture sites now remain active, increased demand for striped bass, coupled with success of its culture, could rapidly lead to even more acreage of Louisiana's salt marshes ending up behind barricades and armed guardposts, off-limits to all residents including sport fishermen, hunters, photographers, birdwatchers, boaters and, of course, commercial fishermen.

Behind those fences, the aquatic feed lots contribute to the already serious problem of nutrient overenrichment in the Gulf. If the projects expand to the extent that all areas of open water are utilized, marshland could begin to mysteriously disappear.

Clearly, New York City is a long way from the Bayou. And so are Houston and Washington, D.C. As the Times Mirror Magazines Conservation Council, the Coastal Conservation Association and other "conservation" groups pursue their shortsighted goal of "conserving" the nation's coastal fishery resources for their own exploitation, what are the additional consequences at the local level, around the coastlines of America?

As the recreational industry excludes the commercial fishermen, it immediately destroys the lives of productive fishing families, effecting the demise of America's unique coastal cultures such as the baymen of Long Island, the watermen of the Chesapeake and the Cajuns of South Louisiana. By refusing to share, it also needlessly deprives the public of its own premier quality, wild-caught fish, at the same time severing what may be the last tangible link between the general public and the coastal wetlands. By severing this link, not only is the public's interest in wetland preservation diminished, but so is the economic value of the wetlands.

These seem like heavy consequences to pay in order that some companies can sell more ads, or more made-in-the-Orient fishing gear. But it gets worse.

The most far-reaching ramification of the national recreational industry's outlawing those whose livelihoods depend on the coastal wetlands is that it removes their uncompromising resistance to those who would destroy this habitat.

Untrammeled, this industry dooms tomorrow those resources which it so ardently pretends today..."to conserve."

THE RECREATIONAL FISHING INDUSTRY: SOMETHING OF VALUE?

In 1986, the Washington, D.C.-based Sport Fishing Institute named Vice President George Bush, Fisherman of the Year. As president, Bush continued to personify the recreational fishing industry's ideal sport fisherman. With a second home on the coast and his 27-foot plastic boat, powered by a pair of V-8s, he burned plenty of gas and cash in search of fish, which he seldom caught.

For the members of this consumption-based industry, it just doesn't get any better than this.

As the recreational industry strives to exclude the commercial industry from any share of fishery allocations, its representatives portray the harvest of fish for food as unwise both on biological and economic grounds. Biologically, going gamefish—taking the fish from "commerce"—say they, removes the "bounty from its head," "protecting" the species from "indiscriminate slaughter" and "exploitation" by "greedy" "commercial" or "market" fishermen. Economically, say recreational-industry spokesmen, it is a "higher" use of a fish to allow it to be caught only for fun.

This is because the sportsmen who fuel their industry are expected to spend far more money in pursuit of this fish than will the consumer who wishes to buy it by the pound.

Interestingly, only the marketing of fish to consumers has been labeled as "commercial" use. This claim is outdated, says LSU economist Dr. Kenneth Roberts.

Politicians currently struggle with the questions: Should netters continue to be allowed to harvest some fish for consumers to eat? Or, should the fish be used instead as bait to lure yet more anglers to the coast?

The results of their decisions are easily foreseen by looking more closely at the recreational and the commercial industries, and at the differences between them. First, it is necessary to be aware of one important similarity:

"No group has an elite position separated from the signals given by money," says Roberts. "*All* uses are commercial."

When he leaves the dock for a day's fishing, the finfisherman carries another man or two to help him haul back the net. Deckhands are paid on a share basis, receiving from one-fourth to one-third of the profits. Daily expenses include gasoline and oil, ice, food and drink, gloves and other incidental items.

Since he's paid by the pound for his catch, the successful fisherman runs his operation as efficiently as possible, trying to bring in the most fish, while incurring the least expense.[1]

When he returns from a trip, the netter hands his catch across the dock to the fishhouse, or "dockside buyer." Workers weigh in the fish, pay the fisherman, pack the fish in ice-filled cartons and load them on trucks for the next move up the market ladder.

The dockside buyer depends on the fisherman's harvest for his survival. No product, no money. Like the fisherman, he too strives for peak efficiency, trying to handle the most fish at the least expense.

THE RECREATIONAL FISHING INDUSTRY: SOMETHING OF VALUE?

His daily expenses include labor, insurance, packaging, fuel for trucks, and electricity to run ice-makers and coolers. Profits are derived from the markup per pound of fish handled.

The dockside buyer moves his fish to a wholesale dealer/processor. Usually located in an urban center, processors may add value by filleting and packaging the fish, which they distribute to retail markets and restaurants in-state and beyond. Competition is fierce; in order to survive, each wholesaler must offer the freshest product at the lowest possible price, for each is competing not only with the other fish dealers but with dealers of other food products such as poultry and beef. Here again, success hinges on old-style American efficiency.

These three interdependent units then—the fishermen, dockside buyers and wholesale dealer/processors—can be said to comprise the commercial finfishing industry.

The value of the commercial finfishing industry to the economy has never been accurately computed. Studies by economists who are employed by the competing recreational industry minimize the value of the commercial industry.[2] The total value of the commercial industry is frequently represented only by the value of the dockside landings—the per-pound price that the fishermen are paid for their fish. But does this represent the total value of this industry?

Obviously not. In addition to their daily expenses and a plague of repairs, fishermen invest in capital expenses including boats, nets, engines and pickup trucks; dealers invest their profits in buildings, large trucks, refrigeration equipment. Workers are employed at all tiers of the industry. Fishermen, employers and employees spend their income locally on the usual living expenses such as homes, personal vehicles, food, clothing, education and recreation.

In an attempt to get a handle on the full economic benefit of the fishing industry, economists have developed sales multipliers. These relate both to the value added to the fish as they ascend the market ladder and to the expenditures made by industry participants.

A multiplier of 3.5 is used to calculate the approximate benefit to the state while dockside values are multiplied by 7 to determine how the nation benefits. The nation? When netters harvest mullet from Louisiana waters and processors export the roe to the Orient, the new money that is brought into the country helps offset the trade imbalance. As for the purchase of goods produced at home, one would be hard-pressed to find a commercial fisherman behind the wheel of a pickup not manufactured by one of the Big Three.

By converting wild fish into cash, this clean little industry clearly enhances the economy at the local, state and national levels. Yet no economist can truly quantify the value of preserving a *local* food-producing industry.

While the commercial fisherman *needs* to catch the most fish at the least expense in order to survive, does the recreational fisherman? Obviously not, because the sportsman fishes only for fun, earning his livelihood by some other means independent of fishing. Efficiency is not his primary goal, enjoyment is.

The lawyer, doctor or carpenter earns more money than he needs to meet his living expenses. This surplus—"discretionary income"— he spends on his favorite pastimes such as golf, skiing or betting on the horses. The angler chooses to spend his extra money on sport fishing; this is the money that those in the recreational fishing industry vie for.

The Sport Fishing Institute lists over 70 categories of goods and services involved in sport fishing. The businesses that produce these goods do so as efficiently as possible.

THE RECREATIONAL FISHING INDUSTRY:
SOMETHING OF VALUE?

Mercury Marine is an SFI member, contributing at least $25,000 a year to the industry think tank. Mercury Marine is a division of the Skokie, Illinois-based Brunswick Corporation. In addition to its bowling, golf and defense-related products, Brunswick is the world's largest manufacturer of pleasure boats, marketing over 15 brands, as well as Mercury and Mariner outboard engines and Zebco fishing tackle. In order to maximize profits, Brunswick—"America's Tackle Company"—must produce this merchandise as cheaply as possible. In the case of its Mariner and Zebco lines, this is accomplished in the Phillipines, Japan, Korea, Taiwan, China....

According to an SFI study, resident and non-resident fishermen spent $538.5 million on *all* sport fishing—in both fresh water and salt water—in Louisiana in 1985. The sale of boats and motors totaled $151 million; nearly $73 million was spent on fishing tackle.[3] Anglers burned $71.5 million worth of gasoline as they drove their vehicles to and from their favorite fishing holes; once on the water they consumed another $45 million of fuel in their boats.

That more than one-fifth of the expenditures made by recreational fishermen consists of petroleum products is not lost on oil companies. British Petroleum, for instance, spent more than $3 million in 1991 to sponsor fishing events and advertise in fishing publications. Other oil companies help finance recreational groups in their efforts to ban commercial fishing.

Oil companies, like the manufacturers of boats, engines and tackle, strive to keep production costs down. In Louisiana this has been accomplished to the detriment of fisheries, by the failure of some companies to repair the immeasurable damage to the coastal marshes incurred in exploration and drilling.

The recreational and commercial fishing industries share the need to operate efficiently, maximizing profits by producing the most goods at the least expense. And by selling the most goods at the highest prices they can.

The commercial industry tries to increase demand both by promoting increased consumption of fish among seafood consumers, and by creating new seafood consumers. The recreational industry also boosts consumption of its products and services among existing anglers, and creates new angling consumers.

Marketing is one way. Because anglers seldom have enough time to pursue their sport, purchasing gear becomes a substitute for the activity. Manufacturers, through sportsman's expositions, magazines and television shows, inundate the armchair adventurer with a never-ending stream of "newer and better."

Fishing rodeos and tournaments also boost recreational sales. According to an article in the Coastal Conservation Association's publication *Tide*, Mercury/Mariner Outboard's sponsorship of the CCA and its 1990 summer-long GCCA/Budweiser State of Texas Anglers Rodeo (STAR), with "$350,000 worth of prizes," resulted in the company's selling more outboards "during these three months than it had in recent years."[4]

Besides selling more and fancier gear to *existing* anglers the recreational industry expends considerable effort boosting the *number* of sport fishermen.

Increasing the number of sport fishermen in a given coastal area is accomplished in two ways: create new anglers locally, and import anglers from other locations.

Casting contests; free fishing days, when people may go fishing without having to purchase a fishing license; urban fishing programs, where swimming pools are filled with fish such as rainbow trout; and other promotional events are conducted by the industry, as well

More than one-fifth of the expenditures made by recreational fishermen is on petroleum products.

Oil companies reduce costs by neglecting to restore marshland—and fishery habitat—to its original productive state. Exploration by "marsh buggy," a large tracked vehicle, may scar the tidal marsh and speed erosion.

THE RECREATIONAL FISHING INDUSTRY: SOMETHING OF VALUE?

Oil companies dig canals to float rigs to drilling sites. As fertile marshland is displaced by open water, fishery production declines.

as state fishery agencies, whose budgets include fishing license revenues. These events target primarily young anglers who, hopefully, will fish—and spend—for a lifetime.

The creation of new anglers among an existing population is a long-term proposition. A more immediate way to enhance sport-fishing-related profits is to promote the coastal area's fishing to out-of-state anglers. These tourist anglers, who may equip themselves with boats, trailers, engines, tackle and utility vehicles before they leave home, are expected to spend liberally on food and drink, fuel, lodging and guide services when they arrive.

In whatever manner the number of anglers in a given area is increased, one thing is certain: The number of fish that each sportsman is permitted to retain must necessarily be reduced.

Bag limits may be slashed and slashed further without affecting sporting activity, but there is an endpoint when the sportsman decides that it is no longer worth his while to spend so much money for so little return.

Managers of wild duck populations are now confronted with this phenomenon among duck hunters.

Hunters are required to purchase both federal and state duck stamps in order to hunt migratory waterfowl. According to a LDWF waterfowl biologist, Louisiana hunters purchased about 120,000 to 125,000 federal duck stamps each season during the 1970s. (The Louisiana duck stamp was not initiated until 1989.) As waterfowl numbers have fallen, managers have attempted to stabilize populations by shortening the hunting season and sharply reducing bag limits. The 30-day season of the early 1990s is about one-half the duration of seasons during the 1970s; bag limits on "big" ducks have been cut to three, less than half of those during the 1970s. Duck stamp sales during the early 1990s have also been reduced by about half, stabilizing at about 65,000.[5]

Funds generated by the sale of duck stamps is earmarked for the acquisition and enhancement of wetland habitat.

Of course, the sport of hunting would not be hunting without at least the prospect of making a kill. Otherwise, it would be merely the activity of observing. It is possible to fish, however, without making a kill. Hooking, playing and releasing a fish is called "catch and release."

The recreational fishing industry already promotes this concept. "The Thrill's The Catch...Not The Keep!" read SFI bumper stickers.

The number of anglers that a coastal region can attract is determined largely by the number of fish in the water. By making it socially incorrect—or illegal—to retain fish, the industry removes this cap, temporarily. While it produces its goods as efficiently as possible, the recreational fishing industry promotes the most inefficient behavior among the consumers of its goods: spending the most money while retaining the least fish.

The commercial finfisherman resides along the coast, catches fish and exports them, cleanly importing new money into his community. The recreational fishing industry, instead, imports tourist anglers to the coastal communities.

To the recreational industry economist or the local booster of coastal tourism, banning the commercial harvest of fish and prohibiting the recreational fisherman from harvesting any, or more than a token fish or two, seems the ideal way to maximize the number of tourist anglers drawn to the coast.

But that is to continue to make the mistake of focusing only on the *harvest* of fish.

Fish are wildlife and, always, the strongest limiting factor on wildlife population is not harvest but *habitat* (though the importance of harvest does increase as the area and quality of habitat diminishes).

While increasingly stringent bag limits are placed upon individual recreational fishermen, in the name of "conservation," never has an attempt been made to limit the *number* of recreational fishermen. Instead, with each member of the diverse—and remote—recreational industry hoping to profit from an increase in the number of sport fishermen in Louisiana's coastal waters, they direct their shortsighted efforts toward accelerating this increase.

By their failure to control, or even consider, limits on "growth," those in tourist-based industries, including recreational fishing, frequently profane and destroy that which made a location attractive initially. In this case, the attraction is the abundance of fish reared in Louisiana's lightly populated expanse of coastal wetlands.

IT'S NOT ME, IT'S HIM!

While the recreationals introduced their 1991 gamefish bill to the Senate Natural Resources Committee, a commercial fisherman and an elderly Lake Charles angler argued outside in the hallway. The angler sported a GCCA redfish nametag.

"How can you say we have anything to do with it?" he asked incredulously. "Where do they get those figures? I've fished 50 years and never been checked by a biologist....Only one in 10, one in 100, one in 1,000 sport fishermen catch any fish. Hardly anybody catches their limit....Huh? The fishin' out my way? My wife and I once caught 1,250 pounds of redfish without even movin'! One on every cast. We was just athrowin' them big fish in the boat."

The reluctance of the individual sport fisherman to acknowledge that he himself impacts fishery populations currently represents the single greatest threat to the long-term welfare of the redfish and speckled trout.

Commercial fishermen kill fish, that's what they do. As the netter ties up at the fishhouse, look in his fish box...dead trout. As he unloads them, two by two, you might count a hundred. Averaging nearly two

The netter's catch may appear large when compared to the sport fisherman's daily bag limit.

pounds, he's made a good day.

To some sportsmen, permitted to retain "only" 25 specks a day, it may look like a lot. But the commercial boy's fishing under a fixed quota—his fish are counted at the fishhouses and when one million pounds are caught, he and his less-than-2,000 partners are cut off until the season reopens.

For each inshore netter, there are now at least 175 saltwater sport fishermen, fishing year round.

Assume that each of the state's at least 350,000 anglers catches just one redfish in the entire year. Each looks at his own single fish..."That's nothing." Now imagine all those reds, averaging, say, a smallish three pounds apiece, in one big heap. That's a helluva pile of dead fish—it weighs over a million pounds.

The collective impact of great numbers of recreational fishermen, each landing just a few fish, quickly adds up.

In 1988, LDWF biologists determined that the state's waters could give up a total allowable catch of 900,000 redfish. They projected that recreationals, fishing under a daily bag limit of five, would harvest 623,000, leaving 277,000 redfish for commercial fishermen and consumers. Unsatisfied with this scenario, the recreational lobby shoved the commercials out of the fishery altogether, claiming that the "endangered" redfish needed to be "conserved."

The recreationals then proceeded to kill 965,000 redfish that year, eating up their proposed allocation, the proposed commercial allotment, and exceeding the total allowable catch by 65,000 fish.

During the first three years that commercials were shut down on redfish, they harvested 3.6 million pounds of speckled trout. Recreational fishermen, during the same period, piled up nearly 12 million trout weighing over 15 million pounds.

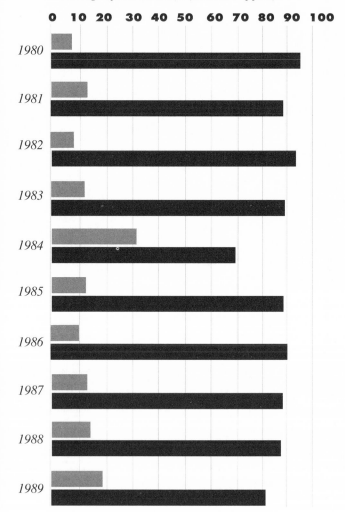

SHARE OF SPECKS
Louisiana landings of spotted seatrout by commercial and recreational fishermen from 1980 through 1989

Commercial   Recreational

Percentage of annual catch (numbers of fish)

0   10   20   30   40   50   60   70   80   90   100

1980
1981
1982
1983
1984
1985
1986
1987
1988
1989

Source: *National Marine Fisheries Service, Washington, D.C.*

SPOTTED SEATROUT
Louisiana landings, 1980 through 1989
(in numbers of fish)

Year	Commercial	Recreational
1980	345,289	5,298,034
1981	335,348	2,415,381
1982	415,775	5,438,020
1983	766,071	5,945,310
1984	556,143	1,228,670
1985	663,770	4,466,242
1986	1,130,307	10,520,190
1987	1,029,642	7,466,073
1988	819,090	5,554,890
1989	850,787	3,859,000

Source: *National Marine Fisheries Service, Washington, D.C.*

During 1986 alone, as the bumper crop of speckled trout following the freeze of December 1983 came of age, recreationals pulled out of the system an estimated 10.5 million, weighing 12.5 million pounds. Commercial fishermen in 1986 took 1.1 million trout, weighing 2 million pounds.

Still, the refrain among the majority of anglers? "It's not me, it's him!"

SHARE OF REDS

Louisiana landings of red drum by commercial and recreational fishermen from 1980 through 1989

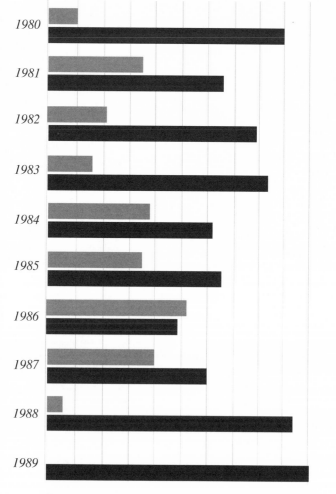

Commercial   Recreational

Percentage of annual catch (numbers of fish)

Source: *National Marine Fisheries Service, Washington, D.C.*

RED DRUM
Louisiana landings, 1980 through 1989
(in numbers of fish)

Year	Commercial	Recreational
1980	181,194	1,704,987
1981	224,646	412,926
1982	363,626	1,405,852
1983	484,654	2,551,358
1984	652,096	1,105,116
1985	733,393	1,359,553
1986	1,954,424	1,814,147
1987	1,142,794	1,705,024
1988	61,341	964,838
1989	0	931,476

Source: *National Marine Fisheries Service, Washington, D.C.*

Long before white settlers arrived in northern Wisconsin, Chippewa Indians spearfished walleyed pike. Each spring, the Indians canoed the shallow waters of the freshwater lakes, using birchbark torches to locate the spawning fish.

Today, they still continue the tradition, but with some changes. Paddles have been traded for outboard engines, and flambeaux for spotlights. Tribal drums still mark the beginning of the short season but, after a night's fishing, the spearfishermen are no longer met by coal-eyed maidens in buckskin. Instead, the Native Americans face a crowd of jeering sport fishermen, some singing, tauntingly, "Where have all the walleye gone?" The "sportsmen" claim that the Chippewa are depleting this species.

A May 1991 *Audubon* article described the ringleader of the recreational contingent: "Dean Crist is a man on a crusade. He is articulate, witty, and creative. And the one thing this forty-one-year-old pizza-maker stretches even better than dough is the truth. Crist is a transplant to Minocqua from suburban Chicago, as are many of the leaders of his protest group, 'Stop Treaty Abuse/Wisconsin.' In the best Chicken Little tradition, he predicts that spearfishing will sound the death knell for tourism and natural resources in the North, despite heavy evidence to the contrary."

About 400 Chippewas participated in the 1990 fishery. They speared 16,000 walleye. An estimated 1.4 million anglers, fishing under a daily bag limit of 3 to 5 fish, took 670,000.

When striped bass populations fell off along the East Coast, Maryland closed the fishery to both commercial and recreational fishermen. The Chesapeake Bay is the major spawning ground for this treasured species.

After a five-year closure, the state reopened a limited striped bass fishery in 1990. Over the strident objections of sport-fishing interests, the Maryland Department of Natural Resources divided the harvest *evenly* between commercial and recreational fishermen.

Of the 750,000-pound total allowable catch, commercial fishermen and consumers were allocated 318,000 pounds, 42.5 percent. Sport fishermen got the same amount, and charter boats were given 15 percent, 112,500 pounds.

DNR officials closely monitored the sport fishery by aerial and launch-ramp surveys and by follow-up phone calls. It was expected that the recreationals would get in about five weeks of fishing before meeting their quota. But on the first weekend of the season, officials were amazed as an estimated 80,000 sport fishermen swarmed out over the Bay. "More people fished any given day of the 1990 Maryland striped bass season than participated in the evacuation of Dunkirk," wrote George Reiger in "Recreational Pressure on Fish Stocks," an article in the April 1991 *Salt Water Sportsman.*

The recreational fishery had to be shut down after just 10 days but not before the anglers exceeded their 318,000-pound quota by at least 20 percent.

Compared with the difficult and expensive-to-monitor sport-fishing season, the commercial season proved easy to control. Each of the 297 netters had to register his day's catch at one of 22 state-operated checking stations before he could sell it, and he was subject to checks by the Maryland DNR police.

By the end of their 30-day season, the watermen had landed only 122,000 pounds of striped bass, a third of their allocation.

"Yet rather than consider the implications of this, private [sport] fishermen immediately began lobbying to get the entire state allotment of stripers to themselves. They argued that this was the only 'fair way' to ensure every angler a fish," continued Reiger, who concluded his ground-breaking article with the admonition, "We as recreational fishermen must begin acknowledging our own considerable potential impact on a number of important marine fisheries." Reiger is conservation (in the old sense) editor for *Salt Water Sportsman* and *Field & Stream* magazines.

The data clearly show that recreational fishermen in Louisiana

Most netters tie up their boats by a roadside fishhouse, rendering the commercial harvest relatively easy to monitor. Receipts are imprinted by a plastic sales card bearing the fisherman's license number.

catch and retain a pile of redfish and speckled trout that is several times larger than the shrinking mound that the state's government allows commercial fishermen to catch for the markets and restaurants. Yet these figures include only those fish harvested *legally*; unfortunately, there are two additional mountains in the shadow of the first—those specks and reds harvested illegally, and those caught and then released into the water to die later.

The activities of less than 2,000 professional netters—most of whom tie up their boats and unload their catch at the same roadside fishhouse—are easily monitored. But how does one keep track of hundreds of thousands of resident and nonresident sport fishermen? Policing this multitude of anglers who each day line the highways, camp across the beaches and barrier islands, and disperse throughout a five-million-acre maze of bays and marshland, is now—and always

IT'S NOT ME, IT'S HIM!

The cumulative harvest of great numbers of anglers is substantial. An educational campaign to heighten a sense of individual responsibility offers many benefits.

will be—an impossibility. While most do obey the law, poaching is rampant, as unscrupulous and irresponsible anglers both exceed their daily bag limits and take home undersized and oversized fish.

These illegal fish are not counted. But, at least, there's a good chance that the poachers' pile of fish will be utilized. Those fish that are too small—or too large—for the sportsman to legally keep, and which are released to die in the water, will not be used.

Even as the recreationals worked to convince the 1991 Legislature to take the fish from the commercial fishermen, the state's waters were thick with the bumper crops of post-freeze-of-'89 juvenile redfish and trout. Most were still undersized, forcing anglers to catch and release several for each that was large enough to retain. By the time a daily bag limit of 25 legal trout and five legal redfish was reached, over 100 of the small and tender fish might have been hurriedly ripped from the angler's hooks and thrown back overboard.

Rep. Johnny Glover was sufficiently concerned that he introduced a bill to help save the lives of some of these small fish. Glover, who operates a sport-fishing marina in Cocodrie, tried to lower the 12-inch minimum legal size on trout so anglers could more quickly fill their limits, thereby reducing the wastage among this particularly strong year-class of fish. "You shouldn't have to throw back a fish that you know is going to die," he said. "We're causing the destruction of these fish."

Glover estimated that less than 30 to 50 percent of the fish recreational fishermen throw back survive. The only way to save the fish is not to touch them with bare hands at all, he said, a precaution he guessed only "one out of 1,000" fishermen takes.

The typical sportsman is well-intentioned and is concerned for the long-term vigor of fishery populations. Not only does he himself deeply enjoy good sport fishing, but he feels that this rich and wholesome outdoor activity should be available for his sons and daughters to enjoy. (A wish that makes him particularly vulnerable to emotional "for-the-future"-type come-ons.)

Yet, in the face of overwhelming evidence to the contrary, the recreational fisherman remains thoroughly convinced that he himself has no impact whatsoever on fishery populations. And that the villainous commercial fisherman, his sworn enemy, threatens the future of his favorite sport by his greedy urge to clear the waters of every last fish. Why?

Aside from the natural human tendency to believe what we want to believe, to willingly take credit for the positive and to blame others for the negative, there is one very obvious reason why the sport fisherman continues to dodge responsibility for his own behavior: He simply is not told otherwise.

IT'S NOT ME, IT'S HIM!

That recreational fishermen take the preponderance of those highly valued coastal species like speckled trout and redfish on the Gulf, striped bass and weakfish on the East Coast, is common knowledge among everyone in the fishery management community. Publicly funded, state and federal agencies are only too happy to supply any data to a sportsman who requests it. Few do.

Some get their earful from sport-fishing guides and charter boat captains, many of whom are quick to attribute a less-than-satisfying day to the predations of the commercial fisherman. But most, for their information, rely on the national outdoor magazines, outdoor columnists in local newspapers,[1] regional outdoor publications, and magazines and newsletters mailed directly from various sporting and "conservation" organizations.

"Simply put, the sport fisherman in this country has not seriously impacted any marine species compared to the damage done by commercial harvest. Most species are not negatively affected at all by sport fishing,..." wrote *Salt Water Sportsman* editor Rip Cunningham, in an April 1990 article "Placing the Blame."

"Our position is that all commercial netting for speckled trout should be stopped indefinitely," commenced a February 1991 *Louisiana Sportsman* editorial captioned "Let's get rid of gill netting for trout." Editor Ann Taylor continued:

My grandfather...fished the Grand Isle surf every summer in the 60s and 70s. I remember him catching between 50 and 100 specks daily, usually before 9:00 am (this was before limits were imposed.) By 1986 he was lucky if he caught any specks at all in the surf. On the very best days, which were few and far between, he might have caught 10. Those days became fewer and fewer until, in 1987, Al had given up surf fishing all together because, "there aren't any more fish."...In 1987, Wildlife and Fisheries said that a 1.25 million pound commercial quota should not reduce speckled trout populations any further. But by all accounts, populations of the popular sport fish had already plummeted to the point where not only surf fishermen, but even anglers with boats at their disposal were not catching fish.

In an August 1992 article in *Florida Sportsman*, the most widely circulated magazine in that state,[2] Mark Weintz wrote, "Early accounts of Florida describe schools of fish so vast that thousands would accidentally beach themselves when attacked by a large predator....Even after the passage of centuries, a youngster could go down to the shore and catch a good stringer of fish."

The article continued:

> But in the last couple of decades, changes have occurred, and much of the decline in fish stocks can be directly attributed to commercial netting....If we do not take action soon, our marine waters will be a vast wasteland. Banning the nets is an excellent step....Commercial net fishing plunders our resources with minimum positive economic impact, while sportfishing's impact is estimated to be larger than that of citrus or cattle. Moreover, sportfishing plays a substantial role in tourism, which is Florida's primary economic base.

Is it any wonder that well-meaning sportsmen have difficulty factoring themselves into the fishery equation?

IT'S NOT ME, IT'S HIM!

The message in such comments has long reverberated through the outdoor community and is now being repeated with increasing frequency by a new breed of money-minded outdoor correspondents. The shrillness of its delivery is directly proportional to the amount of sport-fishing-related advertising within each publication.

Intrinsic to the myth that the commercial fisherman kills the majority of the fish is the promise that getting him off the water will greatly enhance the quality of the angler's sport.

As long as he remains convinced that the commercials are getting practically all of the fish, it is only natural for the sportsman to believe that taking the netter's hands out of the water will allow it to fill evenly, thick as a gumbo, with fish; that whenever and wherever he drops a line in the water, he will be rewarded with a fat fish. And that amid this new-found abundance, his daily bag limits will be generously raised, enabling him to bring home boxes of fish like he did in the old days. Simply put, there will be "More Fish For Me!"

During the 1981 Texas gamefish campaign, *Houston Chronicle* outdoor columnist Joe Doggett found himself in an embarrassing situation. The campaign was being waged on the basis of a scarcity of fish but, while it was underway, Doggett went out on Galveston Bay with a guide who knew how to fish. In a May 3 article he related:

> By scouting carefully and not missing many opportunities, we docked at Pleasure Island Marina with 30 keeper trout in the 3/4-pound to 3-pound class. "Ah ha," the critic might claim. "That's 30 trout, yet you claim that the bays are running out of fish." Let me state that the box [of fish] represented the reward of "hitting it right" with an experienced fishermen. West is a veteran bay guide. He fishes several days a week and it is his business to stay on

fish....West's success is seldom average. His success does, however, reflect a hope for the legions of coastal sportsmen who rarely, if ever, drop an impressive box on the dock. Both speckled trout and redfish may once again thrive along the Texas Coast if the resource they represent is recognized and carefully regulated. Perhaps it was prophetic that on Thursday, the day West and I enjoyed the elusive bounty of feeding fish within easy reach, the Senate voted to re-refer SB 139 and HB 1000 to the Economic Development Committee, thus bringing fresh life to the fish that mean so much to all of us.

Fish are like money and sex—it's tough to get enough. But getting rid of the commercials won't help his sex life; nor will the sportsman make any more money. Will there really be, More Fish For Me?

In 1989, Louisiana's commercial fishermen landed over 850,000 trout while recreationals harvested nearly four million. Out of each 100 trout killed, commercials took 18, recreationals 82. (These figures represent those fish *retained* and disregard those kept illegally and inadvertently killed by catch and release.) If the recreational industry had, instead, successfully elbowed out the commercial fishermen the year before, and the commercial haul was distributed among the state's sport fishermen, each would have received about *two* additional fish.

Appealing to the self-interest of the sport fisherman is extremely useful in attracting his financial support for the recreational industry's drive to monopolize the fish. But keeping the attention of the recreational angler focused intently on the commercial fisherman holds another advantage for the recreational industry.

As the checkbook-wielding anglers march forward, trampling the despised commercial fishermen on their way to "victory," they are less than likely to question how their leaders' simultaneous promotion of their own fishing holes to anglers "from around the world" might affect the quality of their own sport.

The Norco-based *St. Charles Herald*, on May 16, 1991, printed a pro-gamefish article under the headline "Guaranteeing a future: gamefish status for specks & reds now." After stating, "There is no longer enough supply of speckled trout and redfish to both satisfy all current demands and, at the same time, insure a continuing supply for the future," the lengthy article continued:

> There is room for managed growth in the recreational industry. With sensible regulations and relatively inexpensive enforcement, the recreational fishery can be controlled. The Louisiana Legislature authorized the establishment of the Louisiana Marine Recreational Fishing Development Board in its 1990 session. This body...will conduct a needs assessment for the expansion of Louisiana's marine recreational fishing industry, and then develop a marketing plan to bring anglers from all over the world to fish and spend money in Louisiana.

GCCA, in its December 1991 newsletter, celebrated the first meeting of the Louisiana Marine Recreational Fishing Development Board:

> The Board will develop a program to help bring more people from out of state into Louisiana to fish for saltwater species. This will have several positive effects. First, it will help improve the business performance of the guides, marinas

and tackle dealers who have worked so hard in the past to support GCCA. Second, it will bring more money in general into the state. Third, and perhaps most important, it will help increase the awareness within the state of the economic importance of saltwater recreational fishing. That will in turn help give a boost to conservation efforts and to fairer allocations of limited fish resources.

Commercial fishermen should get cracking on their own educational campaign. Convincing the sport fisherman that he himself kills fish may not be easily accomplished, but a preview at how the newly enlightened angler may interpret the above message suggests the possible rewards:

"'Bring in *more* people, from out of state?' Doggone, it already seems like there's a boat everywhere I try to go. And if we sports who live here are already catching most of the fish, then where will the fish come from for these hundreds of thousands of tourist-sports that GCCA wants to bring in? More money for the marinas, boat and tackle dealers? Seems like these guys are already in pretty good shape—they sure get plenty of *my* money. Maybe they ought to learn to appreciate what they already have instead of ruining it for the rest of us. As for 'fairer allocations,' I can't see what could be more fair than sharing the fish 50-50 among the two industries, and among *all* the people of Louisiana. Then maybe we could get started working *together* on our *own* 'conservation efforts'—protecting the wetlands and making more fish!"

ROY LEE YEOMANS

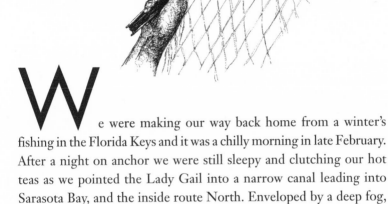

We were making our way back home from a winter's fishing in the Florida Keys and it was a chilly morning in late February. After a night on anchor we were still sleepy and clutching our hot teas as we pointed the Lady Gail into a narrow canal leading into Sarasota Bay, and the inside route North. Enveloped by a deep fog, our entire world consisted of the small clearing that seemed to travel with us as the fog opened about 20 yards ahead and closed in again, just behind us.

Near the bow splashed a manatee, grazing and unthreatened by us chugging along at about eight knots. And then, out of the fog, we were surprised to see a sportsman, wading not 30 feet away by a patch of mangroves. Roy cut back the big Chevy to an idle so as not to run the cold water up his leg or spoil his fishing.

"Good mornin' to ya! Ya gettin' 'em?"

"Not yet, capt'n," answered the white-haired and deeply tanned sportsman, smiling and tipping back his fine old straw hat with paisley band.

"I reckon they can't find ya' in all this fog," shouted Roy as we softly glided by him.

As the fog closed in we left the gentleman angler, the manatee and the mangroves of Old Florida behind. Then it was just this old commercial man and me, until the sun burnt off the fog, opening our little world up to...a Sunday on Sarasota and Tampa Bays.

Six or eight motorized sailers, motor yachts, speed boats and sport fishermen bore down frantically on our stern. And another onslaught attacked from the front, veering off at the last minute, throwing their wakes against our hull. The plastic boats passed us on the left and they passed us on the right. As their wakes nearly beat the planks off our skiff, we, sitting high in the raised cabin, held tight to keep from being thrown right out the doors. Like hawks, the Florida Marine Patrol in their speed boats would swoop in, hail four or five speedsters, "You! you! and you!" stopping them for some reason but overwhelmed as the rising sun seemed to hatch more and more of the plastic craft. Above the roar of the engines and the manmade seas crashing against us, I shouted to Roy, "They don't have a lot of respect for commercial fishermen over here do they?"

Looking straight ahead and clutching the wheel tightly, he answered quietly, "They don't have no respect for nobody."

For 12 hours we took a beating; a thousand boats passed us and not a single one slowed down in simple marine courtesy. But Roy never did complain, never showed any anger or disgust; only occasionally would he shake his head and suggest that it might have been safer to have chanced the open Gulf.

Roy Lee was just as stoic when I sat down with him in his battered waterside trailer in Leeville to ask him about his days in the Ten Thousand Islands of Florida. And about his years in Louisiana, where he moved in the early 1970s after his territory was swallowed up by Everglades National Park.

It was September, 1992, and only a short time after Hurricane

ROY LEE YEOMANS

Roy Lee and Gail Yeomans

Andrew had battered Florida and then come over to hit Louisiana. The trailer where he and his wife Gail lived had been washed with a tidal surge high enough to fill it with more than three feet of water and mud, and strong enough to bust the axles. But he never mentioned it.

Both Roy and Gail are fishermen. From fishing families, they're used to adversity and they don't know what it means to give up. After the storm there was nothing to do but clean up and start over. But a storm is easier to accept than the hail of regulations that time after time have knocked them down, forcing them to cut back and regroup, always with less than they had before.

Roy Lee was a great producer of finfish in Florida and he was a great producer of finfish in Louisiana. He made a lot of money, most of which he plowed back into what he loves to do most—fish. But now it doesn't pay to fish—that's something that even Roy can't accept.

Here, Yeomans describes his years as a fisherman in Florida and Louisiana:

I'm 66 years old and I stayed 35 years in the Everglades. I guess they was some pretty good old days, you couldn't o' asked for anything better.

My daddy had a place, near the old Watson Place[1] on the Chatham River. Long years ago, when grandpa Jim Yeomans was livin' there, they all carried their pistols like Wyatt Earp. All the time, he'd never go nowhere without his pistol, in his pocket or hip pocket.

He shot and killed a fellow over a $10 trade o' tomators, because the man said, "I'll pay you for your tomators there, later on," and he didn't never bring the $10. So Grandpa, he went right there and shot 'im. Had to.

Him and the Daniels, I think, was some o' the first ones to move into that part o' the country. They farmed Fakahatchee Island, and they farmed Russell Island. That was a little island...I lived on it two years when I was first married.

But first we lived on West Pass Island, out on the edge o' the outside white-sand islands. I come out o' the Navy at 21, married this girl, and we went out there to live. We used a little six-horse Briggs & Stratton and we carried tin and lumber and everything else out there and I built a little place and we stayed out there for a couple o' years. I had built it on little black mangrove pilin's that I drove down, and a Nor'wester come in and it lifted it right up off 'em. So we thought we better move back to higher land. And I moved us back into Russell Island there.

Watson? Oh yeah, my granddad used to be one o' his right-hand men. And my daddy and his sister said many times that they would go to Chokoloskee, over to Chatham Bend River, where Watson lived. He had a big two-story house there.

Watson was supposed to have shot Belle Starr long years back. She was some kind o' Western broad or somethin' or other, like a show girl, and she wound up there at Watson's. And he was supposed to have killed her.

But Grandpa would go over there and they would talk and talk and talk. Dad and his sister, Aunt Heddy, went along but they wouldn't get out, they'd have to set in the boat, a little bitty sailboat. Grandpa'd go up there and he'd eat, and do what he wanted to. But they was scared of 'im, a lot o' people were.

Somehow or the other, they always made a trip or two over towards Key West, they'd kill alligators and this and that and take 'em over there to trade at a big tradin' post that had a lot o' stuff you couldn't get around home.

Did my dad fish? Yes. He was Owen Yeomans. He fished mullet, anything he could. Reds? Oh yeah, they caught anything they could. But it was mostly trappin' in them days. Huntin' and trappin'. Fishin' wasn't too popular at that time, you know, only mullet.

In Everglades City, they had a train that run down there, that run right down to the bottom o' the town there, and they would catch mullet and salt 'em in barrels and the train went down there and fetched 'em out.

They'd get brine barrels, you know, like the wood beer barrels from long years back? And they'd cut the top out and they salted it in brine, like regular ice cream salt.

We'd go out there and catch us a load of 'em and we'd take 'em and salt 'em into a skiff. We'd cut 'em, sprinkle 'em with salt and let 'em drain. And when the sun'd come out, it'd dry 'em right there.

And we'd pack 'em in barrels and the train'd take 'em off. It went up to the northern part o' the country, I'd say Georgia.

You'd probably get from a nickel to a dime a pound. You could sell some in the fresh but it was mostly salted stuff in them days— salt pork, salt bacon, salt fish—'cause that was the onliest way you could keep it.

We were usin' just regular old gill nets. Cotton nets. For motors, we used Briggs & Strattons and another old one-lunger, a Palmer.

You'd crank it up a time or two and it'd go, "chhh-chhh-chhh pow!pow!pow!, chhh-chhh-chhh pow!" When my grandpa had one o' them there, every time that he'd want to go somewhere he'd crank that old thing up and she'd fire about every 3 or 4 rpm, "chhh-chhh-chhh pow!" and that's the way they'd go to town. They'd go all the way from Chokoloskee to Key West and it'd take 'em dang near two weeks to make the trip.

Many years ago, at old man Ted Smallwood's tradin' post on Chokoloskee Island, the Indians would come and trade gator hides and coon hides and stuff like that for rice and beans and such. Seminoles.

And there'd be anywhere from 15 to 25 Indians that would be drunk. They'd trade their hides for that firewater and, boy, he would get loaded and he'd get so bad he'd want to fight and cut and shoot and do all that kind o' good stuff and they'd pull 'im off to the side and tie his hands behind the post there underneath the store—it was up on stilts—and they'd tie 'im up there and he'd just stay there and moan and sing and be drunk. Sometimes there'd be 20 or 25 of 'em and their wives would all be sittin' out alongside the road, waitin' for 'em to sober up. And when they'd sober up they'd cut 'em loose and let 'em go back home.

There was a time when they was makin' a bunch o' movies in the Everglades and I helped with a couple, like *Wind Across the Everglades* with Christopher Plummer and Burl Ives. They hired my wife for an extra and I drove 'em around. I was runnin' the Star of Everglades, a guide boat, at the time, around 1958.

Tony Galento was in it, that was after Joe Louis finished 'im off. Burl Ives, he was the main outlaw. He would kill these curlew for the plumes—they used to do that long years back. He was a big poacher and Chris Plummer was the game warden.

And they had a bunch o' prostitutes they brought over from Miami and put on the Star of Everglades. And they had old Gypsy Rose Lee. I walked in on her one time there. She was half undressed and I said, "Oh, I'm sorry, ma'am," and started to get out o' there but, shoot, that didn't phase her a bit. She said, "That's alright, sonny, come on in!"

Now Gentle Ben, the bear that little boy plays with? I caught that bear.

We'd go deer huntin' just about every weekend. We'd get out and walk in the marsh and me and another old boy was out there, and we run up on a big old log. You could see somethin' was goin' in there, and when I looked in I seen there was three little bitty cub bears into it. And the momma was gone. My daddy had always told me, "If you ever get where there is some little bears, the momma would catch ya, she would get ya." But I went ahead and took a chance onto it and I grabbed them three little devils and I put 'em in a sack. We'd always take some sacks out there to tote our deer home. We put them things in there, tied it up and drug 'em, right across the water.

We kept 'em for two or three days and we decided to take 'em to a reptile garden in Bonita Springs. They called it the Wonder Gardens and it was there for years and years. I sold 'em to them there and they kept 'em for years. And they grew up to be huge bears. You could stand there and they'd just put their paws on your shoulders and lick you on the mouth. Tom, Dick and Harry, they called 'em. And I think it was Tom, they started makin' pictures with 'im.

If you ever go to Raymond Wooten's Airboat Tours just outside o' Everglades, you go look at all them alligators. Every one of 'em will run anywhere from no less than seven to 12 feet. There must be 1,500 head in there that I helped catch when they was three or four feet.

Whenever I'd ride my airboat at night I'd pick up four or five and tie 'em up and he'd give me a couple o' three bucks apiece. I caught a hell of a pile o' them gators in that reptile garden.

Later, I had a plane. I flew spotter pilot but I used it for gatorin' too. I done that every dry season, you know, after the mullet run season was over, in the wintertime. I'd hunt these lakes out, further back in the cypress. I'd land it out in the middle o' the marshes there.

By myself? Oh yeah, I'd just run around, just like an old fellow with his head chopped off, with nobody around me. I'd talk to myself when I wanted to and when I didn't want to, I wouldn't.

I had a little Cub, with wheels, and when it dried and the ground was crackin' open, it was hard enough that you could land most anywhere. I'd let the air out o' my tires until you pretty near had a flat tire and they wouldn't roll very far.

I could take off in about 500 feet but every once in a while I'd have to cut down a cypress tree or two, with my axe, if I didn't have enough room where my airplane could jump out. I'd get out and chop one or two o' them trees out and I'd back her up and I'd tie a rope—I always carried plenty o' rope—I'd tie a rope to a tree back there. And the other end I'd tie to my airplane, by my struts right there.

And I'd take my pocket knife and I'd have it good and sharp and I'd get that thing to makin' coffee there and the whole plane would go t' quiverin' and I had my brakes on the best I could and I'd reach down and cut that piece o' rope and keeeeoooom I'd get right out on top of it. With a load o' gators.

I fished a good piece o' the West Coast o' Florida. All the years I was in the Everglades I'd fish down into Florida Bay, just before Christmas to make some extra Christmas money, you know. And I'd go back into January. I first started goin' with my dad and we'd fish out o' Marathon.

We'd drift pompano there. We'd just run our net straight out, tie the boat to it and we'd eat our dinner and go to bed. We'd probably drift five or 10 miles that night, wake up the next mornin' and come ashore by compass. Or you'd see an island, Bay Hondee Island, bridges or stuff like that. And you'd catch anywhere from 100 pounds o' pompano to 500 pounds o' pompano, anywhere from 300 pounds o' mackerel on up to 2,500, 3,000 pounds o' big horse mackerel, every night. It was some good fishin'.

Snook? He used to be a commercial fish too. He's a *fine* fish, with just as pretty as white a meat as you ever seen. They brought as much as 18, 20 cents a pound. And we sold what we could of 'em there, until they made it a gamefish.

Closin' the snook? That was the same deal as with the redfish.
There was plenty of 'em, before they made a sports fish out of it.

They had spawnin' places, just like a mullet, but in the time it'd
take for 'em to all bunch up they'd come settle in these deep holes
around the islands. And you'd see a bunch of 'em just bigger than
this house and just coal black, stacked in there. We used seines on
'em, with real heavy twine, 'cause they'd cut a gill net to pieces. The
males'd run about 17, 18 pounds and the females'd run anywhere
from 18 on up to 32 pounds apiece.

Right after they made 'em a gamefish, in about 1957, you could
catch all you wanted of 'em, but you couldn't sell none of 'em. They'd
go down there and fillet 'em and take 'em back by the hundreds o'
pounds, just like they do here with the trout and redfish.

And pretty soon they thought they was gettin' extinct. That put
an end to it.

That and killin' off the mangroves, like out around Marco Island.
On Marco they just filled 'em in, and the snook, they love them
mangroves.

So they finally cut 'em down to four per person. And it's been
that way for years, the snook never did come back.[2]

We didn't get as much for our mullet as we did for snook but it
was our main fish. I've caught as much as 150,000 to 175,000 pounds
o' mullet in one set. With a seine. We'd pull 'em on Naples beach
there, back trucks down on the beach, shovel the fish in baskets and
load 'em up. For six, seven cents a pound.

About 15 men of us, we could pull 'em down in about 45 minutes,
and all we'd have to do was just back the trucks down the beach
there and take 'em to the fishhouse, seven, eight, 10, 15 truckloads
at a catch.

In them days long back they would ship quite a bit into the Carolinas, Georgia, Alabama, Tennessee, that area there. Mostly for the poor folks because that was a good cheap fish. And a lot of the local people in Florida would eat mullet, just like around here, these old Cajuns prefer a good jumpin' mullet. They'll steam 'em down, or boil 'em. But then they started eatin' this redfish, speckled trout, red snapper, they dropped away from it. But it's a good edible fish.

I stayed in the Everglades until 1971, when they closed the park to commercial fishin'.

Well, they closed it sections at a time. Probably from Lost Man's River south, they closed that first. Then they kept extendin' the park up. The government'd give 'em a few more acres of it, and they would move it on up and they finally got it to where they had forced us out all the way up from Lost Man's River. We fished from Broad River, I'd say Harney River, Lost Man's River and Chatham Bend River, but they just kept on and on and on until they pushed us right on out. They just kept freezin' you out until they actually closed it—only the sports could get the fish after that.

I first come over to Lou'siana in 1972. Claude McCall was the first, I was the second. Well, Fred Shiver was the second and I was his son-in-law at the time and I come over with him. I was married to Hollis, Fred's daughter.

Fred had a fishhouse over there and when he come over to scout around, me and Hollis run it. Then we moved over. Fred opened a fishhouse in Golden Meadow, up there at the old Pelican Seafood place there, but then he was gettin' old to where he wasn't doin' as good as he art to, so he sold the house to Wayland Demere and Delton, and he went back.

The mangrove swamp is an immensely productive type of coastal wetland favored by the snook. Since Florida's mangroves—like Louisiana's marsh grasses—provide shelter and nutrition for a wide variety of marine life, their loss causes fishery productivity to decline.

At least 150,000 acres of Florida's mangroves have been dredged and filled for waterfront developments such as this one on Marco Island, being sprayed for mosquitoes. Anti-commercial and "marine conservation" organizations are frequently directed by developers of coastal wetlands.

Hollis, she moved back with her daddy and left me here. I wasn't goin' back because I seen I was in the land o' plenty right here where I was.

I had come over with a Chris Craft, I brought it from Everglades City. A 26-foot Chris Craft with a Chrysler inboard. And these fellas was doin' so good crabbin' that a hundred cages would produce 1,000, 1,200 pounds o' crabs a day. At eight cents a pound.

Ed Melançon, here in Leeville, he told me that if I'd sell him my crabs, he'd buy me a hundred traps. So he did and right then's when I started.

Then Ted Loupe, who had an outboard place, he fronted me an outboard and I started trout fishin' and this and that until I got set up.

Then I met Gail, and we got together. Gail always did fish with me, she's crabbin' with me right now. She was from Grand Isle where her daddy used to haul seine, until they closed it. Her first year's trout fishin', at 25 cents a pound, we fished 180 days and had $52,000 worth o' speckled trout.

That's when I had the Lady Gail fixed up. A 30-foot redwood Lafitte skiff with a 454 Chevrolet. I paid for her in six weeks' time, just catchin' trout at 25 cents a pound for Wayland.

I was producin' a lot o' fish at that time. I was the onliest one who was doin' it. Me and Claude. Then that bunch from Florida moved in here and they just kept doin' it and doin' it and doin' it. That's when they got that reputation with all these Cajuns of all these Florida guys comin' in here and slaughterin' everything. They'd just come in for the season and go right back to Florida.

The first ten years, it was fabulous fishin'. Fabulous. Anywhere from 40 to 50, 60 to 65 thousand dollars a year...that's just speckled trout, that's not countin' no redfish or anything else.

I wasn't much of a redfisherman, only when me and Gail first got together. Trammel nettin' in the wintertime, it wasn't nothin' to go out there around Fils de Bruce Island and ride around there and whenever you'd come to one o' them deep points and it'd be real cold and they'd be layin' up there in the sun where you'd see 'em glitterin' and whenever you did, just wrap 'em up with that trammel net and that's it...1,500, 2,000, 2,500 pounds.

But you couldn't do two, three things at one time...if you made $500, $600 a day catchin' speckled trout, that's livin' in the land o' plenty. The creditors are really happy over that there...but then we just started gettin' down, down, down.

Right now, you're lucky to catch $10,000, $12,000 dollars worth o' fish of any kind during the whole year. That's how much it's fell right off.

But there's *plenty* o' fish.

A lot o' people just don't understand what the law people are tryin' to do to the poor people. They just don't understand at all.

But if you explain it to 'em, how they're takin' it all away from you, and you can't make a day's wages, I wouldn't be up there lookin' for your danged job. I'd be down here, I wouldn't ask nobody for nothin'. If you'd just leave me alone, I'd go trout fishin', come back, sell my fish, come home, go to bed and go to sleep, and that's how I'd live the rest o' my life. That's all I'd ever do, because that's a good livin'. But I can't even do that.

Now I got to turn around and horn in on some o' your crabbin'. Now, whenever this crabbin' gets bad I got to go and try to get me a boat for oysters and dredge 'em. I've got to try to accumulate enough money to get in on your oysterin', 'cause that's the onliest thing I know to do, is to make it out o' the water.

I know in my mind just as good as anything in the world that a fish is just like a human being. If you take your boat today and you go fishin' and you get there 30 minutes after he's done eat, you can't make that goddanged fish eat. Just like you, if you set up at my table and you eat you a full course dinner and in about 15 minutes I say, "Come on in here and eat these goddanged groceries," I'm gonna have to beat you or do somethin' to make you eat. Because you're just gonna sit there with your goddanged mouth shut, like that old fish. You *ain't* gonna eat.

But the first thing you know, the man goes home and cries, "Goddamned commercial man done caught 'em all up!"

I believe all this fishin's just about to come to the past. Nobody don't never try to do nothin'.

Now I always did think that I could win a battle, but I've been here twenty some years and I've never actually won a battle yet. Never. In the legislature, if you take one step today, you wake up tomorrow and there's a goddanged law passed that says you got to take that one step back. You're still where you were at. Then they pass another law, you got to take another step back, you go to the legislature, take one step up, and you ain't no goddanged further ahead in them two steps then you was when you started!

You know that Gail's fought a lot in legislature. And Jane has too. But they ain't never won a battle, all they done was just compromised. Every year the sports go up there and they ask for more and more and more and we don't ask for nothin'. So when the "compromise" comes, it always says *we* got to give up.

And it's gettin' down so bad now...I've had as rough a winter this year as I've ever seen in my life. Crabbin', me and Gail *both* wound up makin' anywhere from 15 to 20 dollars a day, every two, three, four days. It's *hard* to make it that way, buddy. But we survived it over.

There ain't but one way we're ever gonna get our redfish back...that's if the senators, or the governor, or the president says you got to open somethin' to help these starvin' people.

They don't care how much the people's hurtin', them White Collars up there, they don't care nothin' about a poor man as long as *they* can get that dollar. But they don't know that whenever we're doomed, we're gonna get them sons o' bitches too. 'Cause we got to have some o' their goddanged groceries off their shelves. It's a comin'. I might not never see it but I'll guarantee you it's comin'. They're just too strict, there's too many laws, and they're too damned greedy.

PART V

Fishery conflicts are caused by a basic animal behavioral instinct, aggressive self-assertion for complete territorial and tribal control, rather than mutual beneficial cooperation and compromise. Each must recognize the other has a right to exist if solutions are to be equated.

—Charles H. Lyles, Director, Mississippi Marine Conservation Commission, in "A Study of the Commercial Finfish in Coastal Louisiana,"1979

CONSERVATION THROUGH USE: RESOURCE MANAGEMENT FOR THE TWENTY-FIRST CENTURY

It sometimes happens that, if the water is too clear, then the fish will no longer dwell there. When there are algae and water plants, fish can safely grow by hiding behind the plants.
—"Hagakure (The Way of the Samurai),"
Tsunetomo Yamamoto, 1659-1719

Each autumn, the bull redfish that swim the Gulf return to the beaches. Every year-class of sexually mature fish is represented, from those on their first spawning run, to those that left the marshes 30 years before. The bulls spawn at night, releasing billions of their eggs into coastal waters. As they hatch, the young make their way toward the marshland nursery where they thrive.

But Louisiana has lost one million acres of these grassy waters since 1900. About 25 square miles of coastal marsh wash away each year. So let's assume that, next fall, only a single acre of marshland remains along the state's entire coastline; and that the carrying capacity—the amount of fish or other wildlife that a given area of habitat can support—is such that this single acre will yield ten mature redfish. And let's assume that the spawners in the Gulf will storm the beaches, as indeed they will.

The millions of small redfish that result must all make their way to this single one-acre nursery where they will be preyed upon by other animals, they will prey upon each other, they will starve, they will be infected by disease and they will be reduced in number until the carrying capacity of this single acre is reached...ten adult redfish.

According to H. Dickson Hoese, professor of fishery biology at the University of Southwestern Louisiana and Chairman of the LDWF Red Drum Working Group, a similar though less exaggerated situation may already exist in Louisiana: "Though it is difficult to prove with the existing data, from observation, I would have to say that the brood stock probably does produce more eggs than the marshland can accommodate."

Hoese added that it is not just the *area* of the marsh that limits the population of redfish and other wetland-dependent species; the *quality* of that marsh, particularly as it relates to salinity, is also vital. "We are seeing a strong correlation between high rainfall and strong year-classes of redfish," he said. "The early 1970s were years of extremely heavy rainfall. During the flood of 1972 the Atchafalaya River almost broke through the Old River structure and changed the course of the lower Mississippi. Two decades later we're still seeing exceptionally strong year-classes of reds that were spawned during those years. The last few years, particularly 1990, have also been very wet and we are seeing that extremely strong year-classes of redfish have been spawned across the Gulf Coast, from the Rio Grande River to Florida."[1]

High rainfall may simply increase the area of shallow-water habitat preferred by redfish, or the species may benefit from the increase in numbers of the blue crab—one of its primary foods—that is typically observed during wetter years. Or, since the redfish is well adapted physiologically to reduced salinities, "the enhanced survival rate during periods of high rainfall may suggest that low salinity marsh is simply a more favorable habitat than high salinity marsh."

If the limiting factor in the size of Louisiana's annual crop of redfish and other wetland-dependent fish is not the amount of seed but rather the size and quality of the "field," can that crop be enlarged?

Certainly. How? By enlarging the size of the field and tending it until the maximum carrying capacity of each acre is attained.

Before considering the role that the fishermen themselves might play in such an ambitious undertaking, let's look more closely at Louisiana's coastal marshes and some of the threats that they face.

Louisiana's coastal marshes are relatively new; they were created within the past 7,000 years. As the currents of the muddy Mississippi River slackened off its mouth, sediments that had been carried from as far north as Canada settled out over the shallow waters of the Continental Shelf to create a delta. And each time the river flooded its banks the receding waters left behind a thin layer of silt over an even vaster area. As muddy flats emerged, grasses took hold and the marsh in that area enlarged for about 1,500 years, until the river's course became long and sinuous and it abruptly changed its route to follow a shorter, more efficient path, where the process was repeated. Some of these former riverbeds are known today as Bayous Lafourche and Teche.

Not long after Europeans settled on the flood plains of the lower Mississippi River and its other distributaries, they demanded protection from the annual flooding. The first earthen levee on the Mississippi was ordered in 1717 to protect New Orleans. By 1939, the U.S. Army Corps of Engineers had built high levees along the

Spoil banks along oilfield canals hinder subsurface drainage, causing the roots of salt-tolerant grasses to become waterlogged. As the grasses die, marshland thins and subsides, creating characteristic open areas that Cajun fishermen call *crevées*, "dead marsh" (see arrows). Although emergent vegetation can seldom re-establish itself in these areas, the canals can be plugged or backfilled to establish a useful nursery-ground environment. Costs are great, however.

river, from Illinois to the river's mouth.

The levees prevented the Mississippi's floodwaters from reaching the surrounding marshes; they were shunted instead over the edge of the Continental Shelf, into the Gulf's depths.

After more than 7,000 years of steady growth, Louisiana began to shrink.

Even in a healthy coastal marsh, a delicate balance exists between the accretion of sediments and the dual assault of rising sea level and subsidence. Deprived of sediments, the marsh becomes extremely vulnerable to these natural destructive forces.

Still, a healthy marsh is surprisingly resilient; each year it lays

Freshwater diversions mimic the flooding of the Mississippi River by introducing sweet, sediment-laden water to the marsh. Recently completed, the Caernarvon structure, downriver from New Orleans, is the first—and smallest of three projected diversions. (Mississippi River is in foreground of photo.) On the same principle but a smaller scale, batteries of six-foot diameter pipes that siphon river water over the levees and into the wetlands are being constructed at many locations.

When heavy winds churn shallow waters, sediments may be trapped in brush fences, eventually giving rise to mud flats which are planted to create new marshland. Reclaiming the land with brush fences is a Dutch technique; Louisiana residents donate their Christmas trees for this purpose.

down a layer of thatch that decomposes into soil, just as a forest's fallen leaves compost into a rich humus. If the sea level changes gradually over centuries, the marsh may adjust, slowly creeping inland if it rises, and invading outward if the sea level falls. Abrupt man-made disturbances, however, can easily outstrip this wetland's ability to regenerate, tipping the balance toward destruction.

As the oil companies suck out oil, gas and brine water locked beneath, subsidence of the marshland accelerates. Up to 10,000 miles of canals have been ripped into the marshes for navigation by shipping interests, to gain access to oil-drilling sites and to run pipelines. As the marsh is dug up it is immediately displaced; as the mud and grasses of the marsh tumble into the deep, straight and ever-widening canals, they are whisked away on falling tides. As the canals are dug, the mud is piled alongside in spoil banks; the spoil banks interrupt the normal sheet flow of tidal waters that carry oxygen and nutrients to the grasses and flush toxins away; vast areas of marshland die and revert to open water.

There are many ways to stem the loss of Louisiana's coastal marshes and to reclaim acreage that has been lost. Few are inexpensive.

In the late 1980s, a miraculous coalition of nearly 100 environmental organizations, recreational and commercial fishing groups, church and community organizations, succeeded in placing the state's first-ever environmental referendum on the ballot. Voters overwhelmingly passed the Coalition to Restore Coastal Louisiana's plan to amend the state's constitution to create a dedicated wetlands trust fund.

Each year, from $5 million to $26 million is diverted from the general fund to help restore the state's coastal wetlands. (The amount varies because it, like much of the state's budget, is based upon petroleum revenues.) Though Louisiana residents sacrifice to save the marsh, costs of the massive projects are overwhelming. In 1990, people in the rest of the country came to their assistance when Congress passed the Coastal Wetlands Planning Protection and Restoration Act, which authorized no less than $35 million per year for the restoration of Louisiana's coastal wetlands.

Why is a vegetated area so much more productive than an identical area of open water? The key to the increased productivity of wetland over open water is surface area.

The surface area within an open pond or bay might be compared to that within a glass of water. Slip a single blade of grass into the glass and its surface area within increases as if a single clump of *Spartina* had emerged within the barren pond. Cram a handful of grass into the glass of water and you have the equivalent of a marsh, comprised of hay-like emergent grasses, or of a pond or bay thick with submerged gardens of widgeon or turtle grasses.

Many wetland plants produce organic matter at two to four times the rate of subsidized agricultural crops like corn or wheat. Living stems and leaves provide surfaces for tiny, down-the-foodchain microbial and algal communities to live upon, and they offer nourishment and refuge from currents and predators for a myriad of larval and adult organisms, including shrimp, fish and crabs.

Most of the net primary production of a coastal marsh is plant matter. Plant detritus—particles of broken or decaying vegetation—are the beginning of the food web for most estuarine-dependent species of fish. Wriggling salt-marsh mosquito larvae, for instance, feed upon decaying plant matter; they in turn are preyed upon by killifish and other minnows that help sustain healthy populations of redfish, trout and flounder, particularly during the winter months. Economically important mullet and menhaden graze directly upon plant detritus; both are also forage fishes for highly valued species further up the food chain.

It all starts with vegetation. In order to boost the productivity of the coastal waters, it is the wetland vegetation that must be "farmed."

But, as noted previously, the farmer's success hinges on his control over his lands. In order to "farm" wetland vegetation which, in this case, means only to restore and to maintain coastal marshes in their best condition, the "farmer" must have control over these wetlands.

Of the 3.5 million acres of Louisiana's coastal marshes, roughly 500,000—less than 15 percent—are publicly owned. When Louisiana became part of the United States in 1812, the federal government gained ownership of the coastal wetlands. After passage of the Federal Swamp Lands Acts in 1849 and 1850, ownership passed from the federal to the state government, and then to private hands in transactions which are said to have often lacked the characteristics of pristine honesty.

Some of these private landowners do an excellent job of maintaining their marshland. Most, however, work their extensive holdings only for the non-renewable resources locked beneath, and do little or nothing to maintain the wetlands at the surface. "No Trespassing" signs proliferate as increasing numbers of landowners block public access to tidal marshes by erecting locked gates across waterways or by the construction of levees.

The Legislature issued ten mariculture permits in the late 1980s. The holder of each may isolate up to 8,000 acres of marshland for the farming of fish.

A bill entered into the 1991 Legislature sought the authorization of an additional 20 permits for operations, each of which was "not to exceed 10,000 acres." Rather than farming domesticated fish in pens, holders of these permits could entrap wild shrimp and crabs as they attempted to migrate from the marshland nursery.

Since 1963, fisheries scientist Dr. William Herke has studied the life histories of the fish and crustaceans that use the coastal marsh as a nursery. His dissertation, completed in 1971, was the first comprehensive study in Louisiana of the marsh's role as nursery.

As he testified against the first incarnation of the "capture culture" bill, Herke stated: "Based on the production per acre we have actually measured, use of 10,000 acres of marsh nursery for mariculture would result each year in the loss of export to the Gulf of 400,000 pounds of shrimp, 720,000 pounds of crabs, and over 1 million pounds of other fishes. This amounts to over 600 million individuals of over 100 different species of fish [including redfish]."

An amended version of the "capture culture" bill passed the Legislature and was stopped only by the veto of Governor Roemer.

Louisiana's coastal marshland is increasingly at risk of being developed, either for oil and natural gas or real estate projects such as recreational communities. Some of the largest holders of coastal wetlands are members of the National Wetlands Coalition, the lobbying group of oil-industry giants, mining companies, and real estate developers at the forefront of the aggressive effort to weaken the U.S. Environmental Protection Agency's ability to protect wetlands from development. During the 1991 congressional session, a congressional staffer said, "They are dominating the discussion of wetlands in the House of Representatives, without a doubt."

The National Wetlands Coalition is chaired by H. Leighton Steward, chairman of the Louisiana Land and Exploration Company, which owns about 650,000 acres of Louisiana's coastal marsh. According to the coalition's chief lobbyist, as interviewed in a June 1991 *Washington Post* article, it would be "unfair" to characterize the

Pointe Fourchon is one of the state's first Florida-style recreational developments; when completed it will contain 128 waterfront "campsites." In the September 4, 1993, *Times-Picayune* real estate supplement, Baton Rouge GCCA chapter president Albert Bankston remarked on the success of his coastal development: "It's fishing more than anything else that attracts people because that's the heart of the best saltwater fishing in Louisiana."

coalition strictly as an industry group. The lobbyist noted that its membership included interests as diverse as the city of Los Angeles and the Audubon Institute: "Audubon Institute president Ron Forman says he agreed to join the coalition when asked to do so by Steward, who sits on the institute's board and whose oil company is one of the institute's corporate benefactors. 'Business needs to be part of the solution,' Forman says."

Clearly, both the marshes and the ability of the public to use them are in jeopardy. Considering that the marsh represents the capital of both the commercial and the recreational fishing industries, what are these two industries doing to protect this capital?

CONSERVATION THROUGH USE:
RESOURCE MANAGEMENT FOR THE TWENTY-FIRST CENTURY

The commercial industry has no mechanism in place by which it can acquire and enhance coastal fishery habitat. The recreational industry has a mechanism in place but makes virtually no use of it.

The Federal Aid in Sport Fish Restoration Act authorized the collection of excise taxes on many items used in sport fishing.[2] At the end of each fiscal year, the Treasury makes these monies available to the U.S. Fish and Wildlife Service, Division of Federal Aid, for allocation to the state fishery agencies. These monies are allocated according to a formula based on the states' relative land and water areas and their number of sport-fishing license holders.

Almost any type of sport fishery restoration, management, or enhancement project is permissible under the law, including land acquisition and habitat enhancement. It is mandated, however, that each state *must* spend at least 10 percent of its annual apportionment on development and maintenance of boating access facilities including boat ramps and lifts, docking and marina facilities, breakwaters, fish cleaning stations, restrooms and parking areas.

The apportionment for Louisiana was $561,702 in 1985, $2.3 million in 1989, and, in 1991, the state qualified for $3 million. Marine coastal states must divide expenditures of program monies between freshwater and saltwater activities based on the number of resident anglers licensed to fish these waters. Eighteen and one-half percent of Louisiana's total Sport Fish Restoration funds are designated for saltwater programs.

According to LDWF Assistant Chief of Freshwater Fisheries Don Lee, who helps administer sport fish restoration monies, "Some of the projects we're undertaking have coastal marsh benefits, such as our inland artificial reef program. But none of the funding's been used for acquisition, except to purchase land for boating access, and that's been very minor."

Fishing hole up for sale

Elmer's Island owner [...]nts to get away

★★★★★ 7/24/88

Two large parcels of marshland are being offered [...] the Slidell office of Gertrude Gardner Inc. at $600 per [...] The first is between Bayou Bonfouca and Highway 11 consisting of approximately 1,090 acres. The other has approximately 10 acres of high ground suitable for a camp on Highway 90 at Salt Bayou with the remaining 805 acres of marshland between Highway 433 and 190 East. The listing agent is Elaine Gordon; check the Slidell Gertrude Gardner ads for more information.

The commercial fishing industry, which benefits most directly from an abundance of coastal marshes, could help fund their acquisition for the public's use.

Some recreational fishing groups do contribute time and money to coastal restoration efforts within the state. The Louisiana Wildlife Federation is a charter member of the Coalition to Restore Coastal Louisiana; several local rod and gun clubs are also members. While the coalition's greatest accomplishment was the passage of the wetland restoration fund, this non-profit group continues to influence wetland legislation at the state and federal level, monitor the expenditure of public monies on restoration projects, and maintain a level of awareness among the state's residents.

Some commercial groups also contribute to the coalition. The Organization of Louisiana Fishermen, for instance, is a founding member. Representing 400 independent businessmen whose incomes depend on the wetlands, the OLF pays a paltry annual membership fee of $150.

CONSERVATION THROUGH USE:
RESOURCE MANAGEMENT FOR THE TWENTY-FIRST CENTURY

Many of the finfishermen, particularly the older ones, lack a formal education. Some would be challenged to spell "habitat." But each one knows that it is going—either behind a fence, under an RV park or out to sea—threatening not only his livelihood but his home.

There is frustration at not being able to do more toward protecting his future. But what to do? After all, his job is only to catch fish. When that job is finished, there's not a lot left, either of money or time.

So how to bring in each fisherman? How to bring in an entire industry? How to get this industry to contribute in direct proportion to the benefit it derives from an abundance of productive and accessible wetlands?

With a severance tax on the product, to be dedicated for the establishment of a fund within the Department of Wildlife and Fisheries, for the acquisition and enhancement of coastal marshland.

Placing a severance tax on the products of Louisiana's commercial fishing industry is not without precedent. Both the oyster and shrimp industries are taxed now, with the proceeds going into the Conservation Fund, for the administration of the Department of Wildlife and Fisheries.

Shrimp have been taxed since 1942. Currently all saltwater shrimp are taxed at the rate of 15 cents per barrel (210 pounds). In 1981, the Legislature imposed a severance tax of 2.5 cents per barrel (three bushels) on oysters harvested from leased areas and a tax of 3 cents a barrel on oysters harvested from natural reefs.

In fiscal year 1991-92, the two industries paid $68,745 in shrimp taxes and $15,022 in oyster taxes, a total of $83,767.

How much could be raised each year by the relatively small inshore finfish industry alone?

Dockside prices for the seven major coastal species—redfish, spotted seatrout, black drum, mullet, pompano, sheepshead and flounder—have steadily increased through the years. The redfish closure in the late 1980s precipitated an increase in demand for previously underutilized species such as black drum and sheepshead, spurring an abrupt rise in the value of these fish, which is unlikely to fall.

With a new quota of redfish reallocated to the commercial industry, with inflation, with improved reporting of landings, with better marketing, and with other states destroying their ability to produce finfish—through either political or ecological means—this industry's contribution to the economy can only grow.

The recreationally sponsored referendum to ban all nets, including shrimp trawls, in Florida is just one example. When the commercial season is closed on Louisiana spotted seatrout, many are imported from Florida. Many of the buttery pompano that diners may still savor at the best New Orleans restaurants originate in Florida waters. If Florida voters can be convinced to destroy that state's inshore commercial industry in 1994, demand for Louisiana-caught pompano, trout and other species will immediately strengthen within both Louisiana and Florida.[3] Indeed, if heavyweight Florida should go the way of Texas and destroy its coastal food-production capability, only three states on the Gulf Coast will remain as producers of coastal fish: relatively small Mississippi, with its 60,000 acres of tidal marsh; Alabama, with less than 30,000 acres; and Louisiana.

Though long-term growth in the *value* of wild-caught fish bodes well for the future, for the purpose of taxation, its importance is secondary to the *volume* of fish produced.

The severance taxes on shrimp and oysters are levied on the volume of product sold, not its price. Not only are seafood prices extremely volatile, fluctuating from day to day, but prices also vary from grade to grade and species to species. Small shrimp may be worth only 50 cents a pound while large shrimp may bring the fisherman more than $3.00; sheepshead currently pay the finfisherman from 25 to 65 cents while pompano may bring him $3.50 per pound.

In the ten years from 1982 through 1991, Louisiana finfishermen landed a total of about 117 million pounds of the seven major species (landings for the last three years exclude redfish). In 1982, fishermen brought in a low of 5.9 million pounds; in 1986, the purse-seine harvest of redfish pushed landings to an all-time high of 18.9 million pounds; in 1991, fishermen landed 9.8 million pounds of trout, drum, flounder, pompano, mullet and sheepshead.

Had a one-cent-per-pound tax been in effect during these years, the seven-species fishery would have generated a total of $1.17 million, an average of nearly $120,000 each year. Landings in 1991 would have raised $98,000.

One cent per pound may appear low, but competition within the industry keeps profit margins slim; one cent is still many times greater than the tax currently applied to a pound of shrimp.

To facilitate collection, shrimp and oyster taxes are paid by the "first buyer," usually the dockside buyer. Should a severance tax meet with resistance from this sector, or otherwise prove too difficult to implement, an annual habitat stamp, to be purchased by the fisherman, could prove a simpler payment vehicle. A $50 stamp purchased by 2,000 finfishermen would raise $100,000 annually; if instituted in conjunction with the severance tax on the dealers, about $200,000 could be raised each year.

One or two hundred thousand dollars for the establishment and maintenance of a coastal habitat acquisition and enhancement program may seem insignificant. Yet once such a program is established, a variety of funding sources could arise. Though the relatively small finfishing industry would pioneer the fund, the benefits could soon become apparent to the state's other commercial fishermen, who land over a billion pounds of seafood each year.

When construction is deemed "necessary" in wetlands, a mitigation project by the developer is frequently required. These are often of dubious value. A cash deposit into the fund to acquire coastal marshland for the public's use, or for the purchase of equipment, such as small draglines, to maintain this marshland, might prove a wiser investment. Perhaps residents of wetland-displacing coastal developments should be assessed an annual fee as restitution for the loss to the state's economy they cause by permanently diminishing the production of commercially and recreationally important species.

Genuine conservation, environmental and habitat-oriented sportsmen's groups might contribute to such a fund, as well. After all, areas of intensively managed brackish marsh with a diversified habitat ranging from shallow ponds planted with widgeon grass, to the deep pockets created by the plugging of obsolete canals, will prove attractive to wildlife other than fish. Perhaps the commercial sector's contribution could even be matched by one from the "Sport Fish Restoration" fund.

Taxing any industry is seldom easy; the commercial fishing industry is a particular challenge. By definition, its participants are traditional to the point of reactionary. After decades of attack, they may perceive a tax as simply one more strategy to further erode their financial standing prior to yet another devious attempt to drive them out of business forever.

What collateral gesture could be offered? How to sweeten the deal? A suggestion comes from Chesapeake Bay:

Three seasons have opened and closed since Maryland reopened its striped bass fishery in 1990. In each, the fish were shared evenly among commercial fishermen and consumers (42.5 percent), and private recreational fishermen (42.5 percent). The charter industry received the remaining 15 percent.

Peter Jensen, director of fisheries at Maryland Department of Natural Resources, considers the reopening of the Maryland striped bass fishery under a fixed allocation a real success story:

> We think it's a model program. We've just about negated the gamefish argument up here. We testified against making the striped bass a gamefish in the Legislature. If one user group were destroying another one, we'd have to be against it but, with a fixed allocation, we can't demonstrate that. With an equitable distribution we showed that everyone in the state derives the maximum benefit from this publicly owned resource. And the Legislature agreed.
>
> There are still some holdouts for gamefish—a lot of that is coming from down in your part of the country. Texas. But, basically, we feel that gamefish is obsolete.
>
> How did we determine the ratio? We formed a Striped Bass Advisory Board that included members from each user group. When we looked at the historical data, it appeared that the commercials had harvested the majority of the fish. But that's because we only have good landings data on that sector. If you go back and try to reconstruct the recreational landings, the situation changes.

The advisory board tried to set an allocation but had difficulty arriving at a consensus. The recreationals said, "Hey, we think striped bass should be a gamefish and the commercials should be excluded no matter what." The commercials said, "Heck, if the recreationals are blaming us for catching 80 percent of the stripers in the past, then we should have 80 percent of the allocation." And the guides and charterboat fishermen said, "We're in this thing too, we should get a third."

This went on and on at each meeting until the last, when they still couldn't agree on an allocation. So we [Maryland DNR] just said, "OK, that's it. The commercials and the recreationals each get half." And then we took 7.5 percent from each group and gave them to the charterboats.

The allocation can be altered by consensus of the Striped Bass Advisory Board. We ask them each year, "Do you want to change it?" Philosophically, the recreational and the charterboat industries still think striped bass should be a gamefish, but the consensus is, "No, don't change it, it's working."

All three groups agree that the fixed allocation is fair. It gives everybody the opportunity to go fishing; one group can't catch the other's fish. Once we say, "Here are the allocations," each group can run their own fishery, they can change anything they want without somebody else telling them how to catch their fish.

For instance, we give each group a season, but if they catch their quota before their season is over, we have to shut them down. Now a mortal sin for the charterboat captains is to have to tell parties they've booked, "No, we can't take you fishing after all. Here's your money back." So the charter industry can regulate itself to decide how to make their share last.

The commercials are the most highly regulated, and at first they really grumbled because we made each one tag his fish. They didn't like it but then they learned that if each fisherman had so many tags, it was like he owned that many fish. So it wasn't like fishing under a single industry-wide quota where everybody tries to catch as many fish as possible as fast as they can, which puts a lot of fish on the market at one time and brings down the price. The fishermen can take their time, make it stretch and get more for their fish.

And, if the population data warrants it, the total allowable catch can be raised. We have increased it nearly each year. In the first season the TAC was 750,000 pounds, in the second 1.1 million, and for the third, 1.6 million. For the fourth year, at the request of the Atlantic States Marine Fisheries Commission, we have agreed to hold to 1.6 million, while different analyses and population estimates are conducted.

The recreational industry has spent a fortune on its campaigns to make the striped bass a gamefish. And the commercials have been forced to spend a lot of cash, and lose a lot of productive fishing time, fighting them off. Under a fixed allocation, are these groups in Maryland redirecting their resources to more positive ends?

"If you mean, are the user groups actually doing something to help the fish, I'd have to say no, we're not seeing that yet," Jensen said. "What we do see is a reallocation of their time. Now they don't have to cover the Legislature, lobbying all its members. All the action takes place in the meetings of the Striped Bass Advisory Board where we're getting outstanding attendance. That's where all the decisions are made now."

Recreational industry groups on the Gulf Coast have raised millions of dollars—and are in the process of raising millions more—to be spent on their emotional anti-commercial campaigns that promise immediate gain to their supporters. If, instead, they are forced to share the fish equitably, will these groups redirect these same energies to a long-term campaign against the many threats to fishery habitat?

Regardless of how that question is answered, the commercial industry will no longer be forced to ward off their aggressive advances. The "peace dividend," the resources that they will no longer have to expend on non-productive political battles, will be freed for investment in helping the fish themselves.

Determining a TAC for each of the most hotly contested species of fish and dividing it equitably offers many benefits.

If, for instance, LDWF biologists determine that there are 5 million trout that can be caught in a year, recreational fishermen would be permitted to retain 2.5 million fish. Consumers would also be able to dine on their 2.5 million trout, thanks to the harvest of the commercial fishermen. Since commercially caught trout average two pounds apiece, the commercial harvest would weigh a total of 5 million pounds. At $1.50 per pound, fishermen would pump $7.5 million into their coastal economies as well as generate $50,000 for the marshland fund.

As lost acreage is regained and fishery harvests increase, the average annual TAC is raised.

If some natural catastrophe dictates a reduction in harvest, all user groups are cut, and when fishery populations rebound, everyone's share is increased.

Ironically, sharing the fish evenly among commercial and recreational fishermen assures that the quality of the Louisiana sportsman's angling experience is maintained.

If commercial fishing is eliminated, local anglers can be induced to go to "catch and release." But if netters retain an allocation of fish that they can sell to consumers to eat, anglers will not give up their right to take home some fish. By keeping the commercial fisherman and the consumer locked into the equation, and staving off "catch and release" for local anglers, a fixed allocation limits the growth of the crassly commercial recreational industry which has been overpromoted and overdeveloped in other coastal states.

In the past, when recreational boosters wanted more fish to fuel development, they took them from commercial fishermen and consumers under the guise of "conservation." Under a 50/50 allocation, they will be forced to take them outright from the local sport fishermen: "Uh, fellas, we can't let you take any more fish home because, uh, we need them for these out-of-state fat-cats who spend so much more money than you do."

When the fish are divided equitably between the recreational and the commercial industries, only one way remains for them both to increase the total number of fish they can use, and that's the good old-fashioned way—earn them.

Until these two giants shift the scene of their battlefield from the state legislatures, the halls of Congress and the courtrooms, out onto the wetland habitat of the fish over which they fight, no one will win.

APPENDIX

NOTES

TOOLS OF THE TRADE

BIBLIOGRAPHY & ADDITIONAL INFORMATION

NOTES

PREFACE

[1] Literally, a fisherman who employs a trammel net, the three-layered net known to French-speaking fishermen as a *"tramail."* For a further description of this, and other types of nets mentioned in "Wetland Riders," the reader is directed to the Appendix: "Tools of the Trade."

PART I

TEXAS GAMEFISH FIGHT

[1] Texas is the only Gulf state that reported significant catches of redfish by trotline. A trotline is comprised of a main line to which is attached a series of baited hooks.

[2] Ten bills that regulated fishing gear, methods and harvests of red drum and spotted seatrout were introduced into the Texas Legislature between 1977 and 1981. Between 1975 and 1980, the Texas Parks and Wildlife Commission passed 22 regulatory-powers acts regulating the time, means, manners and places where it was lawful to take or possess red drum or spotted seatrout.

[3] Ducks Unlimited, a non-profit national organization—primarily of duck hunters—is dedicated to the preservation of the continent's waterfowl. "DU," however, concentrates its efforts on habitat preservation.

[4] According to James Presley's "A Saga of Wealth," Fondren's grandfather was one of the original founders and a president of Humble Oil and Refining Company. In 1972, Standard Oil of New Jersey merged with Humble Oil in Houston to form EXXON.

At this writing, Fondren still leads the Coastal Conservation Association, parent organization of GCCA.

[5] Perry Richardson Bass was left a fortune by his uncle, Fort Worth "billion-dollar bachelor" Sid Richardson, who had made his fortune wildcatting in Texas oilfields during the 1920s and '30s. Said to have been the first billionaire west of the Mississippi River, Richardson died in 1959, when Bass took over as chairman of Sid Richardson Carbon & Gas. In 1960, he, with his sons, founded Bass Brothers Enterprises. Interests of the multibillion dollar conglomerate include oil, securities and real estate holdings that range from luxury hotels in downtown Fort Worth to some of the largest developments in Florida, including nearly 20 percent of Disney. Bass continues to support GCCA financially.

[6] The economic argument had been used as early as the 1930s on the West Coast, when California sport fishermen wrested the striped bass from commercial fishermen.

Native to the East Coast, the striped bass was introduced to California waters late in the nineteenth century. Fish culturist Livingston Stone caught 162 striped bass in the Navesink River in New Jersey, loaded them onto a railroad car and hauled them across the country in 1879. He dumped the 132 stripers that survived the trip into the Carquinez Strait at Martinez, upstream of Northern California's San Pablo Bay. Three years later, J.G. Woodbury released 300 more New Jersey striped bass into lower Suisun Bay, three miles above Martinez.

The introductions proved extremely successful; by 1888, thousands of California striped bass were displayed in San Francisco markets. In 1899, a mere 20 years after the first introduction, commercial fishermen landed over 1.2 million pounds of stripers; landings regularly exceeded 1 million pounds until 1915. After 1915, regulations became progressively more restrictive and the annual commercial catch dropped below 1 million pounds.

In 1935, recreational interests convinced the Legislature to take the species off the market. The West Coast sport fishermen's success in monopolizing the striped bass encouraged sport fishermen in Texas to try the same thing with their own favorite sport fish—the redfish.

What follows is a copy of a 1940 letter authored by a San Francisco attorney who was instrumental in the fight to gain gamefish status for California's striped bass. Written in response to a South Texas attorney's request for a blueprint of the strategy employed by the California anglers, the letter contains just that.

Robert L. Mann
Attorney at Law
1020 DeYoung Building
690 Market Street
San Francisco, California

June 12, 1940

John R. Beasley, Esq.
c/o Beasley & Beasley
Attorneys at Law
Beeville, Texas

Dear Sir:

Your letter dated June 4, 1940, to the Associated Sportsmen of California has been turned over to me for reply as the Chairman of the Public Relations Committee of that organization.

I will state that my connection with the Associated Sportsmen dates from shortly after its organization as an unincorporated association on February 19, 1925. I served as Chairman of the Public Relations Committee, also on the Legislative Committee, also during three terms as President and on retiring from the Presidency, I have served as Chairman of the Engineering Committee, and now I am back at my original job of the Public Relations Committee.

Some years ago as an attorney I incorporated the association, the members being the clubs affiliated with the organization. At the present time we have about 80 clubs as members, but our influence has broadened through alliance made with several other sportsmen's councils, likewise consisting of groups of clubs. This confederated organization is known as the California Sportsmen's Council and the total membership of the federation has been computed recently as about 60,000 members.

Commencing with the Legislature of 1927 (our Legislature meets regularly every two years) there has been a striped bass problem. We have carried on the battle gaining a little bit at a time until finally we have reached the point where it is unlawful to buy or sell striped bass, or even to net them, with one exception, that is to say, in order not to cripple the shad industry it is provided that during the three months shad season, striped bass incidentally taken in shad nets while lawfully fishing for shad, must be turned over to public institutions.

The successive steps run something like this: In one Legislature we managed to reserve from commercial fishing, three sloughs in the vicinity of Stockton; one of them was named Whiskey Slough and I have forgotten the names of the other two, very possibly because it was easier to remember the name Whiskey Slough. The next step accomplished at the next session of the Legislature was to reserve from commercial fishing some 50 square miles of mud flats in San Pablo Bay. The session of the Legislature at which this was accomplished was particularly hot. The battle was in the Assembly and the Assembly Committee on Fish and Game was dominated by the commercial fishing interests. Under a rule existing in the Legislature the Committee may be overruled on a petition signed by a majority of the Assembly. Such a petition was circulated and by the time 35 signatures were obtained (the necessary number being 41 or a majority) the commercial fishing interests capitulated and the compromise was reached resulting in an agreement to reserve the 50 square miles of mud flats from commercial fishing.

The next step occurring at the next session of the Legislature was to declare a closed commercial season on striped bass, except during the three months of the shad season, during which striped bass taken in shad nets was permitted to be sold.

The last and final step was to prohibit entirely the sale of striped bass, but still the concession had to be made that the striped bass incidentally taken with shad must be delivered to public institutes.

An abuse and a leak has crept in under this system. In the days when the striped bass was on the market, the fisherman in the boat received no more than 4 cents or 5 cents a pound for his fish, and the retail price to the customer was no more than 6 cents or 7 cents a pound. For some four or five years a secret arrangement has been in vogue of making a profit to somebody on the striped bass incidentally taken. A change in the administration has enabled us to investigate this and a scandal has been brought to light, namely, that it is costing these public institutions according to a contract approved by the State Administration, 12 1/2 cents a pound for fish delivered to them under the incidental clause. We have made our protest to the Commission and have learned that the present contract at this outrageous figure expired May 15 of this year, and before any new contract for the transportation, cleaning or icing of the fish for such delivery is made, the new administration has promised us that we will be given a hearing and the right to protest and urge that the law be enforced.

In as much as the new administration is a Democratic administration and more or less anxious to point out the errors of the previous Republican administration, we have great hopes of success when and if any new contract is proposed.

One of the points on which we have concentrated by way of argument is the showing of the amount of money spent by anglers in pursuit of their sport. A certain sportsmen's organization sometime ago by an extensive survey among its members, developed the fact that each angler spends yearly in the pursuit of his sport an average of $115.00. When this amount was multiplied by the number of striped bass anglers in the state, estimated to be in the neighborhood of 100,000, the resulting figure was extremely impressive and indicated the immense amount of money that was put in circulation in the channels of trade by the angler in the pursuit of his sport. This figure of $115.00 did not include automobiles, gas or oil, or gas or oil used in the operation of automobiles in traveling to or from the fishing grounds.

Another angle of investigation was the extensive development of the bait dealer's business, that is to say, those who supplied bait to the striped bass anglers, and the figures at our command indicate that the business of supplying sardines to the striped bass anglers alone, averaged about $3,000,000 per year. Against these figures the amounts received by the commercial fisherman for the sale of striped bass when it was on the market represented a trifling fraction, and we were able to point out that the equipment of the commercial fisherman, that is to say, the boats used by him in commercial fishing were all capable of being used as sport fishing boats and the commercial fishermen themselves could earn better money acting as guides for the anglers and handling the commercial boats as sport fishing equipment.

You are in error about the Fish and Game Commission being against us. During my connection with the fight we at all times received the active cooperation of Mr. I. Zellerbach who served on the Commission during all the years of the fight to take the striped bass off the market and his influence was sufficient to secure at least a passive support from the other members of the Commission. It is true, however, that the Commercial Fisheries Department of the employees of the Commission appears to have been against us by various recommendations which sounded sincere, but in reality were not. For instance, the Commercial Fisheries Department has at all times advocated a closed season for spawning purposes. This sounded alright but as a matter of fact since the striped bass is migratory and travels between the salt water of the ocean and the fresh water of the rivers, some group of sportsmen would be bound to suffer through the infusion of a closed season, and in consequence the sportsmen would be disunited and fight against each other, which was just the object the commercial fishermen had in mind.

To the argument that it was wrong to take fish during the spawning season, we were able to point out the striped bass was extremely prolific and able to maintain itself without a closed season for spawning and we were able to prove the striped bass were on the increase, through the experts of the Fish and Game Commission. That is to say, we were able to prove that after the stopping of commercial fishing the striped bass that had been very much depleted began to increase materially.

We also called attention to the point that in the case of salt water fish or anadromous fish, the fact that spawn fish were taken constituted no objection; that the very reason that the fish were available was because they had gone out of salt water to spawn. For instance, we pointed out the salmon could be caught because it came into the rivers to spawn. Likewise, the shad, the smelts and the herring, and also the steelhead in the winter season, and therefore, we took the position that conservation should be directed toward the matter of size and number rather than in the case of the striped bass, to proceed on the basis of a closed season for spawning.

The result of our fight is that we are able to offer striped bass fishing whether in the ocean, the bay or the rivers all the year round, provided the fish happen to be present at the time and place that they are sought. Striped bass under twelve inches are not permitted to be caught. A number of clubs have urged that this size limit be increased to sixteen inches, but there is a certain conservative element among us that are afraid of such an increase in the length limit, and recommend that the sixteen inch limit be handled as an individual proposition by the club itself, rather than by making it into law.

We have been more or less interested in the thought that the channel bass [redfish] might be transplanted out here but the scientists of the Commission assure us that our water is too cold. You are very fortunate in having the channel bass there and from all accounts it is a sporting fish equally as good as the striped bass, and our sympathies are certainly with you in any effort that you may make to have the channel bass recognized as an exclusively sporting fish and taken off the market.

By the way, there is absolutely only one way to make it a sporting fish and that is to make its sale unlawful without exception.

We hope that you may be successful, because any progress made by sportsmen anywhere serves as a precedent for their brothers in other portions of the country and helps the cause to that extent.

With best wishes, I am

Yours very truly,

/s/Robert L. Mann
Robert L. Mann, Chairman
Public Relations Committee
Associated Sportsmen of California

Less than 60 years after California sport fishermen grabbed the striped bass, how are the fish doing? "They're doing poorly," said Zeke Grader, executive director of the Pacific Coast Federation of Fishermen's Associations, which represents most of California's commercial fishermen. "The fishery is very poor right now. There have been a lot of restrictions placed on the sport fishery."

Recreational fishermen are limited to two fish per day, which must be at least 18 inches in length. According to a California Department of Fish and Game publication, the number of legal-sized adult striped bass fell to a record low of approximately 500,000 fish in 1990. That estimate represents a decline from about 1 million bass in the 1980s, 1.7 million in the early 1970s, and 3 million in the early 1960s.

Striped bass anglers are required to purchase a striped bass stamp, with revenues to be spent on the "preservation and enhancement" of that species in California. "Originally, they sold about 550,000 stamps a year," said David Kohlhorst, fishery biologist with the California Department of Fish and Game. "But presently the sales are smaller than that, maybe 400,000 or 450,000. The sales probably came down because, in general, the fishing's not good.

"The population is depressed from what it was, say, 20 years ago, in large part because of environmental changes that have occurred as a result of exporting a large volume of fresh water from the estuary," said Kohlhorst.

Although the transplanted striped bass extended its range along the Pacific Coast from Los Angeles, California, to the Columbia River in Washington, its center of abundance—and principal spawning ground—lies in the San Francisco Bay area, particularly the vast delta formed at the confluence of the state's two primary river systems—the Sacramento and the San Joaquin. By 1980, more than 62 percent of the annual historic freshwater inflows to San Francisco Bay had been diverted for agriculture in the arid Central Valley and for industrial and municipal uses in southern California. By the year 2000, the amount is projected to increase to 71 percent.

"A lot of water is being taken from the system and a lot of little bass are going with it. That, as a result, is reducing recruitment to the population," said Kohlhorst.

In addition to causing the death of small striped bass outright, the diversion of freshwater inflow is causing large-scale environmental changes that are proving disastrous to the striper and other species of fish.

"The striper spawns in waters that are essentially fresh, but as they keep drying the rivers up, we're getting greater and greater saltwater intrusion up into the delta," said Zeke Grader. "And it's reduced the amount of spawning area for the striped bass. Also, striped bass eggs float on the current, and when you don't have any current, they sink to the bottom and they die. And so we've had this loss of current plus the loss of a vast area that they once spawned in. And, of course, we in California have allowed more than 90 percent of our coastal wetlands to be drained and filled for development. And many of the wetlands in the Central Valley have also been filled in which, in turn, can affect our fish.

"It's mostly been habitat damage that has caused the reduction in the striped bass. And, arguably, had there been a commercial fishery through the recent years, there might have been more pressure brought to bear than there was to correct some of these habitat problems. And I think that's one of the reasons now where you'll see sports fishermen in this state—at least the wiser ones, the groups that have some credibility—most of the time what they're doing is working in alliances with commercial fishermen. As opposed to just trying to go out and eliminate commercial fisheries or make fish gamefish. Because I think they recognize fairly well that they themselves don't have that much clout and by adding the commercial fisheries—sort of that consumer angle, and the 'working stiff on the dock'—to the mix, it makes for a stronger alliance to protect the fish."

[7] Bass was later voted chairman of the commission, and John Green and Louis Stumberg were replaced by oilman Edwin Cox, Jr. of Dallas and W.B. Osborn, Jr. of Santa Elena. In February of 1981, Gov. William Clements filled the seats of outgoing Joe Fulton of Lubbock and J. Pearce Johnson of Austin by appointing Dallas sportsman and lawyer William O. Braecklein, and sportsman William Wheless III, described in a *Houston Post* article as "a third-generation Houstonian with bank accounts full of old money."

[8] One estimate is that recreational interests spent at least $2 million and commercial interests approximately $300,000.

[9] There was no love lost between commercial fishermen and Clements, whose Dallas company SEDCO had furnished the rig IXTOC No. 1, the Mexican test well that blew out on June 3, 1979, triggering the world's largest oil spill up to that time. The blazing IXTOC spewed up to 30,000 barrels of oil a day into the Bay of Campeche, until it was capped more than nine months—and 130 million gallons—later. A slick of crude began to coat the barrier islands of the South Texas coast by mid-August,

and continued to wash ashore for nearly a year, ultimately affecting 162 miles of beach and a vast area of some of the world's richest shrimping and finfishing grounds. South Texas fishermen joined in a $310 million lawsuit against the governor's company.

[10]National Oceanic and Atmospheric Administration is the U.S. Department of Commerce agency that administers the National Marine Fisheries Service.

[11]A review of the commercial landings since 1887 reveals the extreme fluctuations in population that are characteristic of an estuarine species, whose rate of success of each annual spawn depends upon an intricate balance of conditions including rainfall, salinity, water temperature and cleanliness, available nutrients, wind and currents.

[12]To avoid "duplication," NMFS later discontinued its survey in Texas.

[13]Redfish and trout made up 40 percent to 50 percent of the volume of all edible saltwater *finfish* landed in Texas, including offshore species such as red snapper. The two species acounted for at least 50 percent of the value of the entire Texas *finfish* industry.

TEXAS GAMEFISH BLUES

[1] More than three years later, the "distinction" was still not clear to those in the popular press: "A Texas fish study showed that illegal netters are the largest harvesters of redfish, killing more than 40 percent of a species whose population has already collapsed from overfishing," wrote *National Geographic* reporter Constance J. Poten in her September 1991 article, "A Shameful Harvest."

BILLY PRAKER

[1] A net is comprised of uniform meshes, the sizes of which are expressed either as "bar" or "stretched." A two-inch mesh, "bar," is a square, each side of which is two inches long. By stretching a bar mesh as far as possible, its size is always doubled, in this case to four inches, "stretched." All mesh sizes cited in this book are the stretched mesh size.

PART II

LOUISIANA REDFISH FIGHT I

[1] Fishery resources in federal waters are managed by eight regional management councils within the National Marine Fisheries Service, NOAA, U.S. Department of Commerce. Voting members may include recreational and commercial fishermen, seafood processors, environmentalists, scientists, consumers and representatives of each state fisheries agency within the council's jurisdiction. The Gulf of Mexico Fishery Management Council, responsible for management of marine resources in Gulf waters off Texas, Louisiana, Alabama, Mississippi and the west coast of Florida, contains 17 voting members, 11 of whom are politically appointed. They are nominated by the state governors and appointed by the secretary of commerce for a term of three years.

[2] Fueled by its success in obtaining gamefish status for redfish and speckled trout in Texas, GCCA moved steadily eastward across the Gulf, arriving in Louisiana in

NOTES

1983 and Florida in 1985. In 1985, the Houston-based GCCA changed its name to the Coastal Conservation Association and created a national board of trustees to "coordinate the interaction between states and to address national issues," thereby posturing itself to expand along both the Atlantic and Pacific seaboards.

[3] Connecticut industrialist Baldrige had managed George Bush's campaign against Ronald Reagan in that state's 1980 presidential primary; as president, Reagan appointed him secretary of commerce. Upon Baldrige's death in 1989, President George Bush appointed Houston oilman Robert Mosbacher to the position.

[4] A federal law passed in 1976 that established federal jurisdiction over all waters seaward of the states' coastal waters (usually 3 miles but 9 miles off Texas and the west coast of Florida), to a distance of 200 nautical miles. It also created the regional councils and set policy for them to follow as they managed the fisheries within these waters. Formally known as the Fishery Conservation and Management Act, it is commonly referred to as the Magnuson Act, after a chief sponsor, Sen. Warren Magnuson of Washington.

LOUISIANA REDFISH BLUES

[1] Most professional fishermen purchase these components and, to avoid a hanging fee of about $1.50 per yard, "hang in" their own nets. After stringing corks and leads on separate ropes, the fisherman stretches the ropes between two posts and, using a netting needle filled with twine, ties on the meshes of the webbing.

[2] A bill passed during the 1993 legislative session added a seat for a manufacturer or wholesaler of fishing tackle.

LOUISIANA REDFISH FIGHT II

[1] Scarcely an inch away from this passage, an announcement for one of GCCA's annual banquets did little to dispel the group's "undeserved" image:

"The Delta Chapter of the Louisiana Gulf Coast Conservation Association will hold its annual fund-raising banquet and auction Thursday at the Southern Yacht Club. Cocktails will be served at 5:30 p.m., dinner follows at 7:30 p.m. Tickets are $100 per person."

[2] Later in the year, at election time, Garrity did not survive the primaries, losing his seat—much to his chagrin—to a "housewife."

[3] The severe freeze of December 1989 had killed many of the trout overwintering in the shallow estuary. Fishermen recall at least one, often two, fish-killing freezes each decade within memory, with the last in 1983. Fishermen and biologists have learned that post-freeze spawns of estuarine-dependent species are often immensely successful, rapidly filling the vacuum created by such an event. This phenomenon, referred to as "compensatory recruitment," may result from the absence of competition or predators in the post-freeze marsh. Regardless of how they arise, fishermen anticipate these bumper crops of trout as compensation for having endured the lean times immediately after the freeze. The recreationists, on the other hand, exploited the poor fishing following the 1989 freeze as further justification for the curtailment

of commercial fishing. Indeed, some Louisiana Wildlife and Fisheries commissioners called for lowered limits or closures on both the commercial and recreational fisheries after that freeze. When LDWF biologists stated that such measures were unnecessary, biologists from Texas Parks and Wildlife were brought in to testify in support of such restrictions.

The prediction by LDWF biologists that trout fishing would improve dramatically—without further restrictions—proved correct.

SPOTTED SEATROUT

[1] In the early nineteenth century, many fishermen from the coast of what would become Yugoslavia fled from the political instability of Austrian-controlled Dalmatia, and the overfished waters of the Adriatic. The Dalmatians settled first in port cities on the East Coast but, by the 1820s and 1830s, they had worked their way down to the Gulf Coast. The Slavs first worked the many natural oyster reefs and later pioneered the cultivated oyster industry.

CLAUDE McCALL

[1] The snook is a tropical species that occurs in South Texas and Florida. Never extremely abundant in Texas, the snook supported a major commercial fishery in Florida. In 1952, for instance, fishermen working with runaround gill nets and haul seines landed 156,000 pounds on Florida's east coast and 433,000 pounds on the west coast. Recreational interests in Florida rendered the species off-limits to the public in 1958 by having it declared a gamefish. Bob Jones, executive director of the Southeastern Fisheries Association was there:

"The snook was in trouble. It was all habitat-related but, of course, we got the blame. I thought it was mosquito spray—we can't have a Yankee gettin' bit by a mosquito, you know. I've been sprayed by that stuff and it irritates the skin. But when we complained, they told us that we were just thin-skinned, which in my case is certainly not an accurate assessment!

"Anyway, in those days, it was the Florida Wildlife Federation, the Isaac Walton League. We used to meet regularly and work together to fight things like bulkheads and other habitat stuff. I still have a plaque—it shows a sportsman and a commercial man in his slicker suit....The deal we cut with them, they said that if we gave them the snook, they would never come back and try to take anything else. And they meant it. It worked for a long time, until the 'Moderns' came into it."

PART III

FRANK RANDO

[1] Buffalofish are related to the true carps which, with their deep bodies and large scales, they resemble. The name comes from the bull-like hump which develops behind the head in large specimens. The buffalofish rarely bites a hook and is therefore not an important recreational species. Each year, Louisiana commercial fishermen

harvest up to 5 million pounds of buffalofish from the state's freshwater rivers, lakes and swamps. Although some Louisiana buffalo are sold in local retail markets, the majority end up in urban ethnic markets in Houston, Memphis, Chicago and New York; many are shipped to California where demand is strong among Orientals.

PART IV

THE "CON" IN CONSERVATION

[1] Bulkheads are walls that are built to stabilize shorelines, usually preceding development. Bulkheads bar the entrance of tidal waters—and marine organisms—to coastal wetlands. Often made of treated lumber, they may also leach toxic creosote into the water.

[2] The bill received little support. Rep. Frank Pallone of New Jersey sponsored a similar bill in the 1993 U.S. Congress but it, too, failed to make it out of the House Merchant Marine and Fisheries Committee.

[3] When they outlawed the commercial harvest of ducks, recreationals began the erosion of the financial status of those whose livelihoods stemmed directly from the wetlands. The initiative to ban market hunting was remarkably similar to current efforts to ban commercial fishing. According to *Forest and Stream* editor George Bird Grinnell, writing 17 years before the ban in his 1901 book, "American Duck Shooting," not only were recreationals unwilling to address the main reasons for the species' decline but the initiative was advocated by a national "sporting" magazine:

> Gunning for the market occupies many men during the winter, and the occasional great rewards received for a day's work in the blind or the battery leads many to make a serious business of it...we knew of a gunner who in January, 1900, killed $130 worth of birds in a day, and of another who in February, 1899, killed $206 worth in one day....The constant decrease of the number of our wildfowl is a subject of frequent complaint by [sport] gunners whose memory goes back twenty-five or thirty years. They compare the scarcity of to-day with the abundance of old times, and continually inquire why it is that the birds are growing yearly less and less in number.
>
> Various explanations of the change are given. The blame is laid on the market-shooter, on the supposed destruction of birds and eggs on the northern breeding grounds [by Native Americans], and on supposed changes in the lines of flight by the migratory birds, but most gunners are unwilling to accept the logic of events and to acknowledge that the principal cause of the lessened number of the fowl lies with the gunners themselves, and is an inevitable accompaniment of civilization, not to be changed except by radical measures. Many of the men, no doubt, merely repeat what they have heard other people say, but there are others who advance these remote causes through pure selfishness, realizing that if they admit the enormous

destruction by [sport] gunners they must logically advocate the abridgment of the shooting season, which means the abolition of spring shooting.

The action, first advocated years ago by *Forest and Stream*, and since then made law in a number of States, that the sale of game should be forbidden, is a long step in the right direction. This would put an end to shooting for the market, and would thus cut off one serious cause of the destruction of fowl. If such a law should meet with general favor, if the shooting after the 1st of January or 1st of February should be forbidden, if the bags should be limited to twenty-five or thirty birds a day, new conditions would soon greet the gunner, and birds might once again be seen on their old feeding grounds, in something like their old-time plenty.

THE RECREATIONAL FISHING INDUSTRY: SOMETHING OF VALUE?

[1] Even so, his overhead is high. If, for instance, the weather allows the finfisherman to work 200 days a year, and he catches an average of $150 worth of fish each day, he will gross $30,000. With conservative daily expenses of $45, he will spend $9,000. When these expenses are subtracted from the $30,000 worth of fish that he has put onto the market, he is left with $21,000. After paying his deckhand one-third, he is down to $14,000, out of which must come his repairs as well as his capital expenses such as boats, motors and nets. With the remainder he must support his family which he accomplishes by retaining some of his catch for home consumption, and by utilizing unfishable days to perform his own maintenance on boat, vehicle and home. With his self-image reinforced more by his ability to catch fish than by the accumulation of material goods, the self-reliant finfisherman is content to "just make a livin'."

[2] Studies performed by neutral economists tell a different story. In his "Economics Guide to Allocation of Fish Stocks between Commercial and Recreational Fisheries," NMFS economist Steven Edwards suggests that the economic value of a given amount of fish can be maximized by allocating slightly more than 50 percent to the commercial sector. In a letter accompanying his report, Edwards stated: "It is important that you understand my neutrality on the commercial-recreational allocation issue. My professional concern is that economics not be misused by constituents to sequester resources at the expense of the nation."

[3] Only a few brands of sport-fishing boats are manufactured within Louisiana; a visit to any major sporting goods store reveals that, with the exception of some artificial baits, virtually none of the fishing reels, rods, tackle boxes and other types of sport-fishing gear are manufactured in-state. "If everybody just sport fished, all the dollars would leak out of the state in no time," stated LSU economist Ken Roberts, explaining that "leakage" occurs when money is spent on goods that are not manufactured or grown in the immediate area.

[4] Of the 7,300 anglers that signed up for the event, 3,100 were already GCCA members. According to an article in GCCA's *Tide*, "The remaining 4,200 automatically became new members and now receive *Tide* magazine."

NOTES

[5] In addition to shortened seasons and sharply reduced bag limits, a deepening recession also cut into the sportsmen's recreational dollars.

IT'S NOT ME, IT'S HIM!

[1] Most outdoor columnists are members of both state and national outdoor writers associations. According to its membership literature, "The Louisiana Outdoor Writers Association is an organization composed of some 80 or 90 members, consisting of active outdoor communicators and supporting members (Browning, Stren, Berkley, etc.)."

The national Outdoor Writers Association of America "maintains close contacts with more than 300 outdoor-oriented firms and organizations which joined the association as supporting members." The first canon in the code of ethics of the OWAA reads, "In dealing with the public, we shall strive for honesty, accuracy and truth at all times. Accuracy in reporting, fairness in controversy and objectivity will be our first goals. Facts and opinion will be separate, clearly indicated and attributed."

[2] In 1992, *Florida Sportsman* publisher Karl Wickstrom initiated a statewide campaign to ban most nets—including shrimp trawls—from Florida waters. The "BAN THE NETS! Save Our Sealife" campaign—represented by a logo with a fish, a sea turtle and a porpoise all entangled in net webbing—is coordinated by a "conservation coalition" that includes *Florida Sportsman*, the Florida Conservation Association, Florida Wildlife Federation, Florida League of Anglers and the Florida Coalition of Fishing Clubs. The coalition seeks to gather 575,000 signatures needed to place the constitutional amendment to ban netting on the November 1994 ballot.

According to Wickstrom, writing in his September, 1992, issue:

> Sportfishing conservationists are expected to kick off a major drive for a constitutional amendment...A petition drive is considered likely to be started before year's end in hopes that the issue will go on the general election ballot in two years. A half-million voter signatures will be needed, requiring tremendous support from the public.

A letter to the editor in the same issue suggested that public support for the "BAN THE NETS! Save The Sealife" campaign may be forthcoming. Captioned, EVERY PENNY HELPS TOWARD BAN THE NETS! an earnest young *Florida Sportsman* reader from Lantana wrote:

> I am a nine-year-old who saw the net-ban stories in *Florida Sportsman*....I think we need to stop the netters. I fish with my dad a lot....I am donating to the campaign to help you stop the nets. I made the money by growing plants and doing work around the house.

ROY LEE YEOMANS

[1] Edgar J. Watson was a legendary resident of the Ten Thousand Islands during the late 1800s and early 1900s. For further information, see "Killing Mister Watson" by Peter Matthiessen, 1990.

[2] Research findings indicated a 70 percent decline in the species during a five-year period, from 1977-1981 in the Naples area, historically a center of abundance in the state. At the request of the Florida Department of Natural Resources, the Florida Game and Fresh Water Fish Commission declared snook a Species of Special Concern. Sport fishing is currently banned during January and February, June, July and August; during the remaining months sport fishermen are permitted to retain two snook per day although they are encouraged to release their catch instead. According to a DNR brochure, "Recreational fishing pressure is not the only threat to the snook populations. A significant factor in the decline of the species is the loss of estuarine habitat as a result of coastal development....Use of mosquito-control sprays, such as Baytex and Malathion, in spawning or nursery areas may cause high mortality of eggs and larvae."

Thirty-five years after recreational fishermen took the snook from commercial fishermen and consumers, Southeastern Fisheries Association director Bob Jones concluded, "Gamefish for snook, you can absolutely call a failure."

PART V

CONSERVATION THROUGH USE:
RESOURCE MANAGEMENT FOR THE TWENTY-FIRST CENTURY

[1] Biologists in the early 1990s, speaking with the benefit of a decade of intensive research that made the redfish the most studied finfish in the Gulf of Mexico, point to these large spawns as evidence that data produced by some biologists during the 1980s may have been alarmist. They also dispute claims by gamefish advocates that the red drum "came back," thanks to the ban on commercial fishing:

"In fact, it would seem to be impossible that the ban produced the current strong year-class, as often stated," said H. Dickson Hoese. "First, there are over 20 year-classes spawning in the Gulf and even if the two large catch years [1986 and '87] took *every* juvenile, they would make up a very small percentage of the spawning pool. Second, these classes [spawned since the ban] would be relatively immature and not yet recruited into the spawning schools.

"That the current spawning stocks produced a very large 1990 class would also negate the idea that inadequate quantities of juveniles previously "escaped" into the spawning pool during the 1970s and '80s."

[2] The Federal Aid in Sport Fish Restoration Program was created in 1950 through the Dingell-Johnson Act. Cosponsored by Michigan Rep. John Dingell and Colorado Sen. Edwin Johnson, the act authorized a 10 percent excise tax on some fishing tackle. The proceeds were placed into a special account and apportioned to the states for sport fish restoration.

By the late 1970s, it became apparent that these funds were inadequate. West Virginia Sen. Jennings Randolph introduced legislation to expand the Dingell-Johnson program by lengthening the list of taxable fishing tackle items and by imposing a 3 percent excise tax on the manufacturers of certain boats, outboard motors and boat trailers. Louisiana Rep. John Breaux introduced similar legislation in the House.

Boating industry representatives, however, killed the bill claiming that their industry was already hurting from the increased interest rates brought about during the energy crunch of the late 1970s.

In 1982, the Sport Fishing Institute offered a compromise proposal: Delete the controversial 3 percent excise tax on boats, outboard motors and boat trailers and, instead, tax the fuel used in motorboats. And, suggested SFI, incorporate the duties collected on imported boats and fishing tackle into the fund.

In 1984, co-sponsors Breaux and Wyoming Sen. Malcolm Wallop succeeded in passing the compromise, now called the Wallop-Breaux Amendment to the Federal Aid in Sport Fish Restoration Act. Under the Wallop-Breaux Amendment, the trust fund receives monies from four avenues:

1. A 10 percent manufacturers' excise tax on tackle, including rods, reels, terminal tackle, artificial lures, tackle boxes and most accessories; also, a 3 percent manufacturers' excise tax on electric trolling motors and flasher-type sonar fish finders. These funds are collected by individual companies and are paid into the Sport Fish Restoration Account of the U.S. Treasury.

2. Duties collected on the sale of imported fishing tackle, pleasure boats and yachts. These monies are collected by the U.S. Customs Service and deposited in the trust fund.

3. A portion of the monies collected by the Treasury from the 9.1 cents per gallon Federal tax paid by producers and importers of gasoline on nationwide fuel sales. The Treasury has determined that 1.08 percent of total fuel tax revenues are attributable to the sale of motorboat fuel.

4. Interest earned by the trust fund.

[3] The May/June 1993 issue of GCCA's *Tide* featured a photograph of the 300,000th signer of the petition to put the net ban on the Florida ballot in 1994. (The recreationals need 575,000 signatures.) A working-class black man, Willie Lee Whittey of Fort Pierce, was photographed with pen in hand, with one of his granddaughters looking on. A "retired maintenance worker and lifelong Floridian," Willie said, "I want my seven grandchildren to enjoy catching lots of fish—the way we did when I was a kid. If we get rid of the nets there will be more fish for all the people to enjoy."

The outcome of the impending referendum to ban the "circles of death" in Florida depends on the success of the fishing industry's countermeasures and the ability—and desire—of the state's media to educate the public. But if Floridians should vote to give all their fish to the recreational industry, it can only enhance the position of Louisiana's finfishing industry.

TOOLS OF THE TRADE

TRAMMEL NET

The trammel net is of European origin. The French name for this gear—*tramail*—is a corruption of the French words *trois*, three and *mail*, net. The trammel net is actually three nets in one.

Sandwiched between the two outer "walls," the inner net is fine-meshed and hung with plenty of slack. The walls are nets with extremely large meshes, up to 18 or 20 inches. When a small fish hits the trammel net, it may be gilled in the inner net; when a larger fish hits, it forces the fine-meshed inner net to bulge through a large mesh on the opposite side, neatly bagging itself in a pouch.

The construction of the trammel net enables a fisherman to catch a wide size-range of fish as well as deep-bodied species lacking prominent gill covers such as pompano, flounder and the freshwater buffalo. But it can also be disadvantageous. When he drops his trammel net into a large number of unwanted species, such as saltwater catfish, the fisherman loses valuable fishing time as he disentangles each one. Even desirable species can be difficult to remove from the three-walled trammel net.

This is the net of the Cajun *tramailleur*, but even these most tradition-bound fishermen are abandoning this elaborate piece of gear for the more selective gill net.

GILL NET

Fishermen refer to the gill net as a "straight net," to differentiate it from the three-walled trammel net. "Gill" net refers to the net's ability to enmesh fish by their gills as they try to pass through it. If the fish is the correct size for the net, its head will pass through a mesh but its body will be too large to follow. Unable to go forward and prevented by its gill covers from backing out, the fish is held until removed by the fisherman.

Obviously, the larger the fish desired, the larger the mesh size must be. The selectivity of the gill net can prove frustrating for the fisherman who must often watch helplessly as smaller, yet marketable, fish pass through the meshes. Fish too large to enter the meshes hit the net, back off and escape, as well. Still, the net's light weight and ease of handling and clearing more than compensate for the fish lost through the gill net's narrow latitude in catchability.

Its extreme selectivity makes this net the darling of fishery managers. A minimum mesh size is easily determined which allows all members of a species to spawn at least once before the gill net will stop them. For instance, a minimum mesh size of 3 1/2 inches will not stop a speckled trout until the fish has spawned at least once, often twice, assuring a perpetual supply of this species.

The gill net also enables fishermen to harvest a size "window" of fish. If, for example, managers specified a harvest of redfish averaging 4 to 5 pounds, fishermen would select a gill net with 5-inch meshes; a size window of 8 to 9 pound fish would call for a 6-inch net, etc.

Gill nets may be fished actively or passively. A strike net or "runaround" gill net is a gill net with a weight or buoy attached to one end. It is fished actively: When the fisherman sights a school of fish, the weight is thrown overboard and, as he circles the fish with his boat, the net is pulled overboard. After the majority of the fish have hit, the net is hauled back aboard.

A set net is a gill net fished passively by anchoring it in a promising location, like a spider's web. The set netter runs his gear at regular intervals, clearing it of any fish that might have hit it.

HAUL SEINE

The haul seine is a relatively small-meshed net, usually with a trawl-like "bag" sewn in the middle. Before the otter trawl was introduced about 1912, seines were used to harvest Louisiana shrimp. As huge schools of white shrimp churned the bottom, Cajun fishermen spotted the muddy cloud—*la tache*—and wrapped it up with their seine.

In like fashion, the seine is set around a school of fish and then pulled back to the boat or shore, slowly forcing the fish into the bag. As the bagful of fish is brought to the boat, the fish may be "brailed"—scooped up in a dip net and hoisted aboard—or gaffed individually. Both methods are more efficient than removing individual fish from an entangling net.

PURSE SEINE

The purse seine is a very large and efficient net used primarily to capture schools of fish found near the surface of deeper waters. Typically, trammel nets, seines and gill nets "tend bottom"—their leadlines sink to the bottom to prevent fish from escaping beneath. The purse seine, however, as it is set around a school of fish, floats like a deep curtain of webbing until the bottom of the net is "pursed." Heaving on a wire called the pursing wire, which runs through rings attached along the bottom edge of the net, closes the bottom of the net, preventing the fish from escaping by going deeper.

The net is then hauled in by power blocks or a net drum, until the fish are herded to one end. They can then be brailed aboard or pumped from the net into the boat by a fish pump.

Tuna are harvested in the Pacific with purse seines that may weigh 50 tons. A smaller seine, used for mackerel in the Atlantic may weigh 15 tons. Purse seines are used extensively in the vast Alaskan salmon fishery, but on the Gulf Coast use of this efficient gear is limited primarily to bait and fishmeal fisheries.

Trammel Net

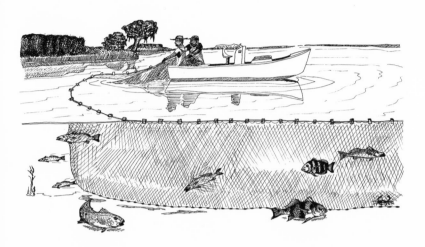

Gill Net (Strike Net)

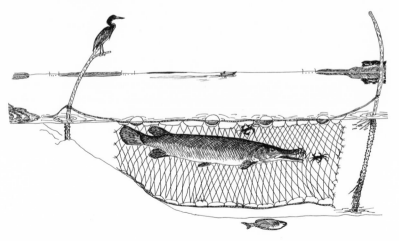

Gill Net (Set Net)

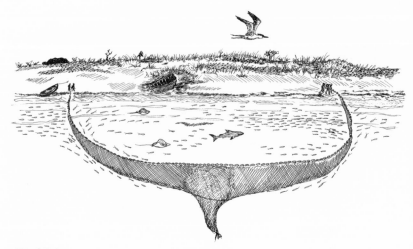

Haul Seine

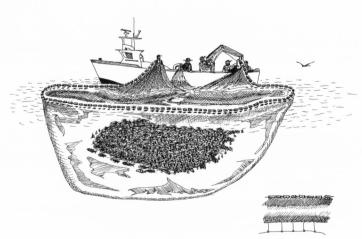

Purse Seine

BIBLIOGRAPHY

&

ADDITIONAL INFORMATION

Adams, Leon D. "Striped Bass Fishing in California and Oregon." Pacific Books, Palo Alto, Ca. 1953.

Adkins, Gerald; Tarver, Johnnie; Bowman, Philip; and Savoie, Brandt. "A Study of the Commercial Finfish in Coastal Louisiana." Louisiana Department of Wildlife and Fisheries, Seafood Division. Technical Bulletin No. 29. 1979.

Barnett, Jane. "Sport Group Uses Conservation to Fight Commercial Fishermen." *National Fisherman*. Vol. 68, No. 6. 1987.

————. "Who Gets the Fish?" *Seafood Business*. Vol. 6, No. 3. 1987.

————. "Battle Lines Drawn in Louisiana." *Seafood International*. April, 1990.

Baumann, R.H. "Mechanisms of maintaining marsh elevation in a subsiding environment." Master's Thesis. Louisiana State University, Baton Rouge, La. 1980.

Belleville, Bill. "Fish Fight: Angling for sport or profit off the Florida coast." *Audubon*. March/April, 1992.

Beno, Mike. "Treaty Troubles." *Audubon*. May, 1991.

Berkes, Fikret. "Competition between Commercial and Sport Fishermen: An Ecological Analysis." *Human Ecology*. Vol 12, No. 4. 1984.

Bowman, Philip; Adkins, Gerald; and Tarver, Johnnie. "A Profile of the Commercial Finfishermen in Coastal Louisiana." Louisiana Department of Wildlife and Fisheries, Seafood Division. Technical Bulletin No. 25. 1977.

Brandt, Andres von. "Fish Catching Methods of the World." Fishing News (Books) Ltd., 110 Fleet St., London EC4. 1964.

Brantly, J.E. "History of Oil Well Drilling." Gulf Publishing Co., Houston, Texas. 1971.

Brister, Bob. "Winning the War on Netters." *Field & Stream*. September, 1981.

Cahoon, D.R., et. al. "Prototype handbook for evaluating drilling site access in wetlands via canals." Final Report, Contract No. 68-03-1962 for U.S. EPA, Region VI, to Lee Wilson and Associates, Inc., Santa Fe, New Mexico. 1986.

Chambers, James R. "Coastal Degradation and Fish Population Losses." Proceedings of the National Symposium on Fish Habitat Conservation, Baltimore, Md. March, 1991.

Christian, Richard Travis. "Decision Making in Coastal Fisheries Conflict: The Case of Red Drum and Spotted Seatrout Legislation in Texas." Texas A&M University. Department of Recreation and Parks. Unpublished Master's Thesis. 1986.

————. "Dingell-Johnson/Wallop-Breaux: The Federal Aid in Sport Fish Restoration Program." Sport Fishing Institute, Washington, D.C. 1992.

Clements, Roland C. "Marshes, Developers, and Taxes—A New Ethic for Our Estuaries." *Audubon*. November, 1969.

Coalition to Restore Coastal Louisiana. "Coastal Louisiana, Here Today and Gone Tomorrow? A Citizen's Program for Saving the Mississippi River Delta Region, to Protect Its Heritage, Economy and Environment." Baton Rouge, La. 1989.

Conaway, James. "The Texans." Alfred A. Knopf, New York, N.Y. 1976.

Cowdrey, Albert E. "Land's End: A History of the New Orleans District, U.S. Army Corps of Engineers, and Its Lifelong Battle with the Lower Mississippi and Other Rivers Wending Their Way to the Sea." U.S. ACOE, 1977.

Cunningham, Rip. "Placing the Blame." *Salt Water Sportsman*. April, 1990.

Dasmann, Raymond F. "No Further Retreat: The Fight to Save Florida." The Macmillan Co., New York, N.Y. 1971.

Davis, D.W. "Louisiana canals and their influence on wetland development." Ph.D. Dissertation, Louisiana State University, Baton Rouge, La. 1973.

De Santis, Marie. "Neptune's Apprentice: Adventures of a Commercial Fisherwoman." Presidio Press, 31 Pamaron Way, Novato, Ca. 1984.

Detro, R.A. "Impact of the marsh buggy on the wetlands," in "Time stressed coastal environments: Assessment and future action." Proceedings of Second Annual Conference of the Coastal Society. November, 1976, New Orleans, La. 1977.

————. "Transportation in a difficult terrain: The development of the marsh buggy," in Hilliard, S.P. (ed.): "Man and Environment in the Lower Mississippi Valley." Geoscience and Man, vol. 19, School of Geoscience, Louisiana State University, Baton Rouge, La. 1978.

Ditton, Robert B.; Fedler, Anthony J.; and Christian, Richard T. "The Evolution of Recreational Fisheries Management in Texas." *Ocean and Coastal Management.* Vol. 17. 1992.

Edwards, Steven F. "An Economics Guide to Allocation of Fish Stocks between Commercial and Recreational Fisheries." NOAA Technical Report NMFS 94. 1990.

Environmental Defense Fund & World Wildlife Fund. "How Wet Is a Wetland?: The Impacts of the Proposed Revisions to the Federal Wetlands Delineation Manual." EDF, New York, N.Y. 1992.

Gowanloch, James Nelson. "Fishes and Fishing in Louisiana." State of Louisiana, Department of Conservation. Bulletin No. 23. 1965.

Gunter, G. "The Impact of Catastrophic Mortalities for Marine Fisheries Along the Texas Coast." *Journal of Wildlife Management.* Vol. 16, No. 1. 1952.

Herke, William H. et al. "Marsh management in coastal Louisiana: effects and issues." Proceedings of a symposium by the U.S. Fish and Wildlife Service and Louisiana Department of Natural Resources. U.S. F&W Serv. Bio. Rep. 89, No. 22. 1989.

———— et al. "Effects of Semi-impoundment of Louisiana Marsh on Fish and Crustacean Nursery Use and Export." *North American Journal of Fisheries Management.* Vol. 12. 1992.

Hoese, H. Dickson & Moore, Richard H. "Fishes of the Gulf of Mexico, Texas, Louisiana and Adjacent Waters." Texas A&M Press. 1977.

———— et al. "A Biological and Fisheries Profile of Louisiana Red Drum, *Sciaenops ocellatus.*" Louisiana Department of Wildlife and Fisheries, Fishery Management Plan Series, No. 4, Part 1. 1991.

Hopkins, S.H. and Petrocelli, S.R. "Limiting factors affecting the commercial fisheries in the Gulf of Mexico." Estuarine Pollution Control & Assessment. Proceedings of a Conference, Vol. 1, U.S. EPA, Office of Water Planning & Standards, Washington, D.C. 1975.

Houck, Oliver A.; Wagner, Fritz; and Elstrott, John B. "To Restore Lake Pontchartrain. A Report to the Greater New Orleans Expressway Commission on the sources, remedies and economic impacts of pollution in the Lake Pontchartrain Basin." April, 1989.

Hwang, Daniel H., et al. "Lipid composition differs in wild and cultured fish and shellfish." *Louisiana Agriculture*. Louisiana State University Agricultural Center, Vol. 29, No. 4. 1986.

Jacobs, Wilbur R. "Dispossessing the American Indian." Charles Scribner's Sons, New York, N.Y. 1972.

Joel, Billy. "Eye of the Storm," videotape from the album "Storm Front." CBS Records Inc. 1990.

Johnson, W.B. and Gosselink, J.G. "Wetland loss directly associated with canal dredging in the Louisiana coastal zone," in Boesch, D.F. (ed.): "Proceedings of the Conference on Coastal Erosion in Louisiana: Causes, Consequences and Options." U.S. Fish and Wildlife Service, Biological Services Program, Washington, D.C. 1982.

Lampl, Linda. "Feeding the People From Generation to Generation: An Ethnography of the Fishermen of Pine Island." Florida State University. Department of Anthropology. Master's Thesis. 1987.

Lawson, Glenn. "The Last Waterman." Crisfield Publishing Company, Crisfield, Md. 1988.

Louisiana Department of Wildlife and Fisheries. "Spotted Seatrout and Red Drum—An Overview." A Joint Fisheries/Seafood Division Task Force. January, 1983.

————. "A Fisheries Management Plan for Louisiana Spotted Seatrout, *Cynoscion nebulosus*." Fisheries Management Plan Series, No. 3. April, 1991.

————. "A Stock Assessment for Louisiana Red Drum, *Sciaenops ocellatus*." LDWF Fishery Management Plan Series, No. 4. 1991.

Luquet, Clarence, Jr.; Roussel, John; Shepard, Joseph; and Blanchet, Harry. "Black Drum Management Plan." Louisiana Department of Wildlife and Fisheries. May, 1990.

Magnuson Fishery Conservation and Management Act. U.S. Department of Commerce, National Oceanic and Atmospheric Administration, National Marine Fisheries Service. 1976.

BIBLIOGRAPHY & ADDITIONAL INFORMATION

Matthiessen, Peter. "Men's Lives: The Surfmen and Baymen of the South Fork." Random House, New York, N.Y. 1986.

McClane, A.J. "McClane's New Standard Fishing Encyclopedia and International Fishing Guide." Holt, Rinehart and Winston, New York, N.Y. 1965.

McGhee, E. and Hoot, C. "Mighty dredgers, little-known work horses of coastal drilling, producing, pipelining, now 25 years old." *The Oil and Gas Journal.* Vol. 16, No. 9. 1963.

Presley, James. "A Saga of Wealth: The Rise of the Texas Oilmen." G.P. Putnam's Sons, New York, N.Y. 1978.

Reavis, Dick J. "The New Rustlers." *Texas Monthly.* April, 1983.

Reiger, George. "Recreational Pressure on Fish Stocks." *Salt Water Sportsman.* April, 1991.

Report of the Legislative Investigating Committee on Salt Water Fisheries and Marine Taxation. Supplement to the Journal of the House of Representatives of the Forty-Fourth Legislature. Austin, Texas, 1935.

Roberts, Kenneth J. "A synopsis of economic impacts associated with recreational and commercial use of Louisiana seafoods (Splitting Atoms is Easier Than Dividing Fish)." Louisiana Cooperative Extension Service, Sea Grant College Program—Louisiana State University, Baton Rouge, La. 1986.

————. "Allocating Spotted Seatrout." Louisiana Sea Grant Program, Louisiana State University, Baton Rouge, La. 1991.

————, Horst, Jerald W.; Roussel, John E.; and Shepard, Joseph A. "Defining Fisheries." Louisiana Sea Grant Program, Louisiana State University, Baton Rouge, La. 1991.

Robertson, William B., Jr. "Everglades—The Park Story." University of Miami Press, Miami, Fla. 1959.

Rockland, David B. "The Economic Benefits of a Fishery Resource: A Practical Guide." Sport Fishing Institute, Washington, D.C. 1985.

Rootes, Rebecca. Politicking for Redfish Legislation. *Practicing Texas Politics.* Fifth Edition.

Ruello, N.V. and Henry, G.W. "Conflict Between Commercial and Amateur Fishermen." *Australian Fisheries*. March, 1977.

Scaife, W.; Turner, R.E.; and Costanza, R. "Coastal Louisiana recent land loss and canal impacts." *Environmental Management*. Vol. 7, No. 5. 1983.

Sikora, Walter B. "Air Cushion Vehicles for the Transport of Drilling Rigs, Supplies, and Oil Field Exploration Operations in the Coastal Marshes of Louisiana." Center for Wetland Resources, Louisiana State University, Baton Rouge, La. 1988.

Simmons, E.G. and Breuer, J.P. "A study of redfish, *Sciaenops ocellata*, and black drum, *Pogonias cromis*." Publications. Institute of Marine Science, University of Texas, No. 8. 1962.

Smith, Courtland L. "Oregon Fish Fights." Oregon State University, Sea Grant College Program. Publication No. ORESU-T-74-004. October, 1974.

Southwick, R. and Hutchison, R. "The Economic Impact of Sport Fishing in the State of Louisiana." Sport Fishing Institute, Washington, D.C. 1988.

Stokes, Samuel N. "Saving America's Countryside: A Guide to Rural Conservation." Johns Hopkins Press, Baltimore, Md. 1989.

Teal, John and Mildred. "Life and Death of the Salt Marsh." Ballantine Books, New York, N.Y. 1969.

Tebeau, Charlton W. "Man in the Everglades—2000 Years of Human History in the Everglades National Park." University of Miami Press, Miami, Fla. 1968.

Terrell, John Upton. "Land Grab: The Truth About 'The Winning of the West.'" Dial Press, New York, N.Y. 1972.

Texas Parks & Wildlife Department. Coastal Fisheries Branch. "Saltwater Finfish Research & Management in Texas. A Report to the Governor and the 66th Legislature." 1979.

————. "Saltwater Finfish Research & Management in Texas. A Report to the Governor and the 67th Legislature." 1981.

————. "Saltwater Finfish Research & Management in Texas. A Report to the Governor and the 68th Legislature." 1983.

————. "Saltwater Finfish Research & Management in Texas. A Report to the Governor and the 69th Legislature." 1985.

Time Magazine. "Walleye War." April 30, 1990.

Turner, R.E. "Intertidal Vegetation and Commercial Yields of Penaeid Shrimp." *Transactions of the American Fisheries Society.* Vol. 106, No. 5. 1977.

————. "Managing Wetlands in Coastal Louisiana For Plants, Waterfowl, Fish and Other Animals." *Bulletin d'Ecologie.* Vol. 21, No. 3. 1990.

———— & Boesch, Donald F. "Aquatic Animal Production and Wetland Relationships: Insights Gleaned Following Wetland Loss or Gain," in "The Ecology and Management of Wetlands, Volume 1: Ecology of Wetlands." Timber Press, Portland, Or. 1988.

Valliant, Joe. "Maryland Watermen: Fishing for Stripers Again." *National Fisherman.* Vol. 71, No. 12. 1991.

Watermen's Gazette. "Rockfish." July 21, 1991.

The author

1998: NEW PLAYERS,
SAME COURSE

The first edition of "Wetland Riders" came off the press in October, 1994. As I stated in the dedication, the book was initially written for the finfishermen themselves, to help them better understand the forces that threatened their way of life, and to give these traditional and productive people more of a voice in what had become a lopsided debate. Additionally, I suggested that the best course for Louisiana's coastal fisheries would be to maximize their value by continuing to share these resources with the public in a meaningful fashion. As the book appeared in bookstores, I was surprised to receive a letter from a high-school friend, whom I hadn't seen in 25 years. After chancing upon the book in a Colorado bookstore, he wrote,

> "...Although it reveals yet another blow against the working man and common sense, I like to think that maybe, just maybe, things have gone so far that (like a pendulum) they will swing back to a more even keel--hopefully before all too many good things are gone forever. Your book should serve to move things more in that direction and perhaps inform those who influence and make legislation."

Frankly, that pretty well summed up my hopes. But it's an imperfect world we live in. Due to a succession of events that began to unfold even before its release, the book has already been reduced to little more than a snapshot of how it was, a mere taunt as to how it might have been. The publication of this revised edition provides the opportunity to note some of those discouraging developments:

Back in 1992, the Marine Fish Conservation Network--bankrolled by the Pew Charitable Trusts, the Rockefeller Brothers Fund, and other philanthropic foundations--started "to coordinate a united nationwide effort to inform, educate, and activate organizations and individuals on the need to conserve marine fish, one of our last great public resources." With a membership comprised primarily of recreational-fishing and environmental groups, the coalition conducted a four-year national media campaign intended to influence the reauthorization of the Magnuson Fishery Conservation and Management Act in the U.S. Congress.

The multimillion-dollar educational effort universally disparaged commercial fishing, without mentioning the effects of recreational fishing.

With this unbalanced media campaign as a backdrop, recreational-industry members on every seaboard and the Great Lakes moved to take an unprecedented amount of publicly owned resource from the seafood-producing industry and consumers. By shifting their strategy from engaging in individual gamefish fights, to attacking the fishermen's harvesting equipment--the net--they ripped at the very foundation of coastal fishing cultures and communities, while continuing to sidestep the issues of allocation and sustainability.

The Florida Conservation Association and *Florida Sportsman* magazine also began their educational campaign in 1992. Two years later, on November 8, 1994, Florida voters overwhelmingly approved a constitutional amendment limiting the size of nets for the harvest of finfish and shrimp to no more than 500 square feet. Although the courts subsequently allowed a workable shrimp net, finfishermen were effectively put out of business.

While the amendment failed completely in 22 rural counties, just seven of the state's most heavily developed counties--in the central, west-central and southeastern areas of the state--provided enough votes to pass the measure.

"First, the 'Save Our Sealife' slogan of the FCA attracted people to the issue," wrote Denise Prodigo, a University of Florida graduate student who polled residents prior to the vote. In her master's thesis, "Developing opinions of Florida residents about the 'Ban the Nets' issue: A test of the situational theory of communication," she continued her assessment of the proponents' campaign:

> "When members of the FCA collected signatures on a petition to ban nets, they explained how nets trap dolphins, sea turtles and seabirds, and kill fish needlessly. This emotional plea distracted people from learning anything else about gill nets--they were convinced that gill nets were bad. Additionally, nearly every *Florida Sportsman* article contained graphic photographs and illustrations, such as dead dolphins or sea turtles tangled upin nets. Many articles also contained quotes from [recreational] fishermen saying there were no fish   to,   catch because the netters were taking all the fish out of the waters."

In 1993 and 1994, Florida fishermen had landed 178.8 million and 176.6 million pounds, respectively, of all seafood types then available to them. Landings in 1995 and 1996 fell to 133.5 and 134 million pounds.

According to an economic report released prior to the 1994 referendum, by Texas A&M University sociologist Robert Ditton, the number of tourist anglers fishing in Florida's salt waters could be doubled--from 3 million to 6 million--by the year 2010.

Following their success in Florida, recreational interests--led by the Gulf Coast Conservation Association--played up the threat of an invasion of displaced Florida finfishermen to neighboring coastal states. The only solution, they proposed to the legislatures of Alabama, Mississippi and Louisiana, was to take the nets from each state's own finfishermen.

As the battles raged during the spring and summer of 1995, biologists from each state made it clear that their fish stocks were in a healthy condition, and that there was no scientific basis for the curtailment of net fishing.

Legislatures in both Mississippi and Alabama found solutions that allowed netting for food fish to continue. Alabama's compromise was hailed by all parties as a "new age" in fishery management.

The outcome in Louisiana, though less absolute than that produced by the Florida vote, mortally wounded the finfish sector. The legislature banned the use of trammel nets, seines and gill nets for the harvest of all coastal food fish except pompano and striped mullet. Pompano may be taken during a three-month season within a relatively small area, east of the Mississippi River. Eight fishermen obtained pompano permits in 1995. Mullet may be harvested for four months only, during the spawning run. Fishermen may not work during weekends, nights or holidays. Only runaround gill nets may be used.

The 1995 legislature created a rod-and-reel-only commercial fishery for spotted seatrout, during the fall and winter. Only 72 fishermen obtained licenses for this fishery in 1995.

The state government also repealed the 1991 "Patti Amendment," which required state biologists to present stock assessments and possible allocation scenarios for the red drum to the legislature each year.

In 1994, state biologists--for the first time since the commercial fishery was closed in 1988--reported that the biological condition of the red drum in Louisiana had improved to a level that the harvest of the fish could be increased without harming the resource.

The biologists stated that if recreational fishermen were held to a daily bag limit of five redfish, commercial fishermen could harvest up to 3.2 million pounds of that species while maintaining the recommended 30 percent escapement rate. An extremely conservative 50 percent escapement rate could be maintained, they said, with a commercial quota of 1.6 million pounds.

In the six years from 1989 through 1994 commercial fishermen harvested no reds, while sport fishermen landed more than 30 million pounds, an annual average of five million pounds.

During 1995, as they clamored to "Ban the Nets!," anglers took an all-time record number of red drum: 2.4 million fish weighing 10 million pounds.

(Biologists attribute these elevated landings to a combination of factors, including the stringent restrictions placed upon both recreational and commercial fishermen in the late 1980s, a dramatic increase in the number of sport fishermen, and environmental conditions in the nursery grounds that have been favorable for both spawning and overwintering. Scientists caution, however, that healthy crops of redfish, shrimp and virtually every other of the state's wetland-dependent species may also be attributed to the *temporary* increase of available nursery habitat, as the interior marshes continue to break up.)

The hysteria generated by the supposed influx of out-of-state net fishermen, in conjunction with the emotional national campaign that sent resonating terms like "overfishing," "depletion," "bycatch," "by-kill," even "commercial extinction," through the media, helped create a climate that made it acceptable for Louisiana's politicians to give the fish to the sport fishermen. At the same time, a booming national economy and an upswing in the state's huge oil industry miniaturized the fishing industry's importance, while pumping up the net-ban proponents, who attended to election-year legislators.

This unique convergence of events created a once-in-a-lifetime opportunity for the recreationals who, with plenty of time for planning, took full advantage of it. As in Florida, their campaign was, to say the least, unsportsmanlike. Since its timing demanded that it be carried out during a period of abundance, sport fishermen claimed that commercial fishermen would, in the future, deplete the stocks. As confirmation, they pointed repeatedly to the temporary overharvest of the 500-year-old northwestern Atlantic cod fishery, which had been reported in nearly every major newspaper and magazine in the country.

On May 3, 1995, as recreational interests introduced their bill to the Natural Resources Committee of the Louisiana House of Representatives, sociologist Robert Ditton, of Texas A&M, testified that the money the family fishermen brought into their rural communities by selling fish to consumers could readily be offset by quadrupling the number of nonresident anglers.

During the fishing year from July 1, 1994, through June 30, 1995, non-residents purchased 35,397 saltwater angling licenses, two and a half times the 14,107 purchased in 1988-89. Resident saltwater anglers purchased 280,360 licenses in 1994-95, nearly 15,000 more than the previous year.

Following passage of the 1995 law, GCCA's executive director touted the economic benefits of saltwater recreational fishing in a letter to a Baton Rouge paper: "Go to the coastal areas of Grand Isle, Fourchon, Cocodrie or Venice to see the construction and tourist boom being generated by sportfishing."

In the Worldwatch Institute report, "State of the World 1990," a sustainable society is described as "one that satisfies its needs without jeopardizing the prospects of future generations. Inherent in this definition is the responsibility of each generation to ensure that the next one inherits an undiminished natural and economic endowment."

As Louisiana's finfishermen take refuge in the publicly owned shrimp, crab and oyster fisheries, it must be re-iterated that, after a few hundred years of harvesting the state's coastal waters with trammel nets, seines, and gill nets, they left an undiminished fishery. This success has to be attributed in part to the natural tension that had existed between the recreational and commercial industries, a sort of two-party system where each "party" limited the impacts of the other, though in different ways. Now there's only one party.

RF

1998